The Big W And A Dog Named Dylan

ISBN 1-58898-832-5

The Big W And A Dog Named Dylan

Napoleon Zimmerman

greatunpublished.com
Title No. 832
2003

The Big W And A Dog Named Dylan

To Joey & Sara, forever shall we love, laugh, learn, play and dream.

CHAPTER ONE
VISIONS OF JOHANNA
"A MOMENT IN TIME"

"Do you have a ruler?"

My mind races, *A RULER. What the fuck does she need a ruler for?*

"Come on, do you have a ruler?"

My mind spins. "Sure, in the top drawer. What are you going to do with it?"

As if it I didn't know.

We are lying in bed, groping each others' bodies. Hot. Hot. Hot. We have our routine. We kiss. I slowly peel her clothes off. Then I get up and strip. Back to kissing, I move to her breasts, sucking, then journeying lower across her belly to the promised land. I tease her. We kiss and my head, The Big Head, as she calls it, gently penetrates. She's wild. She's ready. How long can I hold off before I thrust? Then out of nowhere she asks, "Do you have a ruler?"

My worst nightmare has come true. Every man's dreaded fear. Is the equipment big enough, bad enough? She has never complained. Always had compliments: I love it. It's beautiful. It fits me perfect. Sure. They all say that. She even thinks its cute when not at attention. Cute, not a word one wants associated with his manhood. Monster. Yes. Scary. Yes. Awesome. Yes. But cute, please whisper. My mind plots an escape.

"Oh, here it is. Lie back."

Lying back, I protest. "Why, what are you doing?"

"Come on, I want to measure it."

"Why?"

"Please?"

I protest, but to tell the truth I'm a bit curious. She had the Cosmo Magazine a few months back. I read the article when she was shopping. The average penis is six inches it said. God, I hope I have six inches.

Where is she going to measure from? I don't want to get short changed. Pun intended. Now, I'm just hoping that I remain saluting. I want full credit. She makes it exciting. She plays with me, she cups me, she examines me. It's strangely erotic. But will it remain our secret, our private world; one of secret times, games played, confidential whispers. "Seven inches!" she exclaims. Not shock, not fear, not even like she is surprised.

Me. I'm in shock. Seven inches. Seven inches. My mind does the math. Holy shit, above average. Nothing to be embarrassed about here.

A new confidence comes over me. She has drifted immediately back into our routine. I lay back, head on the pillow, ego being stroked.

I held that nightmare in my mind for many years. One quick measurement and I'm free. No longer a prisoner of a societal "manhood tape" programming my thoughts.

She rolls over. I assume the position with new found strength. She arches. I recognize the moment. I can join her. We let go. Spent. We separate and laugh.

"What time is it?" she says.

I answer, "Seven inch cock. I mean eleven o'clock."

"I love you."

"I love you, too."

She puts her head on my chest.

"Sweet dreams!"

CHAPTER TWO
I AND I
"THIS IS NOT PORN"

This is not porn. Really, its not! Its about the clash between my mind and my heart, the voices within. The programmed, scripted mind voice and the real inner-self heart voice. It's about the spiritual journey from head to heart, the journey to my higher self, my soul.

Funny thing though, nobody watches or reads porn, but it's a billion dollar industry. Then again its not called porn, its adult entertainment. And strippers aren't strippers, their dancers. The magic of words to transform perception.

We lay in each other's arms. Orgasm sleep. Spiritual sleep. Time for the subconscious to play, to encourage us, to remind of us of who we are. They say only five percent of our thoughts are conscious thoughts. The remainder is the domain of the subconscious.

They say! I like the way we do that. "THEY" say it, so it must be true. No facts, no sources. Just, "THEY SAY".

I awake first as usual. My mind, that is my subconscious, is busy. So active it wakes me up. My post dream routine begins. Words, thoughts, theories. I lie there, holding her near. I think, I compose, I write in my head. So much information. So many ideas.

The DREAM. Remember the dream. To write, to share my thoughts, to touch a heart, to encourage a broken spirit, to share the secret, to light the path. My heart whispers many dreams to me. To be a writer is one of them. My mind dismisses these dreams with the speed of a prize fighter.

I want to be a writer. Yet fear stalks me. Terror really. The limiting programmed voices of my mind— "You can't do that", "Who do you think you are?", "What makes you think you have anything to say?", "Besides who would want to read it anyway?".

Quiet. Please be quiet. Pay no attention to those negative ramblings of that disturbed brain. Courage, belief, hope. Listen to your heart. Yes, the dream: TO WRITE.

I lie there. I compose in my head. The thoughts flow, but never make it to paper. Am I just a head writer with one in the audience? Soon, someday, I will scribble it down.

I saw an interview with Stephen King once. He was asked how he writes. He replied, "ONE WORD AT A TIME". One word at a time, what is he in Writers Anonymous?

"Hi, my name is Napoleon, and I'm a writer. Yes, it feels good to admit it. Mostly, I write in my head. I've kept it a secret until now. It feels good to let it out. Even my girlfriend doesn't know. I do it mostly while she is asleep."

I lie and I write. Better than writing lies, I guess.

Actually, Mr. King's words haunt me. They speak directly to my heart. They chase me, imploring me to start. Just one word, start and let it flow. Rise above the limiting beliefs instilled in your mind. Listen to your heart. Write. It's your dream, and we must embrace our dreams, make them real, make them happen.

So you see, its not porn, its spiritual. Yes, spiritual. The journey to the heart begins with a revolution in the mind. Revolt against the nightmares, the fears, the limiting beliefs, the outdated tapes in the head. My penis is my penis. My legs are my legs. My nose is my nose. None of it has to do with the man I am. Connect with my heart. It will lead me to my dreams, to my true self. Release the nightmares of the mind, embrace the dreams of the heart and discover my soul.

I'll give you an example. As I lie with my love in my arms this is what races through my hypothetical writer's head...

CHAPTER THREE
MASTERS OF WAR
"DEPROGRAMMED"

If I were a Jew, would you still let me play with you?
If I were gay, would you let me stay?
If I were black, would you invite me back?
If I had no money, would you call me honey?
If I were fat, would you tell me that's not were it's at?

Why do we judge each other? What are we afraid of? Could it be a weapon? Judge before you are judged. Build up your ego. Validate your existence. Just being couldn't be good enough, could it? No! You have to be someone important. You have to be a success. Bigger, Better, Faster, isn't that the goal?

Why do we judge our insides by others outsides? Why can't I just be me? Everyone has advice, a pointer, a tip. Do it this way. No, not that way. That will never work. Why do people insists on telling us our dreams are out of reach?

Where do all these tapes come from? How did my mind become so cluttered? Born naked, I was perfect. Now, years later, I must MEASURE UP. Lying naked in my crib, just as cute as can be, doesn't cut it anymore.

Scripted. My life has been scripted. Programmed by amateurs. Fear-based lies passed from one generation to the next. Definitions of success, of manhood, of wealth, of prestige, of sexuality, of spirituality, have been instilled in my mind without my consent. Limiting beliefs holding me back, crippling my spirit.

Now, I must filter through the garbage, the bad tapes. The head tapes I let roll constantly. Who am I? Where is my path? Opposing voices dwell within. What is this conflict between my mind and my heart? The mind preoccupied with the ways of the world, the heart with the ways of the spirit.

Go away. Go away. Isolation. Solitude. Aloneness. TIME TO DISCOVER. TIME TO WATCH. TIME TO OBSERVE. TIME TO LEARN. TIME TO PLAY. TIME TO REWRITE THE SCRIPT. TIME TO CREATE. TIME TO DISCOVER ME.

Yes, it's me. Hold tight. Head high. Walk your path. Listen to that inner still voice. No you are not crazy. Keep watch against the programmers, those who are part of the hypnotized masses, the TV addicts, the commercial target audiences, the unhappy herded sheep being led to the slaughter, those who dress the part, those who rely on their cars to make a statement, those who max out their credit cards not to feel and those who chose comfort over character.

It's a war. A revolution. Many fronts. Many battles. A conflict between the limited voices of the mind and the true inner limitless voice of the heart.

The real journey begins when the soul is awakened. Walk the earth. Nurture my spirit. Live my life. Co-create with the Universe. Follow my heart, it speaks for the soul. Scripts lead to ruts. Dreams lived lead to self.

If I didn't like the cold, would we have a chance to grow old?
If I liked to read a book, would you give me a second look?
If I liked to run, would you say I was no fun?
If I liked time alone, would you reject me for your clone?
If I listened to my heart, would we have to part?

HONOR ME. I HONOR YOU. Be free. Follow your inner heart voice, not the programmed, scripted mind. Break free. Dream, live, learn and play.

Johanna and I awake. We start our morning routine of coffee and quiet time. The beach looks inviting today. A ten mile run sounds good. It's sunny, hot and we are in southern Florida. A good day on the horizon, that's the way I remember it. It seems so long ago.

CHAPTER FOUR
I AM THE LONESOME HOBO
"WHAT IS THE BIG W?"

Mr. King would be proud. Words have made it to paper, a small victory for the heart. So now what? I guess the obvious question is, "How did I get here and what is THE BIG W?"

First, The Big W.

As I travel the road, I bring my home with me. The Big W is my home—my sanctuary, my sacred space, my wheels, my RV. Yes, recreation vehicle.

To the average layman, a 1981 Toyota Huntsman, class C, RV with room for a driver, a companion in the cab, and the master bed above. A small kitchen table with a picture window, host to many small gatherings, whether a meal is shared or cards are thrown. To the right is my stove, to the left the sink for dishwashing meditation. In the rear, the emergency toilet, shower and closet. I say emergency toilet as the waste tank is small and what goes in must be dumped. The true road warrior can spot a public restroom a mile away.

To the road traveler it's a home, not just a metal box on wheels. The Big W—a place to dwell, a place to learn, a place to play. A life of simplicity away from the bondage of the complicated world of luxury. Few possessions. Few attachments.

You still wonder what is THE BIG W? It must be more than an RV? Yes, it is. The Big W led me to the road. The road led me to myself. The journey within the journey, the real adventure from head to heart.

Name selection is critical. Words, names in particular give us clues. Clues to the meaning of life and the meaning of love. Who are you? Who am I? The Big W is short. Slang if you will. Wanderer. Wander lodge. Wandering. All of the above. The Big W, The Dub, to those who catch a glimpse of the lifestyle, of the journey.

What is the lifestyle? A lifestyle conducive to battle. To silence the mind and nurture the heart. To awaken the soul and live one's dreams. To take the time to discover one's inner truth, one's inner essence.

The Big W was my chance. Time to go. Time to take off to the unknown. Time to be alone. Time to exorcise the demons in my mind. Time to let the quiet, wise voice of my heart speak the truth to me. Time to wander and discover. Time to just be.

The Big W is not very fast on the road. It has a four cylinder engine. I once went 62 mph. down a hill in Colorado. If you're passing someone in The Dub, something is wrong with the other vehicle (or driver). The Big W is not for racing. Typically, you are on the lookout for minimum speed limit signs. Mostly, we travel in the right hand lane, as others fly by in the passing lane, late for an important engagement, with a total disregard for the valuable cargo aboard. The destination is the journey itself. Never in a hurry, progress not perfection is the goal.

From the outside its looks are deceiving. Older, mature looking. Some would say run down. From the inside a new world expands. Space. A sanctuary from the world, from the rat race, from the Jones's.

The Big W, an RV to the untrained eye, a haven for a restless soul.

CHAPTER FIVE
WORLD GONE WRONG
"HOW DID I GET HERE?"

I moved into The Big W in May 1998 at the age of 36. However, the tugging on my soul had begun years earlier. Born Napoleon Zimmerman on August 1, 1961, in Concord, Massachusetts, birthplace of the American Revolution and home of Walden Pond. Coincidence, I think not. Oldest of four siblings. Public schools grades K-8, private high school, college graduate, and a Masters in Business. Summers on Cape Cod. Hockey player, golfer, marathon runner and an ironman distance triathlon finisher. Married January, 1989. Successful commercial real estate appraiser, husband, father, homeowner, two cars in the garage. I had arrived.

DIVORCE. That's when the voices started.

October 1994, at the age of 33, my world was shattered. My wife no longer wanted to be my wife. She had begun to question her own path. Life as I knew it ended. It was the most devastating period I have ever survived. I did everything my role models showed me and it didn't work. The job, the house, the wife, the kids, I lived the script. Now, I was alone again. Confused, scared and broken. The illusion of "together forever" faded fast. My identity was shot full of holes. My roles as husband, father, provider, homeowner and employee had defined me for so long. Who was I now?

Looking back this tragedy was a blessing. When a man thinks a bullet is an option, something needs to be examined. I was told suicide was a permanent solution to a temporary problem. How true. I went numb for a period of time. I was angry, hurt, scared and lost in a sea of self-pity. It was the dark season of my soul. I had been sober since I was 21 years old and this was not supposed to happen to me. Now I found myself escaping my feelings in all the typical ways: food, sex, gambling, shopping, driving fast, cigars, sleep, music, running. Whatever it took to not feel. The pain and turmoil was intense. Yet I wrote my first poem. Had the heart been pierced? I still remember the poem. It goes:

DIVORCE

Nothing's sacred anymore,
Holy matrimony is a whore.

Wives, husbands, lovers, cheats,
Friends, companions, triumphs, defeats.

Vows of commitment, rings of gold,
Slow detachment, wicked stories told.

Hearts broken, souls battered,
Words unspoken, dreams shattered.

My body is so sore,
It feels like WAR.

My season of suffering lasted a year and half. I've read that pain is the touchstone of spiritual growth. I believe that. When my world was shattered and all the distractions failed to give relief, it was then that I was open to hear my heart, to discover my soul, my higher self. I spent this time relationship-free other than the occasional comfort night encounter with another lonely, beaten soul. During this time the heart begin to whisper, "Napoleon you're okay. There is more. Be still, listen and great events will come to pass." And then a gift.

Forgiveness. My ex-wife's gift to me. I held on to the anger as long as possible. Played the victim. Poor me. I wouldn't let go of the hurt. It became a new identity. My mind told me that to forgive her would be to let her win. How wrong can one be? Forgiveness freed me. What a lesson. What a gift. The childhood St. Francis Prayer made no sense for so long. Why would anyone want to forgive? Surely being forgiven was better. No, the real freedom comes from forgiving. Resentment no longer owns a forgiving heart. The mind could let go. The heart could begin to heal.

The unshed tears could finally claim themselves. Not just with the divorce, but my entire life. The hurt of 33 years could be released. For so many years I ignored my heart and obeyed my contaminated mind. I found an inner wounded boy-child, a warrior-adolescent, and a confused, programmed adult. I had heard these terms before. Always ignoring them as cries of the weak. A copout for those stuck in the past. The pain was surfacing. Once I found myself riding Peter Pan buses for 48 hours to Hartford, Connecticut, New York City and Philadelphia, Pennsylvania. I rode in the rear seat of the bus in the fetal position with headphones on. Literally I could recall crying 5 year-old boy tears, 15 year-old adolescent tears and 33 year-old adult male tears. Again, the un-cried tears of years were claiming themselves. At one point I sat on the ground at Grand Central Station in NYC from four a.m. until nine a.m. just watching the herds of workers rushing by to employment destinations. I was apart from. Separate. Everything was in slow motion. I was lost and life made no sense.

I read Melody Beattie's books, *Codependent No More* and *Beyond Codependency*, and saw myself in those pages. I saw how I behaved in relationships. I connected to this wounded child and this warrior adolescent. At times I felt like I was reliving parts of my life. I discovered the wounded boy-child buried emotions deep. Do not rock the boat. Be seen, not heard. The warrior adolescent shut down and survived. Be a man. Be strong. The heart was hardened early in life. The mind was vulnerable to programming. I became disconnected to myself and to my heart. Time to grow up fast, be responsible, do the right thing, tow the line, live the script, be a success, everyone will love you, and no one will leave you. I lost myself in the pursuit of another's definition of success. But what happens when the programmed adult world is shattered? I now had issues from A to Z. Abandonment, boundaries, care taking, love, shame, and trust issues. The heart and mind quarreled.

As far as the marriage was concerned I could own my fifty percent now. My vision was clearing. Yes, both of us contributed to the breakdown of our union. Both of us brought a "mind set" to the altar. Now my life was my responsibility. I questioned my path. Which road to travel? What to do? Who am I?

With the gift of forgiveness, a season of healing began. Another eighteen month window. Self examination. Who was I? How did I get here? Why did I choose this lifestyle? What made me happy? What was I to do with my life now? My job was just to pay bills. It gave me no inner satisfaction. My life was a routine, a mundane existence of stagnation and boredom. Caught on a tread mill, just one step ahead of the bill collectors. I had all the latest gadgets, but had an empty feeling inside. As Thoreau said, "Most men lead lives of quiet desperation." I was no exception.

The tugging became stronger. A small encouraging voice from the heart was emerging. A questioning voice, weak at first, but steadily getting stronger, as if each time it spoke it grew more daring. Permission to examine beliefs and values held for years. Permission to question the rules of life. Who made these rules anyway? Where did these limiting beliefs in my mind come from?

Gail Sheehey in her book, *Understanding Men's Passages*, describes men in their forties, fifties and sixties looking back on their lives, questioning their paths. They had the house paid for. The career was a success. But their grown children, they knew not at all. They asked questions such as, "Is that all there is?", "Why am I here?" and "Where is the meaning?". I was only 33, yet asked similar questions. It's comforting to discover you are not alone. I wasn't the first to ask these types of questions. Perhaps there was more to life?

A third season began, one of self-discovery and living. I

started to experiment. Try new things. Travel to new places. Taste new foods. Read new books. Discover what I enjoyed. It was like a dead man coming to life. But the ghosts of the mind still haunted me. Deep, deep, messages from the past. "Who do you think you are? This is not the way things are supposed to be done." Negativity would breed negativity. Mind and heart confronted each other in battle. The programmed scripted mind versus the awakening heart voice. As new experiences accumulated with no harmful effects, I could no longer ignore this nudging on my soul. There had to be more.

I remember watching the movie *Shawshank Redemption* and near the end of the movie Tim Robbins' character, Andy Dufresne, says to Red after spending nearly twenty years in prison for a crime he didn't commit, "It's time to get busy living or get busy dying." That did it for me. As Dylan sings, "revolution in the air". The heart could not be silenced. The mind was polluted. What was it to be? Live or die? I knew I needed space. Time to sort things out. Time to explore and find myself. I needed to go. But how?

THE BIG W offered a way out. A way to say, "Enough is enough. I'll walk the earth in search of myself. Free of the constraints of the definition of success lodged within my mind. Free of the bondage of possessions. Free to listen to my heart and discover who I am, what I believe and what is my purpose."

Identification, decision, action. I identified the solution, the decision was made, and now it was time for action. This, I discovered, is where most people drop the ball. Many people identify problems and solutions, some even make decisions to do something, but most never follow through with the necessary action for permanent change and happiness. Identification, decision, action.

The decision was easy. Purchase The Big W and move into it immediately. It would be like paying rent for the next year in advance. Going to pay rent anyway, so why not by a home, a home on wheels. Homeowners say that all the time, "Why rent when you can own?" Theoretically, it could be waterfront property if parked in the right place. If the neighborhood went bad, I could just move. Nothing ventured, nothing gained. Six months working, saving and by November, 1998 I would hit the road debt-free. Buy it. Live in it. Save. I was taking action. $4,500 and she was mine. 48,000 miles she had traveled without my soul aboard. That lifetime was over. A new one had begun.

So divorce, the worst tragedy in my life, became a blessing. It opened the doorway to a new life. A life to be built by me and for me. The decision was made to leave the false comfort of security. The illusion of another's definition of success would be left behind. I would venture into the unknown with my heart as my guide in search of the true self.

Yet, the voices of the heart and mind still fought for attention, and would for sometime. Both wanted to captain the ship called my life. One entrenched in fear, the other faith. Navigating the two contradicting voices would not always be easy. Sailing against the wind would be mastered slowly. As Richard Bode says in the title of his book, *First You Have To Row A Little Boat.*

CHAPTER SIX
MR. TAMBOURINE MAN
"WHO IS DYLAN?"

Dylan is my dog. I say my dog because I feed him and care for him. In reality he is free to leave at anytime. A black Labrador retriever, born April 17, 2000, the day of the running of the Boston Marathon, and now destined to run the beaches of the world. My friend, my travelling companion for my junior term on the road. His namesake is Bob Dylan, poet, songwriter, storyteller, singer and prophet. They even look alike. Especially, when Bob has a beard, like on the cover of *Infidels*.

Dylan is an old, wise, soul, just like Bob. Clearly, they both draw on past lives remembered for their insights. Dylan speaks to the heart, reminds me of the inner journey to my soul, and let's little slip by. He is a welcome ally on the battlefield between the voices of my heart and mind.

Why a dog for the road?

My freshman and sophomore terms on the road in The Big W were marked by several romantic relationships. All loves at a soul level, but not lifetime relationships. Each for a reason and each for a season. Many lessons were mastered and some were ignored. The biggest being solitude. Time to travel alone. While I enjoy visiting friends as I tour, my intention was to avoid intimate emotional entanglements. It was the goal from the beginning. However, the Universe reveals the lessons of life on its own timetable and terms. When the student is ready, the master appears. Sometimes situations or people appear despite our best plans. I was to learn we attract those who will teach us our lessons and sometimes we teach what we are in most need of mastering.

My friend Jimmy and I call it the "Russian Theory". Jimmy was to travel all over Russia. He had all the details worked out. A broken heart now, but Russia would fix it. Then the universe intervened; he received a full scholarship to graduate school. Two years later the job of his dreams in Vermont, a state he loved. He accepted it, went to work and eventually met his future wife. He adores his new baby son and hardly ever thinks of Russia. The Russian Theory. The Universe orchestrating our highest good.

In my case, I ventured out on the road to be alone. Yet, I kept falling in love. New chances to master ignored lessons of the past. I regret none of the time spent with these souls, but the longing to travel and be alone was never extinguished. The struggle between solitude and companionship would challenge me repeatedly. As Anthony Storr in the introduction to his book *Solitude* states, "Two opposing drives operate throughout life: The drive for companionship, love, and everything which brings us close to our fellow men; and the drive toward being independent, separate, and autonomous." These contradicting forces would test me over and over. Were these loves of mine teachers or distractions? Time would tell.

So why a dog now?

I never understood the relationship people had with their pets. The love of an animal eluded me. Often I would watch the master with his pet, fascinated with the unconditional love. Scratch their ears, a little food, take them for a walk, and an undying loyalty, companionship, and love. Forget to scratch their ears, feed them or take them for a walk, and still an undying loyalty, companionship and love. My road relationships taught me much, but it was time for a new companion. Perhaps I could learn something about love at a more basic, simpler level.

Often I refer to the road and life in The Big W as "SOUL SCHOOL-PLAYGROUND EARTH". Dylan would be my junior term companion. As a matter of fact, it was Dylan who suggested I begin writing. He was tired of hearing me talk about writing and with that look in his eyes he sang, *"I believe in you. I believe in you even through the tears and the laughter. I believe in you even though I be outnumbered. I believe in you."*

So we left August 16, 2000 for my third term adventure determined to share the experiences and lessons of the previous two terms. Travel and write. A dream was taking shape, *The Big W and a Dog Named Dylan.*

CHAPTER SEVEN
MAN ON THE STREET
"MAY 1998, ROAD PROTESTS"

Looking back, the lessons began before I even left for the road. I lived in The Big W from May until November while preparing for the road. Our relationship began when I purchased her on May 1, 1998. I had studied the Want Advertiser and knew my price range. There were over 100 RV's on the local lot and it was as if I was led directly to The Big W. The test drive felt right. The transaction was completed and I moved into her and situated her at the rear of the parking lot at my office and began my life living in The Big W.

From the onset no one encouraged me. Negativity was on every street corner, on the lips of all those around me. My sanity was questioned. When told of my plans to travel the country, people actually laughed out loud. Some were as bold as to say, "You can't do that", "It will never work", "Where will you stay", "How will you live", "What about a TV", and "Shouldn't you wait until you retire?". I didn't dare tell them it was to be a "spiritual walkabout", a playground for my heart. No, rather I just said I was in search of the perfect beach. It was safer.

I carry a quote on a small piece of paper in my pocket. It's entitled "Never Quit" and the mouth that uttered it was Casey Stengel. It reads, "They say you can't do it, but sometimes that doesn't always work". Casey, I hear you.

To make matters worse, hitting the road meant quitting my job and breaking up with my girlfriend, Lily. So they looked at me, stunned, confused, and holy than thou. What a nut case.

He quit his job, broke up with such a sweet girl, and now lives in that.

Yet, I knew there were unlived dreams locked safe within my heart. There had to be more to life. The journey couldn't just be about security, comfort, material possessions, and cable TV. I had been sold a bill of goods and my mind bought it. I was programmed without my knowledge. My heart knew better. It would lead me to the key to unlock the dreams within my soul: to run in the sun, to live near the beach, to awake each morning without the aid of an alarm clock, and to be free of living another's code. The dream voice was buried and silenced for years within my heart, but no more. The closer I listened to my heart the more I discovered my dreams. Revolution, the time is now. In this corner, the scripted mind and in this corner, the limitless heart.

Now I was playing with them.

"Where are you going, Napoleon?"

"Don't know."

"How long are you going for?"

"Not sure."

"Why are you leaving?"

"Looking for the perfect beach."

I had to go. To not go would always leave me wondering. The road called and my soul heard the cry. Be strong. Be true to that inner heart voice.

My mind was as polluted as those around me. Fear: a crippling spiritual disease of the mind. "Maybe, I cracked. Maybe, everyone is right. Keep the girl, even though you know in your heart she is not the one. Sure, she is not really what you want. But it's good. Settle for good, because you don't deserve the best. Keep the job. It's good money. You would be a fool to walk away from that kind of security. Who cares that you feel dissatisfied, that you feel like a robot, that you are a cog in a big machine, that you are making no contribution." Yes, my mind was polluted too.

The war had commenced. My mind was not my own. My heart spoke a different language than my head. "There is more.

Don't settle. Chase your dreams. Honor me, I am your real self, your higher self. I will lead you. I will help you cleanse your thoughts and reprogram your mind. You will connect with your soul. Go, Go, Go. The Big W is real. The journey is real. Drive into the unknown. Trust the adventure."

It was as if I was standing at a "sacred crossroad" of my life and I sensed that belief revolution led to soul evolution. Though at times nothing made sense, I knew there would be a day all would be right. My venture into the unknown was the first step preparing me for great events to come to pass. Whether next year or in twenty years, more would be revealed. The time for action was now.

CHAPTER EIGHT
SOMEONE'S GOT A HOLD OF MY HEART
"LILY: THE LESSON OF LOVE"

To chase my dream meant to severe some ties. I gave my notice at work. Was pleasantly surprised that they didn't want me to go. They actually valued my contribution. Imagine that! More difficult was ending my romantic relationship.

Lily was my first serious love relationship after my divorce. Up until her, most women said I had a sign on my forehead, which read "NOT EMOTIONALLY AVAILABLE".

We met in the fall of 1997 at one of those fancy coffee shops called the Java Hut. I prefer black gas station coffee, but I liked this place because they have amateur night. I love to watch first time performers get up and sing or read poetry. The courage is inspiring.

I had been single for almost three years since my divorce. She was a good woman with a six year-old daughter. From the beginning she made it clear she was looking for marriage; a husband for her, a father for her daughter. I made it clear I wasn't thinking about marriage. Ignoring our "declarations of intention", we went forward anyway. A limited pattern I would eventually hit bottom repeating. We shared laughs and good times. We dated. We explored each other. We became a couple and ignored our individual dream voices. Being with someone was fun. It felt nice to be loved and to love. To give gifts at Christmas and Valentine's Day. To celebrate my 37th birthday together with a cake in The Dub. To share surprises. To share a bed. We had fun.

Yet as we enjoyed our last month together we had to get honest. We had different dreams. She in search of a family, me staring out at the road. We realized no one was right, no one was wrong. We were just different. Different visions for our futures. I could no longer ignore the tugging on my soul. Was I to leave or was I to settle down with this woman? To seek adventure and the unknown, or to build a life in New England?

At this point in my life I was becoming more and more open to the concept of how the Universe communicated different messages to my heart, whether from the lyrics of a song, a good book, an encounter with a stranger or a line in a movie. We saw the movie *Titanic* and at one point the main character, Jack Dawson, is seated at the captain's table for dinner while several of the other dinner patrons are looking down at him, poking fun at his lot in life, questioning his path.

"Tell us about the accommodations in steerage, Mr. Dawson. I hear they're quite good on this ship." states Rose's mother.

"The best I've seen. Hardly any rats," says Dawson.

"Where exactly do you live, Mr. Dawson?"

"Well right now my address is the RMS Titanic. After that I'm on God's good humor."

"And how is it that you have the means to travel?"

"I work my way from place to place. You know, tramp steamers and such. But I won my ticket on the Titanic here at a lucky hand of poker. A very lucky hand."

"And you find that sort of ruthless existence appealing to you?"

"Yes, Ma'am I do. I mean, I got everything I need right here with me. Got air in my lungs and a few blank sheets of paper. I mean, I love waking up in the morning not knowing what's going to happen or who I am going to meet, where I'm going to wind up. Just the other night I was sleeping under a bridge and now here I am on the grandest ship in the world having champagne with you fine people. I figure life is a gift and I don't intend on wasting it. You never know what hand you're going to get dealt next. You learn to take life as it comes at you, to make every day count."

This strikes a nerve. That's what I am after. Freedom to live my life, to chase my dreams, to be me. To make every day count.

A decision was made and we let go of each other. Pain again. Ending a love relationship is never easy. Yet, this time I knew I would survive. It was only this relationship I would grieve, not a lifetime of pain as I had felt after my divorce. I was mending. Things would be okay. However, the mind and heart clashed.

The mind was relentless, "Maybe I should stay? She is a good woman. We could make a home, a happy life. Besides who else would want you, Napoleon? You better stick around. Security is good. Plus, the sex is good."

"No. No. No. Don't sell your soul for security, Napoleon", the heart would scream. "You deserve to chase what you want. You are lovable. You can't settle for good when you deserve the best. Go. Go. Go".

"Stay, Napoleon. Who knows what is out there on the road? Wait until you retire to hit the road like everyone else. So what if you don't want to get married again? You don't want to be alone? Stay Napoleon", persisted the mind.

"Go, Napoleon. You don't want to die a slow death, always wondering what could have been if you took a risk. Step out of your comfort zone", encouraged the heart.

They attacked each other.

I remember phoning my friend Jimmy Walker from Colorado. He pointed out that since the time of my divorce three years early he never once heard me talk about getting married, about settling down again. Rather, he said all I shared with him was my dream of heading out on the road, spending time alone, finding myself. I had to look at that. What was my destiny to be? What were my dreams? Did I want to abandon my dreams and begin living another's?

I began trying to learn the habit of getting quiet, getting alone. Letting the Universe guide me. Silence the mind and honor my heart voice. Go within.

"What did you learn from Lily?" came from the heart. The

gift of "LOVE". I could love again. Since the time of my divorce I didn't think it possible to fall in love again. Lily gave me that gift. I was lovable and capable of loving. She showed me love was available. There was no scarcity of love.

Yes, there were many fears. But I could walk through them. I could trust the Universe to lead me to my highest good even though I had no idea what that might entail. Faith was stronger than fear.

Yes, there were many dreams and I could chase them; to spend my days in the sunshine, to run at the beach, to travel, to read, to take time to discover Napoleon. Perhaps someday I would dream of marriage. But for now I would walk my path and each day more would be revealed.

So I let go. I chose to end the relationship, to take a risk and to venture forward. One door needed to be closed before a new one could be opened. And again I wrote a poem.

LETTING GO

The journey to the heart
is difficult to start.

Sex, drugs and rock and roll.
Anything but a glimpse of my soul.

Which path is right?
I'll know in the light.

The separation from my ex-wife,
cut like a knife.

Run, work and hide,
my mind always cried.

Always felt like my hands were tied.
The mind always lied.

I could go and live my dream life.
Then again I could take a new wife.

Hold tight,
with all your might.

Don't sell your soul,
for a big fat money roll.

The journey to the heart,
is difficult to start.

I left for the road thanking Lily for the times we shared
and her gift of Love. Companionship was nice, but at what
price? Yes, it would be fun to share my journey with another, but
Lily was not my match. We enjoyed our time, yet we embraced
different dreams and different visions for our futures. For now
I was to be alone. I left with the knowledge that my heart was
now capable of love again. The gift of "Love".
Thanks Lily.

CHAPTER NINE
STEP IT UP AND GO
"NOVEMBER 1998 – FRESHMAN TERM"

I left Worcester, Massachusetts in The Big W on November 6, 1998, leaving behind the false comfort of security and the illusion of success. I headed north to go south, typical move for me. I had friends in northern Vermont and Burlington was only 235 miles away.

Why Vermont? Over the past few years I went to Vermont many weekends. My good friend Jimmy Day, lived there. Russian Theory Jimmy. I consider him my best friend. He loved me when I felt I was unlovable. He was part of my inner circle. Someone who supported me, encouraged me. A special friend who I kept no secrets from. While many people had negative attitudes and negative advice, Jimmy offered refreshing support. As a result I always felt like a free spirit in Vermont. They call it the Green Mountain State. Jimmy calls it the Switzerland of the U.S. At one time there were more cows than people, I'm told. Jimmy is full of interesting facts like that.

I spent three days in Burlington on Lake Champlain, home of Champ the sea monster. I once competed in a swim across the lake. The previous summer the local YMCA was hosting a swim race across the lake. Eight miles from the shore of New York State to the shore of Vermont. My finishing time was just over four hours. I'm told that the lake has had many shipwrecks due to the battles fought there many years ago. Half way across the lake I felt like there were many souls swimming with me, as if my fallen comrades who made their graves in the water were still treading water. It was a bizarre sensation, which would make more sense later in my journey.

It was nice to see Jimmy as I began my life on the road. He seemed happy with his new girlfriend, Kate. As I left Vermont I began to realize the value of a support system, my inner circle of friends who would encourage me, not pull me down. I was slowly becoming aware how toxic some people could be. So I headed south across New York, New Jersey and decided to visit another friend in Allentown, Pennsylvania.

Don and Patty Kaplin recently bought their first home. Happily married for a few years. They were living their dream and I was living mine. We watched Monday night football. I forget who played, but I'm sure it was a big game. Skeptical and unsure as to what I was up to with my life, they were at least glad I was excited about chasing my dreams. Recently, they had moved to Vermont. I was happy for them and they're great parents to their new daughter Hope.

As I headed south from Pennsylvania to Maryland I stayed a night with my friends, Sean and Dianna. Dianna was a beach fanatic like me. She recently moved up to Maryland from Hilton Head Island, South Carolina. She and Sean were starting their life together in Germanatown, Maryland. I told Dianna that my next stop was Hilton Head Island. Naturally she was jealous. I love to run on that beach. Sean and I used to visit her there. Twelve miles of flat, hard packed, sandy beach. Great for running and biking. Not a beach like it in New England.

After a day's ride of close to 500 miles through Virginia, North Carolina and South Carolina I slept in The Big W at a rest area on Interstate 95 about 30 miles from Hilton Head Island. I had been travelling for a week and all these couples I was visiting had me thinking of Lily.

Once Jimmy and Kate, Don and Patty, Sean and Dianna, and Lily and I had spent a week together on Hilton Head Island. After a glorious beach day we drove 40 miles to Savannah, Georgia and walked around the riverfront. It was a beautiful night. We spent the day at the beach, were all tanned, and had a great dinner. Walking around all the shops I turned to Lily and said, "Anything you want is yours." She turned and said, "Marry me." Wow, were we on different pages. I was thinking fudge, candy, t-shirt, jewelry. "Marry me." She saw the look on my face. The rest of the night was not as romantic. She knew and I knew it was over. We were headed in different directions. We were not a match. The truth could no longer be denied.

The deep heartache was gone now, but being alone was real. I was starting to vacilate between loneliness and solitude. A hunger to be with another and a comfortable feeling of being with myself. Perhaps learning to be alone would be lonely at first. I was happy. I fell asleep, a peaceful sleep. A feeling that where I lie my head is home. I was complete as is. Tomorrow the beach.

CHAPTER TEN
SHOT OF LOVE
"CORRINA"

I awoke at ten on Friday morning (Friday the 13th). I was the last one to leave the rest area. The sun was up. It was a beach day. I think it was snowing back home or at least I hoped it was. The beach was calling. A ten mile run would be fun. Yet, I started to consider skipping Hilton Head and heading farther south. I couldn't get the old haunting memories of my vacation on Hilton Head Island with Lily out of my mind.

"Wouldn't it be sad to go back there? Why go? Why torture myself?" whispered the mind.

"No go," the heart encouraged. "Reprogram Hilton Head. It was yours, Napoleon, before it was hers. Go."

Yes, I would go. I would walk through the fear. My heart voice was guiding me and I was listening.

I made the thirty mile ride to the beach from Interstate 95 East along Route 278 and pulled into a parking lot. As I drove into the lot I noticed a girl. Parking The Big W and getting out I couldn't help but look at her. She was staring at me. Our eyes met and locked. Time and space were irrelevant. Who was this soul?

Soul contact. I have this theory that as we journey through life we might cross paths with some souls only once. What kind of exchange do we want to have? Will it be road rage or an act of kindness? Heated words or gentle encouragement? Do we lend a hand or turn our backs? I love to talk in elevators. Souls trapped in a box of silence.

Corrina, my Carolina sunshine. Our eyes met and took us to a different world, a different lifetime. She noticed my mountain bike hanging off the back of The Big W and suggested a ride. We spent the day together. We biked, talked, and laughed. I invited her to lunch. We hung out around Barnes and Noble Bookstore sharing our favorite books. We talked until two in the morning before parting. I told her of my eventual plans to rent a campsite at the local RV campground on Hilton Head Island and invited her to feel free to come and visit. That night, parked in the bookstore parking lot, I slept tired and content.

I awoke in the morning thinking of this extraordinary woman I had met the day before. It was good to be alone, but my thoughts were preoccupied with Corrina. It wasn't about sex. It was about companionship. I wanted to share my day with her. The night before we discussed my journey in The Big W. She shared that she was bored, and felt stuck in a routine. She was in a relationship that was on-again off-again. She wanted out, but stayed in. She admired that I made a decision and took the action to hit the road and try to discover myself. She was unsure as to what to do with her life. I shared about my past relationship and how we had different visions for our futures. We loved each other, but shared no common vision for a future together. I liked to run and she liked to smoke. I wanted to travel and she wanted to build a home. Parting was difficult, but necessary.

In the local campground, my site was on the water. I paid for three nights, Saturday, Sunday and Monday. Dolphins fed within twenty feet. I counted three. My favorite animal is the dolphin. On my left ankle I have a tattoo of a dolphin. Got it back in '96 after swimming the Waikiki Roughwater Swim in Hawaii. Newly divorced, I went to visit friends and try to heal. I always wanted a tattoo. Thought it would be a shark, a manly tattoo for a swimmer. However, when I was a halfway through the 2.4 mile swim race off Waikiki Beach, a pod of eight dolphins swam by. Minutes later a lone dolphin swam past. This dolphin had cut from the pod. He didn't swim with the pack. Years later I would read Sergio Bambaren's book *The Dolphin, Story of a Dreamer,* and think of that swim fondly. A dolphin tattoo, that's what I would end up getting as a reminder of that period of my life that I survived. A reminder that it is okay to swim at a distance from the pod. It's okay to chase your dreams. Later I would see many more dolphins as I ran the beach at Hilton Head, but for now I was content at my campsite in The Big W.

Corrina was a different kind of woman than I had ever known. She wanted to travel. She biked. She was a runner. She loved bookstores. She wrote poems. She liked butterflies. Who was this woman? Would I see her again? I was so glad I didn't listen to the fear whispers of my mind and head farther south along interstate 95. My heart had guided me safely to this experience. There seemed to be an attraction beyond my control and beyond reason.

I went to the beach and ran. I love to run and hear the crunch of shells beneath my Nikes. To this day, that sound reminds me of Corrina as we would eventually spend many days running together on the beach. The sun was out, the water was warm, and I felt free. My favorite place is the beach. It nurtures my soul. To sit and stare at the ocean is better than any sitcom on TV. Some of my favorite beaches in the states are the many islands from North Carolina to Georgia, the north shore of Oahu, Naples, Florida; Anastasia State Park in St. Augustine Florida; Laguna Beach California; the Gulf Shores in Alabama, Destin, Florida; and Key West. I love the ocean. Perhaps I was once a pirate.

The beach is beautiful to me. Sand, sun, blue sky and the ocean. I can sit for hours and read in the sun, observe and people-watch, run for miles, or just work on a tan. What amazes me the most is that beauty abounds and no one is preoccupied with the death all around. Yes, death. Birds feeding off fish. Shells once homes of living creatures scattered everywhere. Crabs, jellyfish, and other sea life washed ashore. Fisherman stalking dinner. The cycle of life and death overshadowed by the playground of tourists. No obsession with success, possessions, or death. Just the natural rhythm of the Universe – birth, life, death, and rebirth.

Later back at my site in The Big W my thoughts are of Corrina. Will I see her again? Then a knock at the door, it's her.

CHAPTER ELEVEN
IF DOGS RUN FREE
"JUNIOR TERM—THE BIG W AND A
DOG NAMED DYLAN"

Dylan and I spent the summer of 2000 in Barre, Mass., at a local campground called Coldbrook, preparing for my junior year travels. Coldbrook is located in the hometown of my children Joey and Sara who live with their mother Liza, step-dad Paul and baby-sister, Holly. We enjoyed our summer golfing, swimming, playing "catch of the day and home run derby", playing chess, watching movies, reading, and evening campfires with marshmallows. It was a magical summer filled with baseball games, basketball games, football practice, birthdays, trips, and performances.

Leaving New England, our ultimate destination would be Albuquerque, New Mexico where some friends were gathering for the Labor Day 2000 weekend. From there the journey would reveal itself day to day. But for now we had two weeks of roads to get there.

Dylan is a great companion. I didn't realize how much work and what a commitment a puppy would be. I was the victim of the great dog illusion of TV and the movies. Fortunately, once again friends recommended several books. Most helpful in Dylan's training were the two books by the Monks of New Skete entitled, *How To Be Your Dog's Best Friend* and *The Art of Raising a Puppy*. However, it was Elizabeth Marshall Thomas's book *The Hidden Life of Dogs* that allowed me to truly grasp the wisdom Dylan would begin to share with me. His insights were usually precise and to the point. Our relationship blossomed as we spent our days and evenings enjoying each other's companionship.

Having a new companion required some lifestyle changes on my part. No longer was I sleeping late. No, Dylan was up at seven a.m. and ready to relieve himself, eat, and go for a run. During his mid-morning nap he encouraged me to write.

After a summer with full hook-ups of water, sewer, and electric for The Big W we were spoiled. Life on the road was once again a reality. Conserve our limited water supply, make sure the interior light batteries were charged and begin keeping an eye open for toilet facilities.

Campsites are a luxury on the road and not the norm. Searching for a local Wal-Mart becomes a game. Sam Walton and his stores philosophy is to be trucker and RV friendly. Often we awake with a half dozen other RV's and truckers in the lot. A lighted parking lot, often open 24 hours, and most of all – restrooms. To the road wander Wal-Mart is like a Hilton, a Hyatt, a Marriott, or a Sheraton.

Hot showers, now there is a treat. Normally, one is just grateful to find a shower post at the beach. Cold. But great for ending a day and beginning an evening. I once went 21 days without a hot shower. Considering at one time in my life three showers a day wasn't out of the question – a wake up shower in the morning, a post run shower in the afternoon, and a before going to bed, clean up/relaxing shower. My needs were changing. Cold showers and warm soda were both wet and refreshing. On the road I was discovering simple living with simple needs, honoring the resources of the planet and recognizing what my true needs were.

Strangers no longer seem like strangers on the road. I've been told I talk with too many people. In addition to my "soul contact" theory, there is my "road talk" theory. As one travels alone, entertained by the never-ending chatter and noise between the mind and heart, talking with anyone is a welcome relief. Lastly, it is a great way to find the local shortcuts, hot spots and not-to-miss sites. Who made the talking rules anyway?

Bumper stickers are my newly acquired addiction. For the past two years where ever I roamed a new sticker was applied to rear of The Big W. They are a great source of meeting souls for road talk. I've become quite an expert at locating just the right logo to represent the memory of the newly visited location. Gas stations, tourist attractions and local express food marts are ideal. I enter, scan the store, locate the rack, and listen to the heart. Usually the appropriate sticker just reaches out and grabs me. I'm sure I could quit collecting them anytime I want, I just don't want to. No denial here.

The journey of the road is different this time out. Prior to my maiden voyage I received mostly negative feedback and doubt. People thought my dream was crazy and that I should just settle down and live out the script. Now, after two years of actual travel under my belt, those same people seem to expect me never to come off the road. In the beginning people questioned me and had negative comments like "Why are you bumming across the country?". To keep my perspective I would respond, "That's your adjective. I'm on a spiritual adventure." Now, as Dylan and I travel, people are saying, "I want your life" and "I'm going to do that some day". We simply respond, "Why wait? Create and embrace your life now, live your dreams, whatever they may be."

So after spending the summer with the luxury of a campground, Dylan and I left New England on August 16, 2000 and headed south recapturing the life from the road. Me in the driver seat and Dylan riding shotgun with a grin on his face as if to sing, *"Stay free from petty jealousies, live by no man's code, and hold your judgement for yourself, lest you wind up on this road."*

CHAPTER TWELVE
STANDING IN THE DOORWAY
"CORRINA'S RETURN"

Corrina was beautiful beyond words. She had returned. My heart was racing. Not just a physical beauty. Rather, her soul shined through her face.

She stood in the doorway and simply said, "Hi."

"It's great to see you again. Did you have trouble finding me?" I said somewhat nervously.

"No, I just followed my heart."

"Come in."

We spent the night talking. I made coffee. We listened to music. We talked of dreams. We captured the magic of our first day. It was like we were in our own world, our own universe. We laughed the night away. It was a joy discovering each other or was it a rediscovering of each other?

We agreed to meet again tomorrow afternoon. Sunday would be my last chance to see her as she had planned a week-long trip to New York City to visit her sister. The trip was arranged weeks earlier. She wanted time away. Time to clear her head and make a decision about her relationship. She was tired of the on-again off-again status. She would be flying out of Savannah, Georgia Monday morning for a week-long break. I of all people could understand her need to go away and reflect. I slept in peace. Who was this angel? This familiar soul.

Sunday was another beach day. Corrina arrived as promised and we played. We ran together on the beach. We laughed continuously. We read books in the sunshine. I invited her for dinner. Our last night together. She accepted. Dinner in The Big W is never very fancy, but always tasty. Salad, rice and beans. She loved it. She was a vegetarian. My menu was perfect. After dinner we talked of our meeting and of our new friendship. I wanted to kiss her, to hold her, but I held back. She didn't. The night stood still. The stars were out and we held each other for hours. Finally, she had to return home. Parting was unpleasant. I could have held her for eternity. I told her if she decided to make a go of it with her boyfriend I would respect that and love to just be her friend and if she ended it I was available to further discover us. I was totally aware of how genuine this felt. I had no hidden agenda. We kissed goodbye and I was alone.

Monday morning I awoke and watched for her plane overhead. Blowing a kiss upward I wished her luck on her journey and a peaceful resolution to her dilemma. We created memories I would cherish forever.

For me, it was another day at the beach. I would stay on Hilton Head until Wednesday. Then it would be off to Atlanta to see my friend, Tim Hogan. Travelling inland 300 miles wasn't appealing, but Tim was expecting me. Monday night I went to see the movie *Meet Joe Black*. At the end of the movie Anthony Hopkins' character, Bill Parrish, in discussing life with "death" played by Brad Pitt, turns to Joe Black and says, "Its hard to let go. Isn't it?"

"Yes it is Bill", responds Joe Black.

"Well that's life. What can I tell you?" says Parrish.

Life is about letting go. I agreed as I let Corrina go. Friday, Saturday and Sunday we shared and then she was gone. If that weekend was all that we ever shared, I was grateful for it. I would remember her always, but for now I would journey on trusting that the unknown held my highest good.

CHAPTER THIRTEEN
I DREAMED I SAW ST. AUGUSTINE
"COMPANIONSHIP VS. SOLITUDE"

It's about 300 miles from Hilton Head Island, South Carolina to Atlanta, Georgia. Three hundred miles away from the nearest beach. Withdrawal would be short and painless. Besides, I was only a days drive from the coast.

Before leaving I shaved my head. What a freedom. My hair is curly and dark, sprinkled with gray on the sides. However, there is a small patch in the back slowly disappearing. Baldness runs in the family genes. Being clean shaven felt good. Liberating in a strange way. No more "hat head". This was a good travelling look. Low maintenance. No preoccupation with a mirror. It always looked the same. Plus, as I grow older I never wanted to be tempted to do the dreaded "comb over." Acceptance would be the key.

My stay in Atlanta was from Wednesday through Sunday. Tim and I hung out, ran together at Kennesaw Mountain, and even caught an Atlanta Falcons game at the Georgia Dome. Most of all we talked of the women in our lives or should I say the women we met, fell for and had to let go of. Like my fascination with Corrina, Tim was dreaming of a woman named Peggy from Colorado. We both had to let go and trust the Universe to orchestrate our highest good. It felt good to share with someone who was having the same experience. Tim would always say, "She's got it all." I would nod and agree and he knew I meant Corrina and I knew he meant Peggy.

The highlight of my stay was staying overnight at the fire

station. Tim was a fireman and invited me for a night at the station. He worked 24 hours on, 48 off. They called me "the rookie" and all during dinner talked of the rookie's responsibility to do the dishes. Southern fried chicken and biscuits—dishpan hands would be a small price to pay. They had two calls that night, but I slept like a baby and missed the whole thing. Tim has never let me forget it.

One day while Tim was at work I read Nicholas Spark's love story, *Message in a Bottle*. Tim had read it, enjoyed it and recommended it. This was to be a pattern in my travels. People would suggest or pass on books that would reach out and speak to my soul. The Universe Librarian seemed to know exactly what I needed to read. Often as I travelled I would read about what I was experiencing or I would experience something I was reading about (soul school-playground earth). In the book *Message in a Bottle*, the main character is stuck in the past grieving a lost love and as a result he misses the chance to love again. A warning I would heed as I thought of Corrina.

From Atlanta I headed southeast along Route 75 to Route 10 in Florida to Route 95 to the Florida coast. There is nothing like the Florida sunshine to a boy from up north during late November. In northern Florida just off Route 95, they sell the biggest grapefruit I've ever seen. I purchased a bag, had two and studied my maps. Which beach to explore? What did I want to create? Which course to take? St. Augustine looked good.

Pulling into town alone, I was beginning to understand and becoming comfortable with solitude. A quiet peace, an enjoyment of ones' own company. My heart didn't ache. It had been weeks since I even thought of Lily and my thoughts of Corrina were not thoughts of desperation but of treasured times shared. Loneliness had vanished. I was content.

I slept in the square at the center of St. Augustine, which was all in lights for the Christmas season. The advantage of The Big W is its length of twenty feet. She fits in a regular size parking space and for the most part no one bothers me during the night. Eventually I would learn of the town's history, of Flagler College, the historic lighthouse and the fort built on the harbor's edge to protect the town.

Tuesday morning I discovered Anastasia State Park. Securing a campsite within the park, I planned to spend three nights. Like Hilton Head Island the beach consisted of hard packed sand ideal for running and biking. The added bonus was discovering that vehicles were allowed on the beach at the driver's risk. High tide traps a few northerners each year. The Big W looked right at home on the beach. Ocean front property with a million dollar view. Rice and beans never tasted so good.

As the sun set my heart began to whisper, "Corrina would love it here. Call her." She was back from her trip to New York City by now and on Hilton Head only 150 miles to the north. The mind kicked in, "Why call her? She is back with her boyfriend. Besides why would she visit you?" Listening to the heart I made the call about eight in the evening.

She seemed hurried and couldn't really speak. She arrived home the day before but hadn't been able to talk with her boyfriend or should I say ex-boyfriend. She had decided to end it. She took the number of the payphone and said she would call me back at eleven, could I be at the phone? *Could I be at the phone?* Of course I could be at the phone. I was tempted to wait the three hours right then and there.

The Big W was a mess so I decided to head back and clean her up. It only takes a few minutes. Everything in The Big W has its place. If not secured it will be airborne as we travel the road. After cleanup was a little reading and a few entries in the journal (a new habit I was beginning to acquire and enjoy). Time was moving slowly, literally crawling. Finally, eleven o'clock arrived and the phone rang.

Corrina caught me off guard. She was sixty miles south of Hilton Head on Interstate 95 in Georgia heading towards Florida. She was coming to visit and needed directions. Here was a woman after my own heart. She had left without directions knowing she would find me. Something I would have done. She said she would be here in less than two hours. She couldn't wait to see me, hold me. As my thoughts were of her, hers were of me.

One a.m. she pulled into the campsite. She was single. She had broken the news to her boyfriend. He half expected it. According to her it wasn't very emotional. We stayed up until five a.m. talking, hugging and kissing. It was awesome to see her again. She could only stay two nights including the one we just stayed awake through. Exhausted, we fell asleep in each other's arms in The Big W.

I awoke to her tickling me and staring at my eyes inches away from my face. A morning wake up routine to be played daily in time. It was around ten a.m. and I was on coffee detail. We both drank it black. She would eventually buy me my first French Press, one of my few prized possessions. By eleven The Big W was situated on the beach and Corrina, Sadie and I were enjoying our morning run. Sadie was Corrina's two year old black lab. Lots of energy. The three of us ran, swam, played, laughed and enjoyed the sun. Over dinner as the sun set on our waterfront lot she told me of her decision to end her relationship. She said meeting me helped make her decision easy. She was tired of being in a state of indecision. She felt she was settling for less. Seeing me travelling in The Big W inspired her to take action. She knew in her heart it wasn't the right relationship for her but always ignored her inner voice. As I was chasing my dreams she wanted to chase hers. Imagine that, I was a power of example. Lastly, she shared that she couldn't stop thinking of me. Music to my ears. It seemed as if we were on the same page. "Who is this person and why are they in my life?" was a question we both were struggling with.

We stayed up late that Wednesday night around the campfire. We talked of dreams of travel, of adventure, of running the Boston Marathon together, of living on a boat and sailing the east coast, of building a home on a stream in Montana. Tomorrow was Thanksgiving Day and she needed to head back to South Carolina for her family's celebration. By seven a.m. Thursday morning, she was on the road travelling north and I was alone again.

I thought of our last talk. We discussed her joining me on the road in The Big W. We seemed a match made in heaven. A love of the beach, running, biking, reading, travel, and adventure. Spiritually we seemed to be seeking the same path; honor and listening to the inner voice of your higher self. Physically we both loved the outdoors and staying fit. Emotionally, we wanted to love and be loved in a caring way, not a care-taking way. We seemed to share similar visions of life.

Then the voices.

Was this an opportunity to grow, to learn, to share the journey or was it a copout? Was I abandoning my solo adventure? Did the Universe bring us together or was it self-will? A fear-based decision so as not to be alone or a faith-based decision to let the lessons of my life unfold? Should I ignore our newly found friendship or should I see if our love could grow deeper? I've enjoyed being alone. I've enjoyed the solitude, but companionship had its merits too.

I remember reading Hermann Hesse's book *Siddhartha* and how the seasons of a man's life change and unfold as he seeks his spiritual path in life. I identified with his dreams and the restlessness of his soul as a youth and how he lived many lives within one lifetime. He spoke of going into the world to lose oneself as something that could not be taught, but rather something that must be experienced.

Was Corrina to be a new season? We seemed to share similar dreams. The heart urged me to let the love flow. I picked up my pen and journaled. Sometimes I just write and see what appears on paper. This is what was written:

Invite Corrina and I to experience each other and the wonders of life. Yet, at the same time acknowledge we each have a journey and our own lessons to learn. As long as we support each other's journeys, we can love.

My heart was open. I wrote her a poem.

CORRINA

The stars are out tonight. My heart is filled with light.
So many thoughts I want to say, please come out and play.

Do you think of me? Souls are meant to be free.
Why can't we chase a dream, a lover, a boat, a stream.

Too many rusted rules, do I look like a fool.
I want to dance in the rain. There is more than resurfacing
pain.

It's all about joy, a girl and a boy.
Spirits to support, nothing bad to report.

It's about passion, not clever fashion.
Lovers and friends to the end.

CHAPTER FOURTEEN
I WANT YOU
"TWENTY FOUR DAYS"

We left together in The Big W from Hilton Head Island on December 1, 1998. I had been alone on the road less than one month and now had a companion. Actually, two companions; Sadie joined us. The ride from Florida to South Carolina to pick up my fellow travelers seemed strange. Once again I found myself heading north to go south.

Our plan was to go to Orlando. I was registered for a Tony Robbin's seminar called, *Unleash the Power Within.* UPW for short. It was a four-day seminar and then we were off to the east coast of Florida heading south one beach at a time. We were in search of adventure, the sun and the beach.

In Orlando we stayed at a friend of Corrina's. It worked out well as my days began at nine a.m. and ended well after midnight.

The seminar timing was perfect. *Unleash the Power Within,* was exactly what I had been trying to do. My friend, Dean Lewis, from southern California had arranged a scholarship for me before I left New England, as he felt it was something I needed to experience. How right Dean was.

Friday night I completed a twelve foot firewalk. Yes, that's right: a firewalk. Twelve feet long, eight inches wide and three inches high of red-hot burning coals. Really, it was just a symbolic achievement of what one can achieve with the proper "state of mind". The remainder of the seminar on Saturday, Sunday and Monday focused on reprogramming one's mind.

Identifying the limiting beliefs instilled in our minds, creating new limitless beliefs and recognizing the power of our thoughts in creating our reality. It was as if this entire weekend was orchestrated just for me. Then again, perhaps I wasn't alone in my struggles.

I no longer questioned my decision to leave my job, break up with Lily, or invite Corrina on the road. I was co-creating my destiny with the Universe. I was responding to my heart and chasing my dreams. I was discovering my true higher self. The adventure wasn't just the road, but rather the journey to self. The tugging on my soul and the voice of my heart were real. I began to wonder if perhaps I even manifested my divorce on some higher level.

Corrina and I left Orlando and arrived at Cocoa Beach for two glorious beach days. We gave each other space and enjoyed our time together. We nurtured each other. We were falling in love. She taught me to boogie board, surfing on a small board while on your belly. I was in a relationship with a beautiful soul and I wasn't losing myself or giving up my dreams. We traveled, we played, and we loved. It was if we had known each other forever.

At Corrina's suggestion I read Marlo Morgan's book *Mutant Message* about her three-month journey with an aborigines tribe and the lessons she learned. I was most fascinated with their concept of the soul journey. She shared, "All humans are spirits only visiting the world. All spirits are forever beings. All encounters with other people are experiences, and all experiences are forever connections." Corrina shared that we are not humans having a spiritual experience, but rather spirits having a human experience. I was to learn that more would be revealed.

Richard Bach entered my life. Not in the flesh, but his words. His book, *Jonathan Livingston Seagull* reminded me of my own journey. People question you when you fly away from the flock. In his book *Illusions,* Mr. Bach declares, "Argue for your limitations and sure enough they're yours." "No limits" became my saying of the week. I would silence the doubts of my mind and scream "NO LIMITS". I was beginning to believe that no one had it as good as me. I deserved the best and would settle for no less.

Corrina and I ventured farther south and rented a campsite in St. Sebastian Inlet. We went fishing and cooked our dinner on the campfire. The stars were out and after a month of getting to know each other we made love for the first time. We played and explored.

Looking back as I fell deeper and deeper in love with this woman, I never thought of "together forever". I only thought of the day, of the time we were sharing. I was loving like I had never loved before. I was enjoying our season, and it seemed like our season for this lifetime. Wherever it took us, whatever we did, all would be well because our souls would always find each other. Strange thoughts like these were filling my head, or was it my heart? I would often lay with my head on her stomach in a state of bliss.

Our days in Vero Beach, Stuart and Fort Lauderdale were all the same, yet totally different. Eventually there was a cold spell and we decided to head for the Keys. More beaches. More running. More reading. More love making. More adventure. In Key West we found a butterfly store that Corrina couldn't stay out of. As I was fascinated and drawn to dolphins, she loved butterflies. We watched the sunset nightly. One day we raced together in a 5k road race. We cooked oatmeal in the mornings with real Vermont maple syrup and fresh fruit. We shared books on the beach during the day and music, thoughts and dreams at night. Mealtime became a sacred time we shared together. We created our own dishes such as White Man's Mexican (Salsa, rice and black beans) and Mainland Hawaiian (tuna, rice and pineapples). I was in love. I had risen from the depths of my divorce to the heights of passion.

We spent the first twenty-four days of December, 1998 together on the road in The Big W. Then we had to part for ten days. I had made arrangements to fly home for Christmas and be with my children Joey and Sara. Corrina would go home to her family. My friend Jamie and his wife Charlene lived and

Plantation, Florida and graciously allowed me to park The Big W at their home for the holidays. As I flew north to the snow, Corrina rented a car and drove to the Carolina's. She would pick me up at the Fort Lauderdale airport on January 4th and we would resume our road love adventure.

CHAPTER FIFTEEN
THE TIMES THEY ARE A-CHANGIN'
"LETTING GO IN LOVE"

My ten-day visit to New England was awesome. Joey, Sara and I celebrated Christmas of '98 with a shopping spree on the day after Christmas. It was their idea. Sara felt I wouldn't have to mail any presents from the road and they could shop for everything they didn't get the day before. I have never been a big fan of the Christmas season. I let the commercialism get to me. The marketing of gifts makes me sick. Buy, Buy, Buy. Keep up with the Jones's. If you don't have one of these you are less than. The TV ads screamed, "Hey loser. If you don't have this you are a nobody." No I would rather give a gift from the heart on my own timetable, not some date on a calendar. Was it defiance or individualism? Either way, it was how I felt.

Our day shopping was magical. I was a big believer in creating magic times. Quality over quantity. I never wanted to be a Tuesday-at-McDonald's divorced dad. Our time together was always precious. Their mom had remarried the previous April and their step-dad and I each met different needs for them. Our divorce was a turning point for all of us. My ex-wife remarried about four years after we separated. I wish her the best and hope she is happy. The children naturally stayed with their mother after our divorce. My "soul journey" theory of parents and children is that at some point in the lives of their children, a parent must recognize the child's individual soul journey and must release that child trusting the wisdom of the Universe to lead them to their highest good. For most, this probably doesn't occur until they leave the home between 18 and 21. As for me it happened much sooner.

Sara loves dolphins and wants me to move to Hawaii so she can attend the University of Hawaii and we can be close. Joey loves sports and plays basketball, baseball and football. His favorite game is to play "catch of the day" with the baseball. I throw just out of his reach and he makes a leaping, amazing, game-winning catch. While I don't meet their day to day physical needs, I do meet other needs. I am their father and feel I have a great responsibility in helping them develop a solid sense of self, to believe in themselves and their dreams. However, in order to do this one must have it. As the saying goes, "you can't give away what you don't have." Thus, the urgency of my own journey and discovery of my true self. But for now we celebrate the holiday season together.

As for the "reason for the season", I never had a problem with Christ. As a matter of fact I admire him greatly. A wanderer at heart, he seems to love to be near the water, feeds his friends, defended a prostitute while others condemned her, tips over tables in the marketplace expressing his true feelings, likes to hang out with fisherman, lives a life of simplicity, understands the value of forgiveness and enjoys a good story. He rubbed elbows with kings and tramps alike as if the external trappings of a man were of no importance. He spoke of love and seemed to practice what he preached. My favorite theme of his is his insistence on becoming childlike. The innocent hearts and minds of children, free from programming and polluted thoughts and fears directing the mind and smothering the heart. Childhood; when time was for play, and the world was full of wonder to discover. My favorite picture is as he cries in the garden pleading with his old man. Yes, he is someone I can identify with. A revolutionary, he walked his own path, spoke of love, and died a criminal's death at the hands of his frightened fellowman.

So we filled our days with sledding, snowball fights, movies, and hockey games. We hugged, laughed and just hung out. It was ten days of joy, ten days of magic.

I landed in Fort Lauderdale as planned on January 4th, 1999 and Corrina was waiting for me at the airport. We spoke only twice on the phone. Both of us were excited to get back to the life we had created for ourselves during our 24 days in The Big W. We visited Jamie and Charlene in Plantation, Florida, moved into The Big W and headed to the Keys.

Twelve days after being reunited I sensed something was wrong. Corrina denied it. Things were not the same. The weather was mostly cloudy. No beach days. First I was sick and then Corrina was ill. The life we had created in December eluded us. Something deeper was happening. I sensed it. Did we enter the work stage of our relationship? Was the honeymoon over? Something was wrong. Finally, two days later, Corrina shared with me.

She loved me but couldn't ignore a small voice whispering from her heart. She said her whole life she either depended on her parents or had a man in her life. She didn't want to leave me, but her heart was urging her to spend time alone. My emotions were mixed. At least now I knew my sense of dread was real. Something was different and it wasn't just the weather. I was sad thinking of her leaving, but I was joyful that she recognized her heart voice. I realized I loved her enough to let her go. I didn't need to cling. I didn't need to play the victim. I wanted nothing but her happiness, even if that meant leaving me.

I recalled the day I wrote in my journal about inviting Corrina to join me in The Big W. I had written:

"Invite Corrina and I to experience each other and the wonders of life. Yet, at the same time acknowledge we each have a journey and our own lessons to learn. As long as we support each other's journey, we can love."

Yes, as long as we support each other's journey we can love. Support was a choice and her journey seemed to be leading her away. Would I support her?

We decided to split up. We spent a week together grieving our pending separation. We made love for the last time. We held each other and cried. It was if we were two souls in one body of flesh. She would honor her heart and I would honor her. She would always remain special to me.

Coincidentally, she checked her email and had a job offer in the food industry back on Hilton Head Island and a female friend who was looking for a roommate. She accepted both the job offer and offer to room with her friend. Was it a coincidence or was the universe at work?

She left on January 22, ten weeks from the day I met her back in November. Now I was alone. Not a desperate loneliness, but a physical aloneness. I accepted the ending of our season. Some days I cried, but most of the time I just thought of her and smiled. I reflected on the lessons learned and the special love we shared.

They say life repeats itself until we get it right. When my ex-wife suggested a separation, I pouted and played the victim. I pushed her away with my neediness. Did I really love her or was it a selfish, self-centered love? I was immature and childish. With Corrina perhaps I had matured. I could love her and not have to cage her. I was capable of a higher love. My whole life I had known only conditional love. Do better in school, wear the right clothes, have the right hair cut, hang with the right people, say the right things, and you will be loved.

I was given a copy of Chuck Chamberlain's book *A New Pair of Glasses*. Mr. Chamberlain had difficulty comprehending a loving God, one who loved him unconditionally despite the awful things he had done. He describes how, when looking at his children he couldn't imagine anything they did that would stop him from loving them. He realized he would always love them with no conditions. He had a new perspective, a new pair of glasses. I realized God's love was constant with no conditions. Nothing I do will make him love me more and nothing I do will make him love me less. He loves me the same today as the day I was born.

Change your attitude, change your world. What I was unable to do with my ex-wife I was able to do with Corrina. I could let go in Love. I could love her unconditionally with no strings attached. My love did not depend on it being returned.

Did I master a lesson? I was grateful for all we shared. We had a special bond. We were both teachers and students. She taught me that I didn't have to settle for less, I didn't have to lose myself, I didn't have to give up my dreams. I could love. Lastly, I realized I would have built a life with her. I believed in partnership again. I valued companionship.

I wrote a goodbye poem.

You and I have a secret.
It's a secret that cannot be shared,
because it cannot be explained.
The secret is: "You and I".

I think of her whenever I see a sunset or a butterfly.
Thanks Corrina.

CHAPTER SIXTEEN
MOST LIKELY YOU GO YOUR WAY AND
I'LL GO MINE
"TIME ALONE"

It would be a lie to say that I never thought of her. Daily I missed Corrina, but still felt connected. As if our days together in this lifetime were over but we would be reunited again somewhere, somehow.

I settled into a new routine, one of morning coffee, reading, running, beach time and lazy days alone in southern Florida. I was invited to a campout being held at Jonathan Dickenson State Park on Super Bowl weekend by some friends of mine and decided to investigate. It would be good to see some friends and just hang out by the campfire.

It was my first weekend alone after Corrina's departure and I intended to spend my nights that way; single and alone. Time to reflect, time to grieve, and time to heal. I was doing a great deal of reading about love, lessons learned, and soul mates. I was most intrigued by the recurring concept that one attracts those people into one's life that will best teach us our lessons. My mind said Corrina was a distraction not a teacher, while my heart spoke of the lessons of love learned. Either way, I was determined to spend sometime relationship-free exploring my feelings.

There were about forty people at the campout. Tim Hogan from Atlanta and Jimmy Walker from Denver both flew in. Everyone camped in tents in a large circle around the campfire. Off to the side The Big W was like a large hospitality suite. The woman loved the indoor toilet facilities and the fresh morning coffee and oatmeal were a huge hit. It felt nice to have friends visit my home.

My resolve to remain single was challenged immediately. Jane was her name. She flirted and I tried to ignore her. I had met her briefly the year before in Washington D.C. She was dating my friend Reggie at the time. They had since broke up. Reggie was now dating Johanna, a woman from southern California. Reggie drove from Denver and Johanna flew in from Los Angeles for the campout.

As I rejected opportunities to flirt with Jane she finally said, "Why are you afraid of me?" It was about midnight and I was actually preparing for bed. Alone. When she questioned me she looked me right in the eyes. I couldn't look away. I wasn't love struck, rather I was truth struck. I was indeed afraid of her. Immediately I had a haunting memory of meeting her in D.C.. It was a slow motion memory. I remember our encounter and looking in her eyes. I recalled a terror came over me. My soul was terrified of this woman. I was conscious of it now but not then. Instead of brushing her question off and dismissing it as stupid, I found myself saying, "Yes. I am afraid of you. I'm terrified and I don't know why." She suggested we talk. Talk we did. We stayed up until five a.m. sharing.

Jane is a beautiful woman and while most men admire her outer beauty, they consider her somewhat crazy because of some of her beliefs. I became attracted to her inner beauty and those beliefs that others scoffed at. She talked of the journey of the soul and soul mates. She talked of her journey and the inner healing she had experienced based upon overcoming childhood traumas and abuse. We talked of my fear of her, discussing the possibility that perhaps we had conflicts from another lifetime. I hadn't really considered other lifetimes. This one seemed liked it had enough conflict to be sorted out. My mind raced to downplay it. Yet my heart reminded me of my love relationship with Corrina and the strange feelings of familiarity I felt when with her. It was clear that I felt like I knew Corrina before and my terror of Jane in my soul was real. Somewhere deep within my soul I recognized her and was frightened. She said people come into our lives to teach us lessons, share love or resolve conflicts from other times. I was slowly becoming aware of this.

The flirting began again. Unresolved issues from another lifetime or not, meeting her at the campout presented me with an opportunity to master a lesson now. I had decided to spend my nights alone enjoying all the campout had to offer. Clearly, I needed to make a decision now in this lifetime about my current destiny for this evening. Do I jump into bed with a new companion or do I honor my need for solitude? Naturally, my mind was in favor of the immediate gratification offered in this new encounter. My heart whispered, "No. Be alone".

I chose a new path, a higher road. I spent the weekend alone, free from emotional entanglements and sexual gratification.

Jane is from Naples, Florida, and I told her of my plans to explore the gulf coast in March. Perhaps I could look her up and we could talk again. Somewhat fearfully I took her name and number. While my need for solitude was real, I was strangely comfortable with the awareness that our paths would indeed cross again.

Sunday afternoon after the campout my friends Jamie and Charlene Strauss from Plantation Florida, had a Super Bowl party at their home. They had two young daughters named Marena and Kalysta, ages three and one. Additionally, they had two dogs, Levi and Bonnie. Levi Strauss, that always cracks me up. Marena loved The Big W. Whenever I flew home from Florida to visit Joey and Sara I would leave The Big W at their home and usually spend a few days visiting with the Strauss's both before and after my flights. They had a lovely home and large fenced-in rear yard for the dogs. I was the only one to swim in the pool in the winter months. Not sure if it was the northern blood or just a bold adventurer. Charlene always had morning coffee brewing and Marena would wake me up hoping to have a breakfast of raisins in The Big W. Eventually, Jamie and Charlene bought an RV after watching me come and go from there home for a year. Marena named it the Stuffy Old Bear.

Tim, Jimmy, Reggie and Johanna were at the party. I remember watching Reggie and Johanna at the party in each other's arms looking in love and thinking "I want that". Unsure if it was my mind or my heart speaking, I just thought of the road not realizing the power of that thought at the time. Tim from Atlanta and Jimmy from Denver naturally had a bet on the game. Denver beat Atlanta and John Elway retired. The country cheered. I had missed the last three months of the NFL season other than my Falcons game in Atlanta with Tim. Three months with no television and I was amazed at how insulted and offended I felt viewing commercials. It was as if every ad depicted men as childish, moronic, idiots. My senses were awakening.

Relationship-free and travelling in The Big W for the month of February I was reading, writing, running, and reflecting about my adventure of the road and of the spirit. My feelings alternated between the comfort of solitude and the bitterness of loneliness. I had days of peace and contentment and days of fear and isolation. I read somewhere that solitude is feeling one with God and loneliness is feeling apart from God. I was also realizing as Mr. Storr's stated that one's desire for solitude doesn't necessarily translate into the ability to spend time alone. My love for Corrina only seemed to grow as I let her go. Books began to speak to my heart and nurture my soul.

Iyanla Vanzants, in her book *In the Meantime,* spoke of how relationships end when the divine purpose has been fulfilled or the divine season comes to an end and how not all relationships are "The One", that some relationships are valuable as "In the Meantime" teaching relationships. They help us discover the truth about who we are and what we are looking for. Both Lily and Corrina had taught me much about love. As I traveled I would learn more. I understood now that one can accept our seasons with another and let go in love or we can resist and hang on too long, most likely only causing each other pain and destroying the memories that could have been cherished for a lifetime. Ms. Vanzant also talked of inner bells and whistles. How often when we meet someone we ignore red flags or warnings of incompatibility because of our deep desire to be with another. The need for love and companionship is real. Lastly, she suggested that love is about sharing yourself with another, not about giving up oneself for another. I would comprehend more about this further along in my travels.

Depak Chopra, in his book *The Seven Spiritual Laws of Success,* spoke of the wisdom of uncertainty. Allowing the Universe to orchestrate our highest good. There is a divine plan. Control is an illusion. There is no need to struggle. Rather acceptance will lead us to our higher good. Each moment in our loves prepares us for the next moment. There were no accidents. Release the need to know the outcome and let the journey unfold. Trust and listen to one's inner voice for guidance.

Mitch Ablom's book, *Tuesday's with Morrie,* reminded me of how teachers appear in our lives and why I began my journey in The Big W in the first place. Morrie spoke of creating one's own culture. A culture that supports and makes one feel good about oneself. I was creating my own life, my own definition of success. I didn't want to grow old and look back with regret with having not chased my dreams. As Mr. Ablom admits, he traded his dreams for a paycheck and was now questioning the wisdom of his choices. No, I wanted to make each moment count. My heart was leading me to my true self. I was learning the lessons of my life as I lived my dreams.

I thought of the *Unleash the Power Within* seminar I completed in December and how Mr. Robbins stressed how our thoughts create our reality. I was reading more and more about this concept and starting to embrace it. Believe in love and love. Believe in loss and lose. Mr. Robbins spoke of how our values influence our decisions. He believed decision-making was easy when we knew what we valued. What did I value? What were my beliefs? Why did my relationships with Lily and Corrina end? Was it part of a divine plan to teach us lessons or did we simply have different values that made us incompatible for a long-term relationship? What was I trying to create with my life beyond life on the road? Who really was I? Did this time of solitude that I created offer me the opportunity to reflect, to discover, to decide what I value and stay focused on it? I entered the following values in my journal:

Spiritual condition value – To honor my path, my journey, my soul, my inner heart voice. Recognize the journey of my soul, the big picture of life. Identify those people, places and things that distract my soul development and those that support my spirit. Eliminate negative emotions, energy and people from my life. Honor truth, as only the truth will lead me to my deepest desires.

Health/fitness/nutrition value – To honor my body, the home of my soul, my vehicle for this life. I recognized that I enjoyed being fit. Exercise was important to me. I receive both physical and emotional benefits when I run, bike or swim. Nutritionally I became aware of how certain foods effected my overall well being. Food was fuel for my body. If I hang around junk food long enough I will eat it. Rest was important. Getting enough sleep helped my emotional state of being. I would try to surround myself with health conscious people. Recognize that my physical well being effects my spiritual well being.

Financial value – To honor the principle that I make all my financial decisions. I chose to spend recklessly or responsibly. Do not want to live pay check to pay check with the bondage of debt. Live within my means. Live simply, believing in the flow of abundance.

Climate value – To honor my need to be in the sun and near the beach. Growing up in New England I adjusted to the cold. Today I realize that a warm climate helps both my physical needs and my spiritual needs.

Children value – To honor my needs as a father and the needs of my children. At the most basic level I have a financial responsibility to Joey and Sara. On a higher level I have an obligation and I need to be a role model, to encourage them along their spiritual journey to learn their lessons. Make our time together quality time, magic time. To nurture in them a sense of self, a belief in themselves, and a belief that they are worthy and capable of living their dreams.

Travel value – To honor my need for adventure. I enjoy seeing the world, going to new places and trying new things.

Self-improvement value – To honor self-improvement, physically, spiritually and intellectually. To read, to write, to become aware of who I am , what I like, and what are my dreams. To nurture my sense of self. Recognize that the learning never ends and all events in my life, good and bad, offer an opportunity to learn about myself.

Friendship value – To honor the value of the importance of an inner support circle of friends, people who support my journey rather than discourage me. Avoid toxic people. Who shares my philosophy of life? Who do I enjoy being with? Avoid those caught in dysfunctional systems. Remember you tend to adopt the beliefs, values and actions of those you hang around with.

Romantic companionship value – To honor my need for a partner with a similar vision of our future together, similar goals, similar dreams, similar lifestyle. Someone who honors my soul journey and their own soul journey. Do not want to lose myself. Do not want to be a caretaker. Want to love and be loved. Want to support each other's growth but not be responsible for that growth. Want to recognize the need for solitude in a relationship. Lastly, try to remember that I can't find Ms. Right by sleeping with Ms. Wrong.

Lifestyle value – To honor the principle that a lifestyle is created, it just doesn't happen. Value the freedom to live my life on my terms; not trapped in a 9-5 existence. Recognize what I value and when I overextend myself or behave recklessly I lose clarity, focus and vision and get distracted from what I value and from my dreams. I am the only one who can live my life. I am responsible. There are no victims. My time is my time. I must make my own decisions and I must take the action. Practice self-care and listen to my heart voice, it will lead me to my highest good.

Wow! I did have some values. These became my new

standards to live up to. Sometimes they would be directly in conflict with each other. I valued time alone and I valued companionship. I valued a warm climate and I valued my children living in New England. I enjoyed a good cigar after a pizza as much as good run on the beach. I was learning what made me happy and what led to unhappiness in my life. Could I someday find a companion with similar values? My heart was speaking these truths and encouraging me to pursue and honor this part of my discovery, challenging me to live up to these value ideals and find happiness. Yet my mind was telling me they were nonsense, "Go home. This is stupid. You'll never live up to this." I journeyed on while the battle of the voices continued.

CHAPTER SEVENTEEN
ON THE ROAD AGAIN
"DYLAN'S FIRST SWIM"

Dylan was born for the road. He wasn't concerned that each day as he went out to find his marked territory he was hundreds of miles deeper into the journey. He simply marked new territory.

As we headed south out of New England we traveled fast. Well, as fast as The Dub would go. It was approximately 1,100 miles to Atlanta. We decided this would be our first stop on the way to New Mexico for the Labor Day 2000 weekend. Why Atlanta? Love of course. But, I'll go into that later.

We traveled 16 hours and covered eight hundred miles sleeping somewhere in North Carolina along Route 85. Our decision to go to Atlanta meant not exploring the outer banks of North Carolina. Beaches to be discovered at another time.

We awoke around eleven, had baked beans for breakfast, and found the road awaiting our return. By noon the sun was bright and thoughts of a run were tempting me to pull over. We drove 200 miles and near the last exit in South Carolina found Lake Hartwell State Park.

Dylan was now four months old. Still a puppy. But a runner at heart. A two miler was his personal best. At eight minute miles, this was only 16 minutes of running. We completed the run with his eyes upon the fresh water lake. Drinking it at first, he eventually splashed around. This would be his first real swim. He had seen the ocean before, but seemed timid around the waves. I vowed to let him discover the water on his own. So at Lake Hartwell, I dove in and he followed.

At first I thought he was going to drown. He naturally did the dog paddle. Every few seconds, he would stop and begin to sink under. I let him find his own rhythm and love of the water. For a half hour he dove in and ran out. The sun was shinning, the run felt nice, and Dylan had his first real swim.

It was a simple pleasure and a simple day. I was formulating my "Demand Theory". Keep your demands simple and the demands upon you will be simple. What more did we need? A sunny day, a good run, plenty of food in The Dub, and a full tank of gas. So often we get lost in a world of demands. We work just to pay for the unnecessary stuff we think we can't live without. Simple needs, simple demands, that was the life to create for myself.

Dylan was a new companion on the road. We were alone at the lake and enjoyed the solitude. Yet at the same time I felt his companionship. I thought of the last couple of years on the road and the many moments similar to this, but with no one to share it. I thought of the relationships I experienced, the places I visited, the lessons I mastered and how far along the journey to self I had actually come. There was no need for words, he just looked at me as if to sing, *"Ah, but I was so much older then, I'm younger than that now."*

CHAPTER EIGHTEEN
I'LL BE YOUR BABY TONIGHT
"MARCH IN NAPLES"

I made it to the gulf coast of Florida for March 1, 1999 as planned. Looking up Jane, I wasn't sure if it was because I was longing for some companionship or if I was being drawn to her as the result of some conflict from a past life to be worked out as she indicated at the campout. I discovered the beaches of Naples and I discovered more about myself.

Jane and I began a stormy one-month relationship immediately. We dated and I stayed in Naples for the month of March. Parked in her back yard, but sleeping in her bed; more lessons were revealed from the road. On one level I sensed we were not a long-term match. I couldn't decipher if my heart or my mind was encouraging me to stay. I just felt there was something here to learn, so I stayed open and available.

She suggested I read Dr. Brian Weiss's books *Many Lives, Many Masters* and *Only Love is Real*. Both books were about the lessons Dr. Weiss learned conducting past life regressions. I found them fascinating both reflecting on my relationship with Corrina and with what I was experiencing with Jane. Dr. Weiss suggested that all relationships happen for a reason, a season or a lifetime. This concept applied itself nicely to the principle of attracting relationships in order to learn our lessons. However, now I was considering multiple lifetimes of lessons and partners. Life was about growing and some lifetimes offered more growth than others. Dr. Weiss discussed soul mates and soul groups. Souls find each other in various lifetimes to help each other master lessons and discover the true nature of one's higher self—LOVE. My mind tried to remain closed, as my heart whispered, "Stay open, Evolve."

Reflecting on Corrina, I knew we had enjoyed a special season and it felt like we had experienced each other before. As I thought more and more about the relationship I began to have the oddest sensation that Corrina was my mother in another lifetime. I know it sounds strange but I remember how we played like mother and child, how she would wake me up in the morning, how I felt when I rested my head on her belly and breasts and how mealtime was a sacred time as she taught me to cook. Everything was so familiar. I thought of how our eyes met and time stood still. When we parted, she encouraged me to continue on my journey like a mother sending her son into the world to grow up. My mind dismissed this notion as absurd, while my heart gloated like it knew a secret I would someday understand. In the end I wasn't left bitter and full of self-pity, but rather in a state of anticipation of our next season in another lifetime. Often when I would run on the beach or sit and watch the sunset I would say out loud, like a child calling for his mother, "CORRINA COME PLAY WITH ME." I remember writing in my journal to her:

"My tears no longer sting and when I run the crunching of the shells still sing. While my body is not near you, my soul will always feel you. I love you."

On a poster in Jane' s home was a poem entitled *Some People,* reminding me of Corrina. It goes:

Some people come into our lives and quickly go.

Some people move our souls to dance. They awaken us to understanding with the passing whisper of their wisdom

Some people make the sky more beautiful to gaze upon. They stay in our lives for a while, leave footprints on our hearts, and we are never, ever the same.

Another saying (untitled) near Jane's bed reads:

True love cannot be found where it does not truly exist.

Nor can it be hidden where it truly does...

Corrina and I would always love each other for the rest

of this lifetime and perhaps in another. I wished her nothing but happiness as she traveled her path. For now I would walk mine.

Jane's friend Tom Bright and I connected immediately. He had a love for books and a thirst for spiritual enlightenment. He spoke of our spiritual journey not in the context of learning but of remembering. Our soul came into this world and would eventually leave this world. Our physical body was a vehicle for the soul to evolve through a human experience. Was I discovering and learning about my higher self or was my heart helping me remember my true nature? Over time he suggested many books. Two I immediately read were Betty Eadie's *Embraced by the Light* and Dr. Raymond Moody's *Life After Life*. Yes, there was more to this life than accumulating wealth. The journey of the soul was real. The road and "Soul School-Playground Earth" was my present reality. I would embrace each moment and learn my lessons. Each day brought a stronger awareness of my soul's journey. I became focused on the big picture and not stressed out by the details of the little picture of daily life. My new saying of the week became, "Life is good, enjoy the ride."Jane still terrified me, but I was being drawn to her. Would this soul leave footprints on my heart? What lessons could she teach me? Did we have unresolved conflicts from another time or was she simply a new season in this lifetime? Dr. Weiss suggested that relationships are not measured in time but rather in lessons learned.

We fought constantly. It was one continuous power struggle. I had never been in a relationship where you fought all the time. In the past I always tried to avoid confrontation. Deep down I was afraid if I fought I wouldn't be loved. Gradually I became aware that conflict resolution leads to greater happiness. It was better to put issues on the table and discuss them than pretend that they do not exist. Jane and I discussed issues daily. I constantly felt under attack. I was learning about boundaries and wasn't buying into shame tactics. At one point I was so frustrated with the dynamics of the relationship that I left Naples telling her, "I'm going to Key West. I can't take it anymore. This is not what I'm looking for and I don't care if we have unresolved issues or not."

I was impressed with her persistence. I spent my days at the beach in Key West and at night I parked The Big W in the Publix Food store parking lot to sleep. One night as I was laying in bed around nine p.m., thinking of my days running on the beach in Naples and the glorious sunsets over the Gulf of Mexico, there was a knock on my door. Apparently, the customer service desk received a call from a Jane asking if there was an RV with Massachusetts plates in their parking lot and if so could they tell Napoleon Zimmerman to please call Jane from Naples. I was impressed and made the call. Jane had read Ms. Vanzant's book and said I wasn't "The One", but was an "In the Meantime" relationship and should come back to Naples. I drove the 200 miles back the next day and never regretted it. Jane would teach me about the lesson of self-care.

The fighting continued. It was humorous. To be fair I must state we did have some good times and I did love her in a special way, but I never felt like I fell in love with her. Our days consisted of sleeping late and having coffee in bed. I cooked us oatmeal for breakfast after getting my morning run on the beach completed. We played at the beach and shared ideas. Most nights we were up late watching movies or fighting about something I did or didn't do. She had me read Richard Back's books *The Bridge Across Forever* and *One*. She claimed I was a "Richard" and she was my "Leslie". To tell the truth we were both "Richards" in my opinion. She rented several movies she said I must watch. The first was *Sliding Doors* starring Gywenth Paltrow and the second was *Made in Heaven* starring Timothy Hutton. Both were about destiny and soul mates and encouraged me further along my journey. The movies combined with my readings and experiences were altering my concept of soul mates. Up until now I was a victim of the romantic notion of finding that one soul mate. Now I was starting to believe that perhaps we had many soul mates in our soul group and shared many lives assuming many roles in assisting each other in our spiritual evolvement. Additionally, Mr. Bach left me wondering, did each decision we make create alternate realities for us? Were we all creating our own destinies one decision at a time, one moment at a time? And what of time and space? Was my past, present and future, all occurring simultaneously? Could each self meet? Was my soul evolving and learning multiple lessons in multiple lifetimes?

Many people seemed distracted and unaware of their spiritual natures. I was glad to be awake and aware of the journey. I was becoming more aware that as a society we were so preoccupied with our physical needs, we ignore our spiritual needs. Upon awakening we shower, dress, eat and charge out the door, never getting spiritually centered. We worry, stress, and manipulate our fellow man, never considering that perhaps we can be of service to each other's souls. Caught up in man's plan, we forget the divine plan. What started out as love turned quickly to "taking each other for granted". Instead of loving each other and supporting each other's spiritual journeys, we cling to each other for security, for comfort, and for familiarity. When our expectations aren't met, we became bitter and childish. What about our spiritual natures?

I would begin to try to look at people in the context of their soul development or soul awareness, recognizing we are all at different points in the journey. No one was better than or less than, just more enlightened, more aware, more awake. Life wasn't about the accumulation of toys it was about the journey to self, the realization of our higher self, our souls. The saying, "You can't take it with you", was taking on new meaning. People cling to material possessions for security, numbing our awareness of our soul's journey. Our minds are scripted, our hearts are ignored, and our dreams are laughed at. When did we forget our dreams? When did we lose the wonder of childhood? Richard Bach spoke of learning and playing. My new saying of the week became, "LEARN AND PLAY", soul school-playground earth. Later it would become "Love, Learn, Play and Dream".

The negative voice of my mind was silent for now and my heart was in charge. I was committed to this journey and realized only the truth would set me free. Each day I would read, sit by myself and journal. The journey within the journey was real. I was co-creating with the Universe.

Jane and I continued our daily struggles. To make matters worse she had now changed her tune. No longer did she consider me an "In the Meantime" relationship, now she was telling me I was "The One" and should wake up before it was to late. I did enjoy the companionship but my heart knew she was not "The One" for me. I loved her, but was not in love.

Ironically, even prior to our meeting we had both planned on spending Easter weekend in Chicago. My friend, Bobby Coonan, was hosting a bash over the weekend and many of my friends from around the country were flying in. I flew to Atlanta from Naples and drove up to Chicago with my friend, Tim Hogan. While many would question the wisdom of this travel strategy, I valued the time Tim and I would share on the road. Jane flew from Naples to Chicago. Upon her arrival on Thursday, April 1st, our problems began. Apparently, I wasn't paying enough attention to her. We finally had a fight and broke up. She said I didn't love her like she loved me. I told her she was right. Yes, I loved her but wasn't in love. I'm not good with ultimatums and she declared that if I went to hang with my friends it was over. I walked and it was over. Things only got stranger as Jane ran from friend to friend discussing who knows what. I felt alone and vulnerable, but at the same time felt no need to defend myself or attack her. Eventually, one by one my friends approached me and shared that they loved me. Imagine that. Jane eventually slept with a friend of mine that Saturday night. Perhaps he was "The One". Actually, Dan approached me and asked for my blessing as things with Jane and I were now over. At the time I didn't know how to say, "No, Dan. It's not alright. I thought we were friends." Instead, I played it cool, detached myself from my feelings, and said rather manly, "Sure no problem."

After the weekend I made it back to Naples to retrieve The Big W and hit the road. Jane insisted that I give her another chance, that I should wake up and realize how special she is.

My mind actually entertained this. My heart said, "Go. Its about self-care." So I learned a valuable lesson, one of self-care. People will abuse you if you let them. People's actions speak louder than their words. My friend, Eddie encourages me to "listen with my eyes". Only one's self can practice self-care.

What had happened to my value list I had written only one month ago? Sometimes our need for companionship is so strong that we neglect ourselves and what we value and dream of. I still think of Jane. Our season was turbulent and short but she led me deeper into my discovery of myself, my soul journey, the concept of soul mates and the purpose of this lifetime. She taught me the value of self-care. I love her and wish her the best. Perhaps in another lifetime things will be different, but for now another teacher and student must part.

Thanks Jane.

CHAPTER NINETEEN
DRIFTER'S ESCAPE
"RUN BABY RUN"

I departed Naples and drove the 100 miles across "alligator alley",
Route 75, to Plantation, Florida to Jamie and Charlene's home.
I do not believe I was running from Jane, but rather taking care
of myself. It was time to move on, to start a new season.

It was April 10th and the running of the Boston Marathon
was nine days away. I was in pretty good running shape and
thought I'd give it go. I completed the race in 1984 and 1985 and
running it again was always in my plans. I had a plane ticket to
New England and a visit with the Joey and Sara planned. I spent
a week poolside at the Strauss's and reflected on my journey
and lessons learned. It seemed my life was alternating between
time alone with room for reflection and time with a companion
giving me the opportunity to discover more about self through
contact with others. Soul School–Playground Earth was like a
college co-op program: time for study and time for practical
application. I guess if you want to learn how to drive you have
to get behind the wheel of the car at some point. Textbook
knowledge was good, but life experience was real.

Lily taught me that I could love again. Though not a match,
the love we shared was real. Life wasn't over after my divorce. I
was lovable and capable of loving. I didn't need to live in fear. I
could risk loving because love was real. Corrina showed me how
to let go in love. I could enjoy the seasons of love relationships
as they entered my life and when over I could let go in love and
gratitude, awaiting the next season. I no longer had to play

the victim and pout, but rather I could accept the gift of love and recognize that the real gift was in the loving, not in being loved. Jane opened my eyes to the possibility of other lifetimes, expanded my awareness of soul mates loving and assisting each other along the path to self, and to appreciate the value and responsibility of self-care. These interactions with other souls were part of my process in discovering my true nature and highest good. The reprogramming of life long held limiting beliefs was well underway. Not all love was the "together forever" kind. Teachers, lovers and friends were all around. But for now it was again time to be alone.

My friend, Gill Breech, had an apartment in Worcester, Mass., that he let me stay at on my visits home. Gill had moved to the area from Georgia and had been there three years. Currently, he was dating a local woman and never stayed at his apartment. It worked out well for me and became somewhat of a base of operations when up north.

The Boston Marathon is unique in two ways in addition to being the most prestigious marathon in the world. First, you need to qualify. This means one must run another marathon under a certain time limit for one's age group. Second, the marathon caters to bandits. I would be a bandit with no number and no qualifying time. This meant also that I would be at the back of the pack in a special area with about 2,000 other outlaw runners. It was a hot, sunny day, which was fine with me, as I had been running in the heat all winter. Other runners were not as fortunate and the weather along with the 26.2 miles of pavement between Hopkinton and Boston, Massachusetts was an additional hurdle to contend with beyond the distance of the race. Fifteen thousand ran: some for prizes, most to realize a dream.

I ran a 3 hour and 50 minute race. Felt great for twenty miles, questioned my sanity at mile 23, and floated to victory over the last mile. A personal victory, another goal achieved. As a kid I used to watch my dad run while standing at the ten-mile mark of the race. Every year I would say, "Next year I'm going to run." Next year would come and I would find myself at the ten mile mark, repeating my pledge from the year before. While I made the decision to run, I never took the action to train for marathon day. Another victim of aimless dreams with no plan of action. The "talker" versus the "action taker".

My dad and I would have breakfast every Friday. We did this for about a year prior to my venture on the road. Some days we just talked about the Red Sox, while other days we shared a little deeper and grew as father and son. During my visits home from the road we make it a point to meet on Friday for breakfast like old times. I used to kid him that he was responsible for my wanderings. Growing up we spent many weekends and all summer at my parent's vacation home on Cape Cod. Splitting my time between different homes became natural. Now home was were I laid my head.

This week at breakfast we discussed how the marathon is like life. One has to pace himself for the entire race or he will burn out fast. A quick sprint for a few miles won't assist much in reaching the finish line. Many drop to the sidelines after shining for a moment. Furthermore, it requires preparation, determination, commitment, dedication and an honest evaluation of one's self. It's the big picture that counts, not the little picture. The race is run one step at time, one moment at a time. And finally, as Eric Little, the preacher in the movie *Chariots of Fire* says, "Where does the power to finish the race come from? It comes from within." Go within, find the power, embrace your heart, discover your soul, and live your dreams. Run your race.

Corrina and I once shared a dream of running this race together. I mailed her my finisher's medal. I ran for us and I ran for myself.

My visit in New England was for a week. A very busy week. The kids and I played, saw the Red Sox, had breakfast with Dad, and I ran the marathon. Exhausted, I headed back to Florida, The Big W and new adventures in living.

CHAPTER TWENTY
LIKE A ROLLING STONE
"HEADING WEST"

The end of April found me back in Florida. My friend, Matt Vine, from Houston, Texas, was hosting a get together over the weekend of May 1, 1999; a good way to celebrate one year living in The Big W. I decided to drive north along Interstate 75 to Atlanta and pick up Tim before heading west to Texas. Together we shared The Big W as we headed south from Atlanta on Interstate 85 through Alabama and west on Interstate Route 10 through Mississippi and Louisiana on our way to Houston. We played for a day in New Orleans smoking cigars and walking Bourbon Street. The energy in New Orleans felt similar to Key West – everybody just doing there own thing.

While my relationship with Corrina was over physically, his with Peggy was too. Together we loved from a distance and knew they would always be in our hearts. I was grateful for my time on the road with Tim and the sharing the lessons we had learned.

We spent a week in Houston, mostly sunning by the pool. The temperature was in the high 70s – low 80s. The highlight was when Matt brought us all to the Houston Astrodome for a baseball game; my second major league game of the season. Tim flew home to Atlanta after four days in Houston. Jimmy from Denver had flown in to attend the Houston festival and had made plans for me to drive him to Denver in The Big W unbeknownst to me. I agreed and we spent twelve days together on the road playing and sharing about life and love.

Jimmy had seen The Big W at the Florida campout he attended over Super Bowl weekend earlier in the year. He had some vacation time and wanted to see a little of the southwest and enjoy life in the slow lane for a few weeks. Driving west across Texas to New Mexico and then heading north on Route 295, we hit a head wind and averaged 32 miles per hour over a distance of 300 miles. Literally, he was spending time in the slow lane.

One memorable moment occurred when we stopped at a Dairy Queen restaurant for some refreshments. Jimmy was big on snacking. Especially ice cream. It was May 3rd, Joey's ninth birthday. I knew I would be out of town for both Joey and Sara's birthdays and we had a big three way celebration planned for when I returned over the summer. Sara's birthday is June 12th and mine is August 1st. While in the Dairy Queen they had a baseball promotion going on – five dollars for a Nolan Ryan ball. As soon as I saw the ball, I missed Joey. I bought one and gave it to Jimmy and explained that if I was home I'd be giving it to my son. He held me while I cried. I vowed next year I would be home for the birthdays. On a side note, the following year on Joey's tenth birthday I watched him pitch two innings for his little league team. He walked three and struck out six. It was a magical day.

We stopped for a few days in Santa Fe, New Mexico, visiting some friends we knew. Teddy and Nate were both Michigan born and now living in New Mexico. I had met them earlier in the year while in Chicago. Teddy was an outdoorsman. He loved to hunt and fish. Someday he would show me the ropes. Another friend of theirs from Michigan named Alan decided to take Jimmy up on his offer to join us in The Big W. Alan was a tall, thin guy, who everyone called "Slinky". While in Santa Fe Jimmy spent $600 and picked up three boxes of cigars and we found ourselves smoking Feuntes in the morning, Montessinos for lunch, and Avos in the evening. No one had been to the Grand Canyon so we traveled west to Arizona and cooked T-Bone steaks by the great hole in the ground. Between the cigars and red meat, I managed to get a few runs in. Temporarily neglecting myself, I knew in a few days I would be back to rice and beans and daily runs. Hanging with Jimmy often reminded me of kindergarten. I watched as he threw rocks and boulders into the Grand Canyon for over three hours. Some say he's a little manic, I just love the boy in him. We heard of a campout in Joseph, Utah some friends were having so we headed north stopping for a swim in the ice cold water of Lake Powell. Once again The Dub was the perfect hospitality suite and the campout was a blast. After a few days of soaking in the hot springs of Utah it was off to Las Vegas, Nevada. We parked The Big W at the Circus Circus Hotel RV parking lot and explored the pools by day and the casinos by night. The World Series of Poker was being hosted the four days we were in town. Jimmy held his own in a side game for most of the trip, but ultimately made a rather large donation, while Slinky and I watched and tried to figure out the game. After twelve days in the warm weather of the southwest and with the temperature being in the low fifties in Colorado my plans were to continue to the coast. Jimmy took a plane to Denver, Slinky a bus to Detroit, and I steered The Big W to southern California along Route 15 out of Nevada and dreaming of the ocean once again.

California in the middle of May was perfect. I spent my first day at Laguna Beach and that evening I looked up my friend Dean Lewis, from Dana Point, for dinner. After dinner I slept Thursday night parked in front of Dean's house. Jimmy had given me Johanna's phone number. She had since broken up with Reggie and I was thinking some female companionship would be fun. The boys were great, but now I was thinking of quick visit to Mexico and some companionship. Not a relationship, just some female companionship. I mentioned this to Dean and he said he knew who Johanna was. A mutual friend of ours named Lyle Christopher had previously dated Johanna. I was unaware of this and wasn't sure if I should call her. Lyle was a good friend of mine. We had both attended Tony Robbins' seminars and supported each other as we chased our dreams. I decided to call Lyle and run it by him. He assured me that Johanna and he had parted as friends and it would be no problem if I wanted to give her a call. Loyalty to a friend. I remembered when my ex-wife and I split and how many people I thought were my friends began asking her out on dates. Lyle and I chatted for a while and he said he had just read the Dali Lama's book, *The Art of Happiness*. I assured him I would pick up a copy and telephoned Johanna.

CHAPTER TWENTY-ONE
HILLS OF MEXICO
"A WEEKEND OF COMPANISONSHIP"

Johanna was young, 22 to be exact. I was 37. At first I would say, "What is age, when souls are eternal?" Eventually, I would learn the difference. Time. Life's lessons take time to unfold.

I called her on a Friday morning at work and told her I was in southern California and was thinking of driving to Mexico in The Dub for the weekend, and was wondering if she was interested. She was excited to hear from me and told me she had never been to Mexico. I was surprised, I thought everyone in southern California had gone to Mexico at least once. A plan was formulated.

I picked her up after work at her house in Pomona about a half an hour east of Los Angeles off Route 10. We had dinner and within three hours were naked in her bed. So much for just companionship. We agreed sex wouldn't get in the way of our friendship. Denial of course. Sex is just too powerful, I was to learn. We got out of her bed and hit the road sometime after eleven p.m. We made it as far as San Diego and pulled over to sleep. In the morning: Mexico.

It's funny, Californians always say everything is twenty minutes away. In reality, its always an hour and twenty minutes.

We awoke on Saturday and crossed the border into Tijuana, Mexico. The Dub was now an international vehicle. We visited the beaches, had some lunch, and of course walked the shopping district. The big negotiation was for a $75 guitar. Purchased for $25, with a hat thrown in. I'm sure somebody still made a profit, but I was happy with the deal.

We listened to music and shared each other's day. We opened up and talked of our pasts, our presents, our dreams, and who we were. Does sex cloud your vision? Should you talk first, then have sex? Answers to questions like these would eventual come. Sex is indeed very powerful.

Saturday night found us back in San Diego walking the streets and dancing to a lone, romantic, street trumpeter. Sunday we drove back to Pomona and spent the night in Johanna's bed. It was the middle of May and I had plans to drive from Los Angeles to San Francisco along the coast starting on Monday.

I awoke late while Johanna had already left for work. We agreed the weekend was the weekend. There were no expectations by either of us. We shared time, Mexico and her bed. So it was to the north I headed with fond memories of my new friend Johanna, southern California and Mexico. As I drove I had a sense of pride: I was able to spend a weekend with some female companionship and not get distracted from my journey. I was now heading north to San Francisco.

CHAPTER TWENTY-TWO
MAMA YOU BEEN ON MY MIND
"FOLLOW UP WEEKENDS"

Heading out of Los Angeles I took the 5 to the 101. I was in no hurry to get to San Francisco, which was 400 miles to the north. My first stop was Santa Barbara. I was pleased to find a beach parking lot with a few other vehicles parking overnight. In the morning I awoke looking out at the ocean, made some oatmeal and did some reading. A few hours later and I was ready to explore. My favorite method is running. It's amazing what you can see and learn about a place on a run.

As I ran along the coast, my thoughts were of the past weekend. I wasn't in love. But I certainly enjoyed playing. I was very comfortable with Johanna. It was nice not to be needy and attached. I began to envision a series of playful relationships around the country. Fun, travel, play, sex. No commitment, no attachments, no expectations. Yes, that would be the life. Of course that wasn't how my relationships normally went. Usually, I met someone and there was some type of soul connection, some lesson to be learned. Lily, Corrina, and Jane all had their seasons, all taught me lessons. Yet, separation sometimes brought heartache. Maybe, I had turned the corner. Maybe, I could just play and move on. My mind encouraged this line of thinking; just play and travel on. My heart whispered, "Be careful."

Wednesday morning I awoke in Morro Bay. It was windy and cold. I still managed to get a beach run in. My thoughts were more and more of Johanna and the past weekend. I didn't feel that soul connection. I just missed playing. Or was it the sex? I tried not to analyze it.

As it was cold, and not a beach day, I headed north along Route One and the coast. Big Sur offered views of the Pacific unlike the Atlantic coast. In Monterey I couldn't find anywhere to park, so I rented a campsite at the Monterey Pennisula RV Park. A hot shower and campfire would be nice. Later, thinking of Johanna, I decided to give her a call.

It was nice to hear her voice. Like me, she had thoughts of our weekend in Mexico. We both agreed it was nice to play and not feel any pressure. I had left her a copy of Marlo Morgan's *Mutant Message*. She had read it and enjoyed it immensely. Then out of nowhere she suggested that she fly up to San Fran for the weekend. Great idea. Make the arrangements and I'll call you Friday at work so you can let me know your flight information. It was a date.

The next day, still heading north and finding the 101 again, I pulled into San Francisco. I drove straight to the Golden Gate Bridge. I love to run over and back across the bridge looking down on the bay. Plus, I was hoping to park there overnight. No one bothered me and I awoke around eight a.m. with over 200 Japanese tourists flashing photos. Not of The Big W, but the bridge.

Johanna and I spent our second weekend together. We visited with several friends. Daniel was from San Francisco, Marilyn relocated from Pittsburg, Jack relocated from Cleveland and Darren from Vermont. It was nice going to dinner with everyone. Johanna and I played tourist. She had never been to San Francisco. We walked Haight Ashbury, had breakfast in the Golden Gate Park, explored beaches, slept overnight at the Golden Gate Bridge, had chowder at the wharf, and on Sunday we caught a Giants game at Candlestick; I mean 3-Com Park, my third ballpark of the season. I like San Francisco. Its energy reminds me of Key West and New Orleans. Everybody just doing their own thing.

After the game we just hung out in The Big W and were the last to leave. Nearby was a public park. I found an outdoor shower hookup. The water was ice cold. It was a new experience for Johanna. I often would call her a blowdryer babydoll. Perhaps condescending, but true. Later that night I dropped her off at the airport for her flight back to southern California and was on the road heading north.

I had made plans to be in Denver for the following weekend. Jimmy Walker was hosting a little get together over Memorial Day weekend. My plan was to travel Route 80 East and visit friends in Salt Lake City on the way. I headed north, out of San Fran, out of California, across Nevada, and into Utah.

Two days of driving with lots of time to reflect, analyze, and navigate the voices in my head. My mind boasted, " Good job Napoleon, two playful weekends in a row. No commitment. No attachments. No care-taking. Yes, while Johanna is young, she has her own place, a job, friends, money to travel, no expectations, no sexual hang-ups, likes to play and most of all she seems to have experience beyond her years." At least that's the way it appeared. My heart took notice of one difference between Mexico and San Fran. While in Mexico we played and explored new territory for both of us. In San Fran I felt a little pressure to entertain, to play the tour guide. I rationalized that I had been there before so this was only natural. Yet the pressure to entertain was real, and it slightly annoyed me. Later, it would haunt me mercilessly.

Johanna and I talked of our past relationships, lessons learned, and future dreams. Johanna was one year out of a three year relationship in which she was engaged to be married. They lived together, but eventually called the wedding off. In my mind, from what she told me, it was like going through a divorce emotionally. So while she was young, she had been through the emotional wringer. She talked of going to college and having a career. She hoped to someday marry, have a home, and a couple of children. Of course she reassured me that this was not for a few years. For now, she wanted to play and travel. Naturally when she suggested we meet in Las Vegas in a couple of weeks, I agreed. She would drive the four hours from Los Angles and I would fly in from Denver. A third date was in the works.

I visited the Mormon Temple in Salt Lake City, Utah, on Tuesday. After successfully touring the Temple and avoiding the sales pitch, I headed out of town and journeyed across Wyoming. When I got to Cheyenne I turned south along Route 25 and cruised into the Denver area late at night with the bright lights of the city acting as a beacon for those wandering in the Rockies.

Denver in May is ideal for running. Sunny, but not the extreme heat of the summer. Jimmy thought I was nuts spending time with Johanna. He knew of some of her past and was a good friend of Reggie's. Reggie, with a gleam in his eye, just said, "You'll see." The big issue was a legal issue. Seems when I met her back in January in Florida she had just been terminated from her job. The legal aspects had since been sorted out and she was now making restitution and putting it behind her. While my heart whispered, "be careful", my mind assured me it was in her past and not to worry. I didn't push her for details and she didn't volunteer any.

The highlights of my two weeks in Colorado were the running of the Boulder Boulder Road Race in Boulder about forty minutes from Denver and attending an NHL playoff game between the Colorado Avalanche and the Dallas Stars. My friend Peggy (who had dated Tim Hogan from Atlanta) and I ran the road race together. We broke no records, and just had a blast running with 40,000 other runners and finishing in the University of Colorado's football stadium. My friend Christina's dad had season tickets to the Ave's and invited me to a game. Dallas won and eventually went on the win the Stanley cup that year.

While in Denver I met several woman who just wanted to play, sexual play. While I had previously fantasized about this, from the heart came one word: HONOR. Honor what you started with Johanna. She is fun and you enjoy her company. Honor her. Honor yourself. We had plans to meet in Las Vegas the following weekend. Perhaps we had something. I would never know if I didn't honor what we started. I declined the Denver temptations and flew to Las Vegas as planned.

We stayed at the New York New York Hotel for three nights. A mutual friend of ours, who visits the casino from L.A. on a regular basis, made arrangements for us to have a room in his name. If you lose enough money you get free hotel rooms for your next visit. We explored the city at night, tanned at the pools during the day, saw the musical Chicago, and of course lots of sex. Was it lust or love? Confused and blinded we made plans to see each other in three weeks at the end of June.

My friend, Dean Lewis, from southern California was hosting a men's weekend on a few boats off of Catalina Island, 24 miles off the California coast the last weekend of June, which was also Johanna's birthday weekend. My plan was to leave The Big W in Denver at my friend Chris Wheelman's house for the month of June. Chris lived with Reggie who had previously dated Johanna. Their place was a classic bachelor pad. The Big W was right at home in Chris's driveway.

June was a busy month. I flew from Denver to New York City for a friends wedding on the 12th. Craig and Julie were getting married on the Coney Island Boardwalk. I spent a week in the city at my friend Clay Bordo's place on the upper west side. I hadn't seen Clay in a few years. He was originally from Worcester, had moved to San Fran and was now making a go of it in New York City. We went for several runs in Central Park. After the wedding in the city I rode a bus up to Worcester and visited with the kids for a week. Again I was able to stay at Gill's house while he slept at his girlfriend's. As the Catalina weekend approached, I flew back across the country to Los Angeles. I was to spent a few days at Johanna's, go to Catalina for the weekend, a few more nights at Johanna's, and then the two of us would drive her car to Denver for the 4th of July weekend, pick up The Big W and attend a campout in Breckinridge, Colorado, in The Dub.

CHAPTER TWENTY-THREE
TANGLED UP IN BLUE
"RED FLAGS IGNORED"

Red Flags. Red Flags. While my heart pointed them out, my mind ignored them. Was I blinded by the sex? Looking back, I think so.

Things just weren't the same. The playful weekends of Mexico, San Fran, and Las Vegas were a lifetime away. Reality was setting in. Johanna and I were great playing, travelling, and making love randomly. But the pressure of everyday living offered new challenges.

I agreed to visit Johanna at home because I was curious. While I valued my time on the road alone, I also knew I enjoyed companionship. I suppose we all look for a partner. Deep within there is the longing to connect with another, to share oneself and one's adventures, to love and be loved. I was no exception. Perhaps Johanna could be that one. Sometimes we want it so bad we ignore the billboards saying, "turn off at the next exit." My heart tried its best to light the way. My mind rationalized. Romantic love feels good and one will do almost anything when blinded by its bliss. In other, words sex is powerful.

My visits at Johanna's home both before and after the Catalina weekend were tension-filled. For the first time in our relationship Johanna was preoccupied with responsibility and stress. She worked 9-5 plus had to negotiate the L.A. traffic. Money was tight and she lived paycheck to paycheck. Her plane ticket to San Francisco was purchased on a credit card. She had mounds of debt and the stress of dodging the bill collectors. Red

Flag. Red Flag. Her female housemate was uncomfortable with a male visitor in the house and they were having a silent fight with me in the middle. At night she was tired and depressed. Our love making was obligatory and mechanical. Our days resembled little of our weekends on the road. Red Flag. Red Flag. I shared a little with my friend, Rick Wood, about it one night after he took me to a Dodgers Game (my fourth ballpark). He knew Johanna's history and a few of the men she had dated. He encouraged me to enjoy the weekend and get back to the road. He indirectly implied things about her age, her legal problems, and some of the other problems his friends had had with her. I simply ignored what he was saying. We had so much fun on the road and I wanted it to work so badly that I lied to myself.

The weekend with the boys on Catalina was a welcome diversion from the "Process of Discovery" with Johanna. A couple of days on the high seas, fishing, exploring Catalina Island and just hanging with the guys gave me time away. My heart encouraged me to move on. We had fun, but were we really a match? She was young and eventually looking to go to school, get married, have children and settle down. I on the other hand had no nesting instinct at all. Continue your journey, came from my heart. You and Johanna had three great weekends. It is time to move on. Your season is over. My mind fought. Go back, next week will be different. You didn't know what you were getting into. Now you can be prepared. The battle raged within and I kept it all within.

On Sunday after the weekend with the boys Johanna picked me up at the dock in Newport Beach. She looked tired. She was up all night with a close friend talking. Coincidently, this friend was a past lover. Red Flag. Red Flag. I questioned her, but she simply said they were just friends now. TRUST. I lost it in an instant. Deep within, from that moment on, I never trusted her again. My heart knew that trust was the foundation of a solid relationship. Without it there was no chance of success. Did she sleep with her friend? I may never know. But, I would always think she did. I would never trust her again. "Red Flag.

Red Flag," my heart shouted. My mind turned down the volume and home to her bed we went. Blinded by sex again. Red Flag. Red Flag.

That week brought the same tension of the week before. Only now it was worse. No trust. Surprise. Surprise. We had tickets for the Bob Dylan & Paul Simon Concert at the Hollywood Bowl for Johanna's birthday. Each day my heart would encourage me to leave town. Yet I wanted to see the show. I called Jimmy in Denver. He simply stated, "Get on a bus now!!!"

The Dylan show was fantastic. *Time out of Mind,* his latest album was probably just what I needed. That night a true Dylan fan was born. We danced all night at the Hollywood Bowl in the warmth of the L.A. summer under the open sky far removed from the problems of our budding relationship.

Later in the week I finally verbalized to Johanna that I didn't think things were working between us and perhaps I should leave alone. We seem to be a lot different off the road than our time on the road. She admitted that she was stressed and depressed. Things were different than our time on the road and she pleaded, "if we could just get through the week and on the road to Colorado, the campout in Breckinridge would be different." Red Flag. Red Flag. I was proud of myself for voicing my concerns. At least now I knew it wasn't just myself. She knew there were problems too. Why I kept silent for so long would be a lesson in itself.

Breckinridge and Colorado were different. Of course they were. We were back on the road. My world. Time away and time on the road. We weren't one hour out of Los Angeles and the old Johanna was back. We drove the 14 hours from L.A. to Denver in Johanna's Honda Del Sol, singing, talking and reminiscing about Mexico, San Fran and Las Vegas. There was no stress, no roommate, no time clock, just the open road. We stopped and picked up The Big W at Chris's house. It was good to be home.

My friends in the Denver area always had a Fourth of July campout in Breckinridge. Deep in the woods about 75 people gathered in tents nestled in the mountains near a stream. After navigating the dirt roads to the site, The Big W was a luxury suite providing fresh coffee, toilet facilities and a table for the card players. So we hiked, sat around the campfire, made love at night, and played. Things were like old times between Johanna and me. Mexico, San Fran, Las Vegas, and now Breckinridge. Four magical weekends. My mind boasted of success, while smothering the heart's barely audible warnings of "Red flags, Red flags". You have different dreams, different lifestyles, different economic circumstances, and different ages. Sure the sex is great, but what about your journey to your higher self. Conquer the lower self urges and journey on."

The magic moment of the campout was when Teddy Reilly, my friend from New Mexico, took us trout fishing. We caught about a dozen fish between us and Teddy cooked them on an open fire. It was a perfect weekend.

Back in Denver we caught a Rockies game at Coors Field. My fifth ballpark and Johanna's second. The next day, as Johanna was preparing to leave Denver for Los Angeles, confusion was the word of the day. Johanna and I were falling in love. Or at least what appeared to be love. Life was good. But was it her I loved or just having a road companion to share the journey with? We talked of our times on the road and our times at her home. I shared that I had no nesting instinct. I still wanted the road life. I was not willing to sprout roots in southern California, but if she was willing to travel, she was welcome in The Big W. I knew she wanted to go to school, she wanted to get married someday and she wanted children someday. These were not things I was interested in now. Someday maybe. But not now. So as she returned to southern California and I drove east we talked on the phone of her joining me on the road. We had each recently read Antoine de Saint Exupery's *The Little Prince,* and as I traveled she called me her Blue Eyed Price and I called her Flower.

CHAPTER TWENTY-FOUR
WHAT WAS IT YOU WANTED
"FRESHMAN TERM COMPLETED"

The last leg of my freshman term began as I headed east towards New England alone in The Big W. Yes. I left the Denver area in The Big W alone. Johanna wanted to come, but had responsibilities and a life in Pomona to attend to. I would have liked for her to come, but I knew in my heart it was time to drive alone again. I started the year alone and needed to finish alone. This was to be the end of my freshman term on the road. I needed to put some closure on it and reflect on the time I spent travelling and the lessons offered. Perhaps in my sophomore term there would be a companion. But for now, I drove alone.

Two days driving across Nebraska and Iowa along Route 80 and I found myself back in Chicago. I thought of the weekend back in April with Jane. How was she? She introduced me to the idea of multiple lifetimes and had taught me the value of self-care. Did I forget? I arrived around midnight and my alternator had just broken. I pulled into a parking lot of a small retail mall to read a map and The Big W wouldn't start. The alternator light had been flashing. Twenty minutes later The Big W started. Across the street was a full service gas station. I pulled in and parked for the night. By ten a.m. and $158 later I was underway again. I arranged a visit with my friend, Bobby Coonan. Vikki from Nashville was in town and we all went dancing at a local Chicago jazz club called Blue Chicago. During the day we caught a White Sox Game with Kevin Callahan and Bobby

Fricca. It was my sixth ballpark of the season. Bobby shared with me that the summer before he had completed a baseball park tour. He caught at least one game at each major league park in the United States and Canada. Later, I was to share this fact with my son, Joey. A father-son dream had been born. Someday we would complete a baseball park tour together. We tentatively planned it for the summer of 2003 when Joey would be thirteen. Naturally, Sara would join us.

From Chicago I stopped in Detroit. Parked in my friend Amy Shearson's driveway I couldn't convince anyone to go to a Tiger's game. On Sunday I attended the game by myself and then headed east into Canada. It was an historic day. My seventh ballpark and my third country in The Dub.

It took nearly two hours to cross the border as the drug search was conducted. It was the third search of the trip. I guess I fit the racial profile. Young man travelling cross country, older vehicle with too many bumper stickers, no job, no home, two earrings, and Mardi Gras beads from New Orleans hanging from the mirror. My first search was in New Jersey. They kept threatening to bring the dogs. Knowing that I don't use drugs and had no drugs in The Big W I kept saying, "Bring the dogs on." After an hour the let me go. The second search was in Panguitch, Utah, while travelling with Jimmy and Slinky. Parked at a restaurant the police pulled in and began to question us. Not being familiar with the smell of fine cigars, they suspected marijuana and searched the vehicle. Finding nothing but premium Dominican smokes we offered both officers a cigar. They accepted. Three stops, no drugs. Ironically, the only problems I ever encountered on the road were the police. Why? The answer still eludes me.

Travelling east across Canada from Detroit, I eventually stopped on the Canadian side of Niagara Falls for a quick visit as I had been there once before, and then proceeded back into the country. Wearing a goatee, two hoop earrings, Mardi Gras beads around the neck, and a shaved head, the smiling custom agent just winked and said, "Have a good day." I think he liked me. I guess I just fit the profile.

The drive across New York State to Massachusetts was filled with many reflections and projections. What had I learned this past year? What would the summer hold? Where would I go next? Would I travel alone or have a companion? How was Lily? Had she found a husband? Where was Corrina? Was she honoring the voice within and spending a season alone? What was Jane doing? Who was she fighting with now? Was Johanna in my past or to be part of my future? Why had I taken to the road in the first place? What was it I wanted?

Sometimes I feel like I have shed many selves, many past lives within this lifetime. The seasons of my journey led me to who I am today. With each rebirth I am led to my highest good, my higher self. Clothes that were once my identity no longer feel comfortable. Places that were home, feel empty. People who I played with seem far away. Beliefs that once guided my life were no longer embraced by my heart. What did each season have to offer me? What lessons were mastered? What lessons were to be repeated?

Life is an adventure. Change is constant. We are always in a process of discovery and as we journey we must be the masters of our lives, not the victims of life. I ventured to the road to discover myself. Time away, time to silence the battle between the mind and the heart. Yet, the conflict still persisted. Perhaps I was just a newcomer. Solitude alone didn't guarantee the heart's message would be heard. Daily we struggle to be true to ourselves. The programming and fears run deep. When I left Lily, left my job, left my home, and explored the unknown I had made a beginning. My external journey brought me from New England to the southern beaches of Florida, the California coast and Mexico, across the Rockies and the Midwest plains, to Canada and back to New England. My inner journey brought me lessons of love with Lily, Corrina, Jane and Johanna. Freshman term was over and my summer session with the kids was about to start. Yet the tugging on my soul was still growing stronger and stronger. The heart and mind would battle. What was it that I wanted?

CHAPTER TWENTY-FIVE
IN THE SUMMERTIME
"SUMMER SESSION"

After only having visits of a week or so over the past year the kids were delighted I was going to be around for the summer. I rented a campsite in their hometown and we played. We toasted marshmallows, went to Red Sox games, visited my sister's home at the beaches on Cape Cod, swam in the campsite pool, played golf, played chess, set up Joey's VCR in The Big W and watched movies, played board games, and just enjoyed being together as father and kids.

Johanna and I continued to talk on the phone and write each other letters in July. We missed each other and eventually decided she would fly to New England on my 38th birthday in August and we would leave at the end of the summer in The Big W for adventures together. I asked about her dreams of school, marriage and kids, and she said, "Yes they are my dreams, but not for a few years. For now I would love to travel and see what you and I have." We would put the negative times of southern California behind us and would set out to recapture the spirit of our weekends on the road as we created a life on the road.

I told myself there were no wrong choices. There is only my path to walk, only my lessons to learn. I have the power of choice and re-choice. If Johanna and I were in love, we would need to create an environment for this love to blossom. If it was not love, at least there would be new lessons learned. Ignoring the red flags from the stay at her home, Johanna and I began to prepare for the road together. I told her she should save some money, eliminate her debt and have a fall back plan in case she didn't like the road.

By now my dream to write was emerging. I had filled about a dozen journals as I traveled and was now envisioning a life on the road with a travel companion and dreamed of becoming a writer. My friend, Dianna from the D.C. area who loves the beaches, had met Lily, Corrina, Jane, and Johanna. She was like a soul sister to me and was always willing to share her point of view. When I mentioned to her that I was thinking of writing about the road and the lessons of love she responded both enthusiastically and somewhat sarcastically saying, "I can't wait to hear this tale." Others scoffed at my dream as they did when I started my dream of travelling in The Big W. As I dared to say out loud that I was thinking of writing, people just rolled their eyes in disbelief. Why do people fail to encourage each other to chase their dreams?

One of my favorite activities, as I travel, is finding used bookstores, and wandering aimlessly up and down the rows and rows of books. So many books have been written. Why couldn't I write one? Of course I could write one. While the mind encouraged me to believe the eye rollers, my heart said, "Keep learning, keep playing, keep journaling, keep dreaming and keep driving."

That summer I read Rainer Maria Rilke's *Letters to a Young Poet*. Rilke responds to the young poet's question as to whether his works are of any merit, "You ask whether you're verses are good. You ask me. You have asked others before. You send them to magazines. You compare them with other poems, and you are disturbed when certain editors reject your efforts. Now (since you have allowed me to advise you) I beg you to give up all that. You are looking outward, and that above all you should not do now. Nobody can counsel you, nobody. There is only one single way. Go into yourself. Search for the reason that bids you to write; find out whether it is spreading out its roots in the deepest places of your heart, acknowledge to yourself whether you would have to die if it were denied you to write. This above all – ask yourself in the stillest hour of your night:

must I write? Delve into yourself for a deep answer. And if this should be affirmative, if you may meet his earnest question with a strong and simple "I must", then build you life according to this necessity; your life even into its most indifferent and slightest hour must be a sign of this urge and a testimony to it. Then draw to nature." These words spoke to me. Look within. Perhaps I could be a writer and support my lifestyle. Looking forward to my sophomore term I told myself I would teach, I would learn, I would play, I would laugh and I would love. Soul School–Playground Earth would continue, more would be revealed. The heart would have to reprogram the mind. Believe and miracles will happen. The heart whispered, "Live your truth."

In July I attended Jimmy Day's wedding in Burlington, Vermont. Jimmy was happy and I was happy for him. As he shared about buying a condo and plans of children, I shared of my adventures of the road and of love. I shared about the romantic weekends on the road with Johanna and the not so romantic times at her home. We talked of the power of sex. He pointed out that the bible said something to the effect, "when the flesh is joined, it must be torn apart." Ouch. The red flags about Johanna or not, Jimmy was always willing to let me walk my path and learn my own lessons. He could tell me, but knew experience was the best teacher and led to true wisdom. No one could learn our lessons for us, we each had to master our own. I realized that as Johanna and I continued to have sex we became more and more entwined.

Does Johanna fit into my path? Do I fit into her path? Do we have an 'our path?' The world of southern California and the world of the road presented conflicting outlooks. I had questions. I had pondered the lessons to be learned. I yearned to travel alone and to play with another, to share the adventures of the road with another and to rejoice in solitude. Johanna would come on the road. I wrote in my journal:

Johanna and I are free to love each other, to have our hearts and souls entwined. To love and be loved. Yet, we each must be true to our inner voice, our highest self. We must honor each other and each other's path. Like a gentle flower, we must hold each other, tend to each other, but if we cling too tightly we will kill each other and our love.

Later, looking back, I wonder if I was foreshadowing our ultimate demise.

A week before my 38th birthday on August 1, 1999, Johanna called and let me know she had moved out of her apartment, was staying at her parents for the final week in southern California and had finished her last day at work. Financially, she had no money and still had about $5,000 of debt. My heart couldn't believe what my mind voiced, "Don't worry we will work it out." On my birthday she arrived penniless, with debt, and no fall back plan. This situation would haunt us over the next several months as I tried to live on the road and she was on vacation.

RED FLAG. RED FLAG. Something was wrong. The woman I enjoyed travelling with in Mexico, San Francisco, Las Vegas and Breckinridge did not step off the plane that just arrived from Los Angeles. No, Johanna was scared. She just left the life she had created and knew so well. She gave up her home, her job, her friends, her family, and all things of comfort. This was no weekend trip, this was a new lifestyle. Reality was setting in for her. She was scared and depressed. It was as if a little girl landed in New England. Why I volunteered to be the caretaker, why I ignored the red flags, why I needed her, why I invited her, why I loved her, why I ignored my heart, would be sorted out over the months to come. For now I did my best to entertain her. RED FLAG. RED FLAG.

CHAPTER TWENTY-SIX
SIMPLE TWIST OF FATE
"RETURN TO ATLANTA"

Dylan likes to ride up front with his head out the window and the breeze on his face. It's hot and within an hour he is dry from his swim and we have crossed the South Carolina-Georgia border. Less than one hundred miles to go to Atlanta and my lover Josephine.

Johanna and I dated for ten months, from May of 1999 until March 2000. Then there was a playful season with Angelina during March and April. In May I was reunited with Josephine.

We had known each other since 1992. Our paths crossed numerous times with no recognition at a soul level. She was married. I was married. She was divorced. I was divorced. Whenever our paths crossed we were always dating others. Then in May, 2000 at a party hosted by my friend, Tim in Atlanta, the recognition occurred.

Like in slow motion our eyes met and I knew. All the previous lovers led me here. All the previous lessons would be applied here and new lessons would be presented to be mastered. There was no sex. There was no come travel with me. There was no move to Atlanta. There was just a knowing. It was time to do things differently. There was a window of opportunity to get to know each other, to share, to laugh, to discover, to not be blinded by sex. But I'm getting ahead of myself.

We shared a weekend together in Atlanta as Dylan and I continued on our journey to New Mexico. Later Josephine would be flying in from Atlanta for the Labor Day 2000 weekend festivities in New Mexico. For now Dylan and I traveled west and as I would write, Dylan, with his head out the window, would sing, *"the same thing that I want from you today, I would want again tomorrow."*

CHAPTER TWENTY-SEVEN
MIXED UP CONFUSION
"SOPHOMORE TERM WITH JOHANNA"

After Johanna's arrival on my birthday we spent three weeks in New England before departing for the road. Joey, Sara, Johanna and I enjoyed the last remaining days of the summer of 1999. We caught a Red Sox game at Fenway. Johanna's third ballpark. Joey was entering 4th grade and Sara 2nd grade. For me it was the road and sophomore term with my new travelling companion.

I continued to journal throughout the summer. But it was just reporting. No creativity. It was as if I was suffering a block. Was it the hustle and bustle of being a dad? Was it my new companion's blues? Was it the energy of New England? I felt trapped, confined, suffocated. I had read Thich Nhat Hanh's *The Miricle of Mindfulness* and was trying to learn to meditate, but was making little progress. Perhaps someday when I stay in one place long enough, I could join a meditation group. For now I would just breathe in and breathe out.

While I cherish the weekends we shared together in Mexico, San Francisco, Las Vegas and Breckinridge, they became a curse. The time spent at Johanna's in southern California and the three weeks we spent in New England pointed out many reasons that Johanna and I should go our separate ways. Yet, I clung to the memories of the times on the road, hoping with an obsession for more romantic times and ignoring the warnings from my heart. Deep within I sensed Johanna was not for me and I was not for her. There were large differences in our beliefs, dreams and visions. Yet my mind persistently and desperately tried to recreate our weekend getaways.

I convinced myself that we were still discovering each other. Looking back I believe I misunderstood our sexual connection and compatibility for love. Believing I was in love, I discarded negative discoveries and focused only on the few rays of sunshine of romantic times we would share. While I was suspicious that this was not a together forever love, I would at least try to enjoy and extend our season together. Was it just a mind trick to numb the heart voice?

My running was going strong and I decided to run the Honolulu Marathon on December 12, 1999. We would travel in search of the perfect beach until December and then fly to Hawaii from Los Angeles for a month, run the race and celebrate the millennium making love on the beach. We, or I should say, I bought two round trip tickets for Hawaii before we left New England.

We headed south and I drove all night. It was real. We were on the road together. Out of New England, past New York, New Jersey and Pennsylvania, our first stop was Rehobeth Beach, Delaware. I awoke Johanna at sunrise. We played on the beach and went for a swim. While I ran five miles, Johanna ran one. She was contemplating quitting smoking and wanted to start running. I thought of Corrina. Was I trying to recapture what I had with her on the road with Johanna? Did I think any companion could replace her? As we traveled, more and more I would make this comparison. But for now we played like our times on the road and the romantic weekends we previously shared.

During the late night drive to Rehobeth Beach Johanna slept. I listened to music and became intoxicated with the adventure of the unknown sacred road. I had left New England again and was becoming alive again. I drove and the words flowed. In the morning I wrote the following in my journal.

PEACE OF THE NIGHT

Peace of the night
Beautiful as sunlight
Lost in my thoughts
My memories have all been bought
Why do I hide from myself, Oh child come out in the
     peace of the night.

Eternal soul from ancient times
Gifts of words that sometimes rhyme
Unlock the mystery of who I am
Bring forth the child and reveal the plan
Oh child shed light in the peace of the night.

Embrace the child and the wild warrior too
At times the path is clear
Yet often clouded with fear
The journey of the soul unfolds
Wondrous stories to be told
Like a bright shining light, Oh child come out in the peace
     of the night.

Somehow in the night, alone and driving my heart began
to speak. There was a voice that would not be ignored. Did this
voice go back to the time of innocence as a child? Who was I?
Where was I going? Why was Johanna here? The road was real.
I knew we had plans to be in California around Thanksgiving
time before our departure to Hawaii on December 1st. Would
the red flags haunt me? Could I stay true to my vision? Would we
grow or go? For now she has no money, no home, nowhere to go.
Learn your lessons. Let the path unfold. Enjoy the good times.
If things don't work out we will be in California in a few months
and you can deal with it then. Nothing like procrastination to
deal with a problem.

Our plan was to head down the Atlantic coast and then
west to Houston, Texas. My friend Matt Vine was hosting a

Labor Day 1999 weekend get together and The Big W was expected to be there. After that we would explore the coast of the Gulf of Mexico from Texas to Key West, Florida.

Heading south we stopped in Ocean City, Maryland. I knew a hotel with an outdoor hot tub we could sneak in and have a relaxing bath in. From there it was Virginia Beach and rinse off showers along the boardwalk at the waterfront hotels. Next, Myrtle Beach, South Carolina for a run and swim, dinner in Charlestown and then we headed southwest across Georgia and onto Route 10 West in Florida. We spent a day in New Orleans and had french toast at the Trolley Stop Restaurant. We entered Texas and drove along the coast. The Big W took its first ferry ride to Galveston. I didn't like the Texas beaches. They seemed dirty and dark. I was told to go farther south where they were clean and blue. I would have gone, but our plans were to meet friends in Houston. So we headed inland as friends flew in for the weekend.

About 30 miles outside of Houston we stopped at a mall. Johanna wanted to get her hair colored. We had been on the road about two weeks. While she was adjusting to a new lifestyle, I was free. The road, travelling, and adventure, made my soul soar. Whatever problems we had I ignored. We traveled and I felt alive. No hot showers for ten days was something I was used to. Johanna was not. Getting her hair done would give her comfort she said. The complaints of life on the road were starting. We pulled into the mall.

The Labor Day 1999 weekend in Houston with our friends was fun. We slept in a real bed and had hot showers in the morning. Everyone loved Johanna's hair and asked how life on the road was treating us. Johanna shared that she had started to run and tomorrow was giving up smoking. I confided in Tim from Atlanta. I told him many of my concerns about my relationship with Johanna. He pointed out that our age may be a major block to the success of our life together. While I had been on my own for twenty years and was looking within for answers as I traveled the road, she was young and dreaming of settling down, getting married, having children, going to school and having a career. Did we talk about any of this before jumping into bed? No. Well, a little. Okay, Tim, I get your point. But, I did tell her I had no nesting instinct. That's why I didn't go to southern California. That's why she came on the road. The sex was entwining and powerful. What had I created? The mind and heart battled. But for now we were together. We were travelling.

At one point all the girls were going out shopping for dresses for the big Saturday night dinner we had planned. Out of obligation, not love, I gave Johanna $100. Red Flag. Red Flag. My friend Dianna, soul- sister Dianna, called me a Sugar Daddy. Ouch. Was that what I was doing? Was I buying companionship? Was I settling for less, so as not to be alone? Was Johanna trading sex for money? These questions really started to eat at me. Could everyone else see it but me? Or did I see it and ignore it?

The road and sex distracted me. Now it was off to the gulf coast. Heading east we left Texas late in the afternoon and didn't stop until New Orleans. We slept on a side street near Bourbon Street in The Big W. During the day we walked around and explored. At night we went to the House of Blues and saw Jim Belushi as he made a guest appearance with The Sacred Hearts. Good jazz, good dancing. We laughed and played. The next day it rained and I took an outdoor shower. Johanna wouldn't join me and just pouted as I told her I had no money to go shopping.

We stopped at the beaches of Mississippi and the Gulf Shores of Alabama. Being from New England, I never really thought of Mississippi and Alabama as beach states. From there we explored Navarro Beach and Destin, Florida. We were having glorious beach days. While I was running 8 to 10 miles, Johanna was building up to 2. She didn't run everyday, but was trying. She had quit smoking for about a week and was miserable. The only times she seemed remotely happy was while sleeping, shopping, or going out to dinner. While I considered the road a lifestyle, she played tourist. I enjoyed cooking in The Big W. She enjoyed eating in restaurants. I enjoyed reading.

She missed her weekly comfort television shows. I enjoyed the challenge of seeing how long one can go without a hot shower. She missed her blow dryer (okay I'll give her that one). While I enjoyed the beach all day, two hours was all she could take. While I enjoyed running, she enjoyed shopping. Sex was the only distraction. It seems all day I would count the reasons why we should end this relationship, why she should just go home to California, and then sex. The inner battle between my mind and heart raged. I now felt like it was my job to entertain her, to fix her, to make her happy. Also, I think I felt obligated. She had no money, no home, and nowhere to go. It was like taking care of a child. And I kept it all inside.

We ventured farther along the Florida coast and explored Treasure Island and St. Petersburg. In Tampa Bay we caught a Devil Ray's game. Johanna's fourth ballpark and number eight for me. We stayed in Sarasota, Venice, Fort Myers and eventually visited my friend, Tom Bright, in Naples for three days.

Tom had a roll-out couch and we stayed indoors. Tom and his girlfriend Hillary lived together. She was pregnant and they were building a home and a life together. From Naples we went to the east coast of Florida to Jamie and Charlene's home in Plantation. Hot showers and a bed. Hanging with the couples Johanna started to talk about marriage, homes and babies. While she was thinking of engagement rings I was thinking of the Keys and the road.

Jamie and Charlene had purchased a used RV since my last visit. Malena, their eldest daughter at age three named it the Stuffy Ole Bear. They had watched me for a year and thought they would try life on the road: a week here and a week there. It was the end of September and they were planning on their first adventure; a 17 day trip to the mountains of North Carolina beginning on October 1st. They said we were welcome to stay at their house if we liked. No, No. The road, the beaches, the Keys, we must be going. We left and caught a Florida Marlins game on our way to the Keys. My ninth ballpark and Johanna's fifth of the season. We stayed in Islamorada, Marathon and Key West. My plan was to stay the month of October in Key West.

But after one day in Key West I looked at Johanna and knew she would never make it. I knew deep within the road was not for her. While my heart was happy to be in the Keys, I knew we had to leave. I told her she looked unhappy. She agreed she was tired, depressed and missed the comforts she left in southern California. Perhaps the road lifestyle wasn't for her. I suggested that maybe we should take Jamie and Charlene up on their offer to housesit. She looked relieved. I justified it, hot showers, a phone and TV for her and a pool for me. After dinner at the Waffle House we drove 200 miles north to Plantation. Jamie and Charlene left the next day; excited we would watch their home and dogs for the next couple of weeks. We played house for seventeen days.

CHAPTER TWENTY-EIGHT
HURRICANE
"PLAYING HOUSE"

Johanna was more relaxed. I knew deep within my heart the road was not for her. Romantic weekends and vacations are easy. Life in The Big W, no frills, but minimum bills, is not for everyone. The lifestyle requires discipline, faith, and a desire for adventure.

Hurricane. Is there a divine plan? Southern Florida got hit by a hurricane after we arrived at Jamie and Charlene's home. The Keys were evacuated but we were safely parked away from the beach and the brunt of the storm. We rented movies and played house. After the storm passed we had our routine of morning coffee, reading by the pool, and afternoon runs. I was re-reading Scott Peck's *The Road Less Traveled*. In it Mr. Peck talked of falling in love, falling out of love, and then making a decision to love.

Johanna and I eventually had to talk about our situation. While I was temporarily happy with being poolside and enjoying my daily reading and running, I was also relieved that I didn't have to entertain her. Video rentals were cheap and they kept her occupied. Johanna was able to call home and reconnect with friends and family. A settlement check arrived at her parents from a car accident she had suffered the year before. She was to receive about $5000. Of course she had about $5000 that bill collectors were hounding her for it.

I was thinking this was our opportunity to end our relationship. I voiced my concerns and eventually suggested that she fly home, pay some bills and keep a little money to find an apartment and job. I asked her if she was happy on the road. She agreed the fantasy of travel and a life on the road is a lot different than the reality. She missed the comfort of a home. She missed little things like being able to bake, watch TV, shower daily, call a friend, get dressed up, and have her own pictures on the wall. She felt like The Big W was my home, my space, and she was only visiting. She was realizing the road was not for her. She asked me if I was happy. I had hit bottom. I let it all out. I told her I felt obligated to take care of her. While I realized that the Universe brought us together for a reason, I felt responsible for her happiness as she had given up so much to be on the road with me. But taking care of her was getting old. If she was hungry she looked to me to feed her. If she was tired she looked to me for rest. If she was bored she looked to me to entertain her. I was disappointed she quit running two weeks ago. Not for me, but for her. I was disappointed she starting smoking again. Not for me, but for her. I was disappointed she didn't really like to spend the day at the beach, but rather only a couple of hours. I felt obligated to take her shopping and out to dinner. To entertain her. To me that was not what the road was about. She seemed always to be depressed and have a negative attitude. Her toxic emotions were hard to be around. It seemed like the only real thing we had in common was sex. We had fun in Mexico, San Fran, Las Vegas and Breckinridge, but the road wasn't for her. I did enjoy driving and talking with her. Often I felt like a teacher and shared what I had experienced in my life. It was fun to teach and share, but entertaining was getting old. Overall, I was unhappy most of the time. Perhaps our season together had ended. Perhaps our season together was only to have been four romantic weekends. She agreed that she had been depressed and lonely and that she was expecting me to entertain her. She started to talk more of marriage, family and of having a home. The road was not for her. She said she loved me and didn't want to leave. She said she gave up everything to be with me. I said we fell in love, now it feels like we have fallen out of love. What do we do now? It appears we have different dreams, different visions. Are we holding on too long? Are we killing each other's spirits? It was a great, honest and open talk. But we took no action.

For me it was the same uneasy feelings I had in June at her apartment, in August in New England at the campsite when she arrived as a scared little girl, and on the road in September. We had watched the movie *Pretty Woman*, starring Richard Gere and Julia Roberts. It was Johanna's favorite movie. I should have realized: Prostitute rescued by knight in shining armor.

Now it was all out on the table. What would we do? Johanna was talking more of marriage and giving up the road. She had begun reading some books on Midwifery and thought perhaps this could be a career for her. But for now, she said she wanted to give the road a try until Hawaii. We decided to keep at it. She paid about $3,500 in bills and kept $1,500 for the road.

For her the decision to stay was based on conflicting reasons. She said that she wanted to be with me and build a life, but also she felt she couldn't go back to California. She was worried she would look like a failure. She said she loved me and wanted to try the road some more. Maybe this time would be different. I made it clear marriage and kids were not on my agenda. Did she not believe me? Did she think she could change me? But why did I agree?

Work. We had reached the work stage of the relationship. I always avoided this. Perhaps there were lessons to learn, relationship skills to master. I was aware of my heart voice. I was hearing my heart voice. Yet that wasn't enough, I was still learning to trust this voice and to express this voice. I committed to speaking my truth within the relationship. You can't go backwards in your evolvement and live in peace. Once the journey to the heart is started, the voice will never go away. You can ignore it, you can pretend it doesn't exist, but it will never be silenced and you will never be happy until you honor it. I recognized that sometimes I withhold my truth in relationships because I think I am sparing the other person pain. But in the long run only the truth will set us free. I recognized that discovering one's truth is different than expressing and living one's truth. I now had the opportunity to do this in the context of a relationship. We had identified many problem areas and now had the opportunity to grow and work through them. I had made the decision to try to love. Dr. Peck suggested that there was a spiritual freedom in a relationship when people have agreed that each is free to leave the relationship, but chose to stay. We agreed we now were choosing to stay but were free to leave. I had shared many of my secret thoughts and would try to love. Yet, one thought deep within still haunted me, "Did she stay because she chose to stay or because she felt she couldn't return to California?" Plus, we did have those Hawaii tickets.

CHAPTER TWENTY-NINE
NEW MORNING
"TECUMSEH "

We stayed seventeen days at Jamie and Charlene's home from October 1st through October 17th 1999. Our time together there was not road time, but enjoyable nonetheless. Johanna had the comforts of a home and I ran and played in the pool. With her newfound wealth and the sharing of inner held secrets and thoughts, the pressure to entertain was off and we felt reconnected. Johanna had read some of Brian Weiss's books and was as fascinated as I was with them. She went online on Charlene's computer and found a one day Past Life Regression seminar to be conducted by Dr. Weiss and to be held the following weekend in nearby Fort Lauderdale. It was $150 per person and she offered to take me. That night I suggested we watch the movie *Made in Heaven,* which I had previously seen while with Jane in Naples. She loved it, but it left me wondering. At the end of the movie the two main characters meet and their eyes lock with a deep recognition that they had found their soul mate. I never had that with Johanna. I felt certain that we were in the same soul group, here to help with lessons of this lifetime, but, lifetime companions, I was not so sure of that. A season of lessons was all I could hold onto. I remember when I met Corrina, my thoughts were, "Oh kind spirit we meet again." I decided to investigate Mr. Weiss's seminar and see what I could learn.

While I didn't recognize Johanna in any of my regressions, I did have a fascinating day. We performed several different exercises.

In the first meditation two men from my past, who had since past away, appeared to me. As a boy of fifteen, I used to caddy at the Dennis Pines Golf Course on Cape Cod where my family spent our summers. I once carried the golf bag of a man named Mike O'Leary. He reminded me of my dad's dad, my grampie. The following summer I would be sixteen and would be looking for my first job. Mr. O'Leary said to call him over the winter and remind him to talk with Mr. Brown from the local supermarket chain. I did and eventually went to work as a bundle boy in the summer of 1977. Mr. O'Leary's face came to me and he simply said, "Napoleon, you were a good boy." Next, Father Fred Hawkins appeared. Fred was a retired Jesuit priest at the college I attended in Worcester, Mass.. After graduation we stayed in touch and he answered many of my spiritual questions over the years. Some I agreed with and some I disputed. Father Fred's face appeared and he simply said, "Napoleon, you're a good man."

In the second exercise we held an object of our partners and told them the thoughts and images that appeared. We were instructed to share any image, no matter how absurd it seemed. I held some of Johanna's jewelry. Gradually, I had an image of a man on a ride-on lawn mower waving a hat and holding a child about 2 years old. I saw a metal clothesline behind him and to the side the asphalt shingle siding of a home. Johanna thought it may have been her grandfather who had died years ago. The image was black and white, but very vivid.

Lastly, Dr. Weiss conducted a guided mediation were he conducted a past life regression. After relaxing us, he told us to descend a staircase where we would come upon three doors. Instructing us to open a door and enter a past life. Immediately, I found myself frantically paddling a canoe. I had big brown hands and large strong legs. I was an Indian. I was sweating, panting, and scared. I could see the water and feel the pressure of the paddling. I was racing back to my village. I arrived and found the village completely burnt to the ground and my family and friends slaughtered. Falling to the ground I wept. I couldn't save my family. **I couldn't save my family**. I was full of sorrow.

Progressing in the mediation I had images of wandering the country, mourning and searching. The regression progressed to the end of that lifetime where I found myself as an old man surrounded by a new tribe. I was a chief and I was happy. Then my funeral. Dr. Weis instructed us to ask for a name. The name Tecumseh appeared in my mind. I had the distinct feeling I was a Seminole Indian somewhere in Florida near the water. As I saw my body lying there my children, Joey and Sara appeared. They were in their present-age bodies. Each spoke and each said, "Don't worry, Dad. We've been together before and we will be together again." And then I was back.

Needless to say this made quite an impression. Had Joey, Sara and I been together before? Had I in the past, like in this present incarnation, been unable to save my family? Was I reliving my wanderings as Tecumseh in this present lifetime? I was filled with a great peace. While physically separated, we would always be together.

Johanna asked if I saw her. I wish I could have said I did, but I didn't.

Shortly after the seminar I went to the library and researched Tecumseh. Turns out he was a highly educated Indian from the Ohio area. He was Shawnee and tried to unite the various Indian tribes as they fought the whiteman as they were stealing Indian lands. He did a great deal of travelling and was a chief. With all my research I never really felt that this great chief was the Tecumseh that I had regressed to. Plus, I had a strong sense that it was the Seminole tribe and not Shawnee tribe. So I let it go for now.

Poolside for another week I began to read some of Shirley MacLaine's books such as, *Out on Limb, Don't Fall off the Mountain, You Can't Get Here From There, Dancing in the Light, It's All in the Playing,* and *Going Within.* I had purchased them for one dollar each in a used bookstore in Denver months earlier. While Ms. MacLaine received a lot of ribbing from the press and society, I was fascinated with her journey, transformation and beliefs. One man she mentioned was Edgar Cayce. I read his biography *There is a River* by Thomas Sugrue and another book *My Life With Edgar Cayce* by David E. Kahn as told to Will Oursler. I was becoming fascinated with reincarnation, soul mates, life after death, and teachers from beyond this plane of existence. More would be revealed.

Eventually, as our pattern was, Johanna and I had a fight about something. I don't recall what it was, but I'm sure it was really important. We sat in silence for a day. I entered the following in my journal:

It is a glorious sunny day by the pool in southern Florida, and we sit in silence. Who will make the first move, to leave the ego, to touch their soul, to love? Has it become a game with no winners, only losers? No scoreboard, no fans, just silence, just brooding. Each mind plays it over and over. Surely each is right, each is justified. To waste the moments. To stop the flow of love. When do we awake from this tragedy? When do we cry no more? How much suffering? How much isolation? Two hearts just words apart, yet worlds apart. A lovers quarrell. A lovers game. Why do we play it? Will it rest? No it has a life of its own. Kill the beast, heal the wounds. When will love reappear? Two hearts, two minds, two journey's. Did we miss the lesson?

The next day it is forgotten. Over coffee I ask Johanna what she would do if we broke up. Her response would haunt me for months. She said, "I would get a one way ticket to California, get my stuff out of storage, find an apartment in Hollywood, start stripping in a bikini club, pay off my bills, work my own hours and go to school." Did she say start stripping in a bikini club? Now school had its merits, but stripping? My stomach sank. I don't know if it was jealousy or a concern for her, but my stomach sank.

Jamie and Charlene returned from their road adventure and it was time for us to leave. I was missing the kids and asked Johanna if she wanted to take a ride north. We could travel slow, visit friends with beds and showers, and see the kids for Halloween. I promised that we would get a hotel room while in New England.

CHAPTER THIRTY
TONIGHT I'LL BE STAYING HERE
WITH YOU
"FRIENDS, HOTELS AND PLAYING
TOURIST"

Our first stop was only an hour north along Route 95 at our friend Linda's in West Palm Beach. Some female companionship for Johanna. The next day we drove 300 miles and played on the beaches at St. Augustine, Florida. From there we stopped at Jekyll Island in Georgia. Beaches to run on and not a lot of driving. We stopped at the "South of The Border" tourist trap at the South Carolina—North Carolina state line on Route 95. Later we stayed in a hotel and explored J.R.'s Discount Shopping in North Carolina. As you travel north in South Carolina you can't miss the "South of The Border" billboards. In North Carolina you can't miss the "J.R." billboards. We drove to D.C. and stopped to visit Sean and Dianna. From there it was a day ride to New England and the kids. The trip north and later west was like a game of balancing the road with the comfort of friend's homes and low budget hotels. With her own money to spend, sleeping in a bed, and being able to take a shower in the morning, Johanna was somewhat appeased on the road.

We spent a week or so in New England both at my friends Gill's apartment and in a hotel as promised. Visiting with the kids, the four of us caught a Worcester Ice Cats Hockey game, swam in the hotel pool and went trick or treating. Halloween was a blast. Though at times it felt like I had three children, not two. Sara was a bunny, Joey was a clown, Johanna was a cat and

I carried a baseball and an electric fan. No one could guess that I was a baseball fan. After Halloween we took a quick visit to Vermont and visited with Jimmy Day. We went to the Vermont Teddy Bear Factory and the Ben & Jerry's ice cream plant.

We were getting along great and really talking. Johanna was still talking about marriage and I was as noncommittal as ever. She said she would move to New England and settle down if I was interested in that idea. She didn't like the road, and wasn't crazy about marrying a man with kids, but if she could have some of her own, she thought she could do it. She suggested that I get my old job back and be near my kids. Did I want more kids? I didn't say yes, but I didn't say no, and that was all she needed. She had hope and I gave it to her by my silence. This too would haunt me. As far as my old job was concerned, she knew it was an option. One night at dinner we bumped into my old boss. He asked when I would be done with this nonsense of travelling. If I could wrap it up by February, my old job was waiting for me. Apparently, one of the female appraisers was pregnant and due February first. She was planning on taking six months off and they needed to replace her. Johanna thought it was a great idea. We could get off the road, get out of The Big W, and get an apartment. I could work. She could go to school and work. And eventually marriage and kids. I reminded her of our Thanksgiving Day plans in California and the Honolulu Marathon in December. We could talk about it, but we still had some travelling to do before February.

In early November, 1999 we left New England and stopped 300 miles away in Philadelphia at my friend Billy Doyle's home. Billy lives a block from the two most famous cheese steak places in Philly, "Pats" and "Genos". Naturally we had one at each place. From there it was back to Sean and Dianna's only 125 miles south in D.C.. Bob Dylan was playing in Baltimore and Sean had four tickets. The show rocked and Johanna and I danced the night away. After sleeping at Sean and Dianna's, the next day we toured the White House, the Lincoln Memorial and the Vietnam Veteran's Memorial Wall. This made a very strong impression on Johanna. She wondered if she was killed in this war in a previous lifetime. She was excited to be travelling and finally having some of her own experiences. From D.C. we headed northwest and had a visit with my friends, Craig and Julie in Cleveland. They were married in New York back in June and settled in Cleveland where Craig was originally from. Real estate was a little cheaper than San Francisco where they were previously living. Watching the newly married couple move into their first home was making Johanna's commitment to get off the road even stronger. No trip to Cleveland would be complete without a stop at the Rock and Roll Hall of Fame. Heading west to California we drove Route 70 through Indiana and Illinois and stopped at the Arch in St. Louis, the Gateway to the west. For dinner we dined on the floating McDonalds on the Mississippi River.

Driving west across Missouri we laughed as Johanna flashed her breasts the whole trip every time I reminded her we were in the "Show Me" State. Johanna's parents grew up in Kansas and attended the University of Kansas. We stopped and toured the University campus in Lawrenceville and Johanna bought Christmas presents for her family. Heading south along Route 35 we stayed in a motel in Ottawa, Kansas, and laughed, as we couldn't believe that the pizza we ordered for delivery in our motel room was indeed a grocery store frozen pizza. It reminded me of the pizza I would devour after a hockey game in a cold New England Ice Skating Rink. Two slices was all I could eat. The next day we drove to Hutchinson, Kansas. Johanna's grandparents lived there before they died. She wanted to go by and see their old house and also to visit the family plots in the cemetery.

I nearly fainted when we pulled up to the house. I couldn't believe it. There it was, the metal clothesline and asphalt sided house I saw in the vision when I held Johanna's jewelry at the Past Life Regression seminar back in Florida. Johanna had a camera with black and white film so I snapped a picture. Later I would just stare at that photo in disbelief. How did I see that vision? We knocked on the door and explained to the new owners who Johanna was and she graciously gave us a tour of the house. Johanna couldn't believe what she found in the basement. As a child when she would visit, her granddad would measure and mark the kids height on a wooden pole in the basement. Her name and the date were marked several times alongside her sisters'. She was in tears. Later we visited the cemetery and after about an hour of wandering she found the grave markers and sat in silence for an hour. It was the highlight of the cross country trip for her. I was happy for her, happy to be with her, and had hope that maybe we could make this thing work. Of course I forgot that meant coming off the road, getting a job and an apartment, getting married and having kids.

From Kansas we drove to Denver, Colorado, for a three-day visit with Jimmy. He couldn't believe we were still together. I had told him of my many concerns earlier in the year, but for now we were moving and we were happy. After Denver we headed south to Arizona. I drove through the night and we slept in The Big W at the four corners where Colorodo, Utah, New Mexico and Arizona all meet. In the morning we took photos for Joey and Sara and then spent a day in the Grand Canyon. That night it was another hotel in Flagstaff on the historic Route 66. We were eating out and not cooking in The Dub. We were staying in hotels and not sleeping in The Dub. We were pissing through money, but she was happy, so I was happy.

We spent three nights in Scottsdale, Arizona. Johanna was an adopted child and in the past year she had located her biological mom who was now living in the Phoenix area. While they had talked on the phone and met once in California, Johanna had never met her half brothers. She contacted them and made plans to see them. She was overjoyed to be able to watch her younger half brother's BMX off-road bike race on one of the evenings there. Again, I was happy for her and happy to be with her.

From Phoenix it was Route 10 West to California once again. We had spent the better part of October and November either sleeping at friend's homes or in hotels. On November 22, 1999 we arrived for Thanksgiving at Johanna's parents home in Ontario, California, forty minutes from the coast.

CHAPTER THIRTY-ONE
STUCK INSIDE OF MOBILE WITH THE MEMPHIS BLUES AGAIN
"GRACELAND"

Dylan and I left Atlanta after visiting Josephine and decided to visit Vikki from Nashville. We headed north on Route 75 and picked up Route 24 in Tennessee. Vikki was the first person to read anything I had written. She was presently in the middle of five different novels she was currently writing and showed me some of her writing. I took a risk and shared some of mine. We made a deal, we would encourage each other's dreams.

She took us to dinner and downtown Nashville on Broadway. I filled her in on my current lover, Josephine. She lives outside the Atlanta area, is 31 years old, a nurse, has her own apartment, is three years divorced, and speaks her mind. She is very independent and not someone who needs to be taken care of. Furthermore, she is not interested in a life "on the road". While she does enjoy travelling, she loves having a home to come back to. More importantly, she is not interested in dragging me off the road until I have finished what I set out to do. While I search within on the road, she searches within at home. When the time is right we will see where it goes. Spiritually we share similar beliefs and both have a deep knowing that we share a soul connection. Vikki said she was happy for me and said, "It sounds like Josephine challenges you to grow, Napoleon, and you truly crave the challenge." Perhaps she is right.

The next day we drove east on Route 40 from Nashville

to Memphis and toured Graceland. The King is gone, but not forgotten. Literally, his face is on everything from ashtrays to lunch boxes, teddy bears to shot glasses, salt & pepper shakers to coffee mugs, radios to toy soldiers. If obsessed enough one could own nothing but Elvis souvenirs and completely furnish one's home.

Before leaving Nashville, I purchased Joey an NFL jersey from the Tennessee Titans. It was an Eddie George shirt, Joey's favorite team. As I traveled this year I picked up game jerseys from around the country for him. A new father-son tradition was born.

Heading west, with a new Elvis Presley Boulevard bumper sticker on the rear of The Dub, Dylan and I drove into the sunset, ready to drive late into the night. The music played and Dylan smiled as if he was singing along, *"Everything passes, everything changes. Just do what you think you should do."*

CHAPTER THIRTY-TWO
EVERYTHING IS BROKEN
"LYING TO MYSELF"

Johanna was happy to be back in California. We spent four days, Monday to Thursday at her parent's house with The Big W parked out front. I was in the guest room. She was in her sister's bedroom. We had the luxury of showers and a bed for a few more days.

House-sitting in Florida and playing tourist on vacation as we traveled from Florida to New England and New England to California was easy. We were distracted from any of the real relationship problems we had. It didn't take long for me to start to question the sanity of what I was creating once in California.

Johanna's money had run out as quickly as it arrived. To make financial matters worse, the $1,000 check she was expecting to find waiting for her at her parent's home had never materialized. Apparently, the insurance company took it as reimbursement for a rental car she drove for over a month after her car accident. This was the money she was planning to live on while we were in Hawaii. I told her we would manage somehow, but in my heart knew we had done this before. To make matters worse, there was a bill from a chiropractor for $1,700 who was going to seek legal action in a small claims court in one week if the bill was not paid. Johanna had put this bill off hoping it would go away. Further deepening the problem, her mother was also listed on the bill for some reason, and both of them would be dragged to court. Her parents kept trying to talk to her about it, but she always changed the subject. To my disbelief on the day we flew to Hawaii she gave them a check for $1,500 to mail to the chiropractor while having no money in her account. Did it really matter $1,500 or $1,700, there was not a nickel in the account. Red Flag. Red Flag.

Her parents loved me and why not, I was as close to their age as hers. While Johanna visited with her girlfriends, I had my morning coffee with her parents and focused on my running. They were a little skeptical of my lifestyle and wondered why it was taking us so long to get to Hawaii. Apparently, when Johanna had originally left California in August she had told them it was to start a life in Hawaii with me. Red Flag. Red Flag. Additionally, they wondered when I was going to get her to quit smoking. This is humorous for two reasons. First, she sneaks her cigarettes when they are not around thinking they are none the wiser. More deception. Second, when did it become my job to help her quit? Other oddities included my instructions not to mention her meeting with her biological mom in Arizona, as her adopted parents who have raised her since she was six weeks old knew nothing of her research and discovery of her biological mom. While I didn't understand this, I did respect it. Red Flag. Red Flag. My biggest challenge was avoiding the Amway sales pitch about every couple of hours or so. Her parents were full- time distributors and didn't understand why I didn't stop all this travel and start a business and a financial empire. All in all though the biggest eye opener was seeing how Johanna was still the black sheep of the family. Her sister was an elementary school teacher and engaged to get married. Johanna was the closet smoker, with some recent legal problems, bill collectors, a travelling boyfriend, and no Amway business. The shame hung heavy in the air. These family dynamics were not for me. Seeing one's role models often sheds light on that person's behavior.

I got ahold of my friend, Rick Wood, and made plans to leave The Big W parked at his home while we were in Hawaii. At this point I was considering going alone. The plan was to bring a tent and find a beach to camp on. My friend Kevin lives there, so at least I had one contact. Watching Johanna lie to her parents makes me wonder what lies she tells me. No trust. We are disconnected as she visits friends.

I wonder, does the fact we are not having sex under her parents' roof give me time to think about the relationship without the distraction of physical contact? My friend, Lisa Davies, from Colorado jokes that God blessed man with two heads. The problem is he can only use one at a time.

The last two months on the road have been easy in hotels and at friends. How will she handle camping? Our history would tell me, not well.

As Johanna visits with friends I decide to call a few myself. Wednesday, Lyle, Johanna's old boyfriend and my friend, and I spend the day walking the streets of Hollywood. I expected a little more glamour. Basically there are shoe stores, t-shirt stores and stripper stores. We stopped at Mann's Chinese Theater for a quick photo. Lyle and I talk. I share with him about the road, about Johanna, and some of our problems. He agrees that the road is not for everyone. I tell him of my dream to write and he says he can't wait to read it. Positive encouragement, I love it. Lastly, I share with him two things about my relationship with Johanna. First. Marriage and kids. I tell him I'm not sure this is what I want to create. He points out Johanna is young and many woman her age have this dream. Nothing is wrong with it. It's just not your dream, Napoleon. He is right. Second, I tell him that throughout the entire relationship I feel as if I've been waiting for Johanna to just hold me and tell me she loves, she wants me, and she appreciates me. Funny, how life works. He shares the reason he called it quits when he dated Johanna was that he felt she wasn't available emotionally. Did I have emotional needs? Was this longing to be loved, to be wanted, to be appreciated, part of what I was searching for in a relationship? Travelling and playing was fun, but did I need more? A sexual connection was pleasurable, but how deep was it? Could it really be that I had emotional needs that were going unmet?

Thanksgiving dinner goes well and we are off that night

for three nights in Salt Lake City to visit friends. Valerie is hosting a Thanksgiving weekend get together and several friends are flying into town. We take Johanna's car and make the ten hour trip from California to Utah straight through the night. The ride is long and tense. I voice some of my concerns about the way she deceives her parents. Especially, how she avoids the whole chiropractor bill conversation. She tells me not to worry. She will handle the bill and is looking forward to camping in Hawaii. I voice my reservations about marriage and kids. I tell her I think we have different visions of our futures. To me, October and November was not life on the road, it was vacationing. We played tourists, were distracted from our problems, and played. We fight the whole weekend. I feel just like I did when we decided to go house-sit in Florida. On the way back, we stop in Las Vegas and have dinner at the Hard Rock Café. While she wants to reminisce about our romantic weekend here back in early June, I tell her I'm thinking of going to Hawaii alone. Money is tight and we will be roughing it. My heart pleads with me to go alone, but in the end I lie to myself and we both go.

CHAPTER THIRTY-THREE
DEATH IS NOT THE END
"TECUMSEH, OKLAHOMA"

Dylan and I left Memphis, Tennessee, and drove 400 miles across Arkansas and slept at the Seminole Travel Plaza at mile marker 200 on Route 40 in Oklahoma. I have my morning coffee, some quiet time for me to journal and a little outdoor time for Dylan. As I sit and journal I question why I am heading west. I feel drawn to spend some time out here. I told Jimmy from Denver that after the Labor Day 2000 weekend party in New Mexico, I planned to spend some time in Colorado after travelling for a while. Why not the beach is what is confusing me. We fuel up and hit the road.

At mile marker 185 I start crying for no reason. I'm looking out at the land and getting very sad. This is odd. It looks so ugly with all the advertising billboards and travel plazas. I started to feel like this was once my land and it has become very ugly. I was sad and for some reason felt like an Indian who's land had been taken from him. This lasted for only a few minutes and went away as quickly as it came. Strange, I thought, and drove on. Then I couldn't believe my eyes. I see a sign to exit for TECUMSEH, OKLAHOMA. Tecumseh. I couldn't believe it. I exited and was in a town called Shawnee. I drove south for ten miles and found myself in Tecumseh, Oklahoma. I drove around the small town and found the public library. In the hallway is a giant statue of Chief Tecumseh, who the town was named after.

I stayed in Tecumsah for over two hours researching

Tecumseh. It appears the town was named for the chief from Ohio whose Shawnee tribe was relocated out to this area by the white man. Tecumseh himself never lived here, but his tribe was relocated to these lands. I was also to discover that the Seminole tribe from Florida was relocated to this area also. Was my past life regression real? Perhaps the name Tecumseh came to me in my regression not because I was Cheif Tecumseh in a past life, but because this is where the Seminole's were relocated to from Florida. The name had something to do with the place, not the man. I was floored. Why had I started to cry just moments before reaching this area? Was this my tribes land? Was this why I was drawn out west and not to the beach? The whole morning was surreal. Eventually, I purchased a copy of the book *A Panther in the Sky* by James Alexander Thom and was able to read about Chief Tecumseh. For now I was just in awe.

We drove farther and stopped at Foss Lake for a run and a swim. It was a sacred day. It was good to just play, be in the sun, and reflect on all that has happened on my journey. Dylan is really starting to enjoy swimming. As we continue our journey west, with me lost in my thoughts of the times in southern Florida and the Past Life Regression Seminar and Dylan with his head out the window, I thought I heard him sing, *"I'm a-thinkin' and a-wonderin' all the way down the road. I once loved a woman, a child I'm told. I give her my heart, but she wanted my soul. But don't think twice, it's all right."*

CHAPTER THIRTY-FOUR
DON'T THINK TWICE, IT'S ALL RIGHT
"WINDOWS OF OPPORTUNITY"

On December 1, 1999, Johanna and I boarded a plane for Hawaii.
Her parents drove us to the airport and were happy to have a
check in their pockets to pay the outstanding chiropractor bill.
Or at least that is what they thought. The plane trip from L.A.
to Honolulu is about six hours. She was excited. I was confused.
What had I created, or recreated? We were to spend five weeks
on Oahu. My plan was to rent a car at the airport for the first
week and find a place to sleep when we arrived. To me it was a
pure adventure of the unknown.

Arriving in Hawaii, the weather was beautiful and I couldn't
wait to run and swim. We pulled out of the Honolulu airport in
our rented car and headed straight to the beach. Waikiki Beach
is where most of the tourist go to tan and swim. But I love it
anyway. The water is blue and Diamond Head offers a great
back drop for the beach. Johanna was exhausted and not feeling
very well. She would fall ill for our first three days. As she would
lay on the beach and rest, I went for an eight mile run. The
marathon was twelve days away and with all of our travelling
I was only running about four days a week. My typical runs
were between eight and ten miles. Not in the best shape, but
confident I would finish. As I ran, I explored. Near the end of
my run I spotted a youth hostel called the Banana Bungalow.
After a swim and a little beach time I told Johanna I was going
to check this place out. She was really sick and couldn't move.
My dreams of camping on the beach were evaporating quickly.

The Banana Bungalow rates were $16 per night per person. If you paid for seven nights, you got the eighth night free. Two blocks from the beach and eight nights for $112 sounded like a great deal to me. Of course it was $224 for me as Johanna was penniless. Parking became a real problem. I did enjoy the car for trips to the north shore, but now that we were staying at a youth hostel we really didn't need it. Johanna was grateful just to have a bed. There were six to a room and each room had a private shower.

Each day I would arise and run while Johanna slept late. After my run I would drag her to the beach. I like to get there about 10:30 a.m. and leave about 4:30 p.m. Dinner each night was a little sushi at sunset by the water. I was looking forward to five weeks of this. While my camping adventure never materialized, I was happy with the youth hostel. The added benefit was it was three blocks from the finish of the marathon.

Johanna was frustrated that she was sick and felt bad that she was no fun. I ran up to the top of Diamond Head, I went swimming in the beaches of Waikiki, I explored the area on my daily runs, and entertained myself. After a few hours at the beach Johanna headed to the room as I read in the sun.

It was interesting staying at the youth hostel. I was meeting people from all over world who loved to travel. People who didn't need to stay in fancy hotels and eat in fancy restaurants. People who loved the beach. People who loved to travel. As Johanna anticipated settling down, my travel bug was growing larger. Sitting on the beach, I knew this is where I wanted to live someday. Not necessarily Hawaii, but the beach. Going back to the winters of New England was not very appealing to me. I wasn't ready to settle down. Not yet.

By day four in Hawaii Johanna was starting to feel better. We went snorkeling in Hanauma Bay. She had never been snorkling. Later we drove up to the north shore and watched a surfing contest. On the way back we stopped at the Dole Pineapple Plantation and sampled the goods. A day of tourism and she was happy.

Problems. While they were always there, they began

surfacing again, as I was content to dream of a life at the beach and she of a home and a family.

Financially, it gets draining always doling out the money. To be fair, I have to own my part in the creation of this situation. When she called back in July and said she had none, I said, "Don't worry." When we arrived in California and her money never materialized before leaving for Hawaii, I said, "Don't worry." Why did I say don't worry? Why did I continue to spend and entertain? Why couldn't I be true to myself? What did I learn? When one person has money and the other doesn't, an imbalance of power is created. There is no give and take. Things become one-sided. In Hawaii there was no money to go shopping with. The car, the hostel and food, was as extravagant as it got. Window shopping bothered me immensely. I always felt like I was obligated to buy gifts. It was like being with a child. Back on the Catalina trip there was a guy named Ricky who said, "I don't mind giving, it's just hard to do when they have their hands out constantly." I was learning the lessons of giving of love not of obligation. Giving out of love feels good. Giving out of obligation creates resentment and victimization.

Sexually, the fire was dying. The romantic weekends and the two month cross country tourist trip were behind us. We were dreaming in different directions and were disconnected. I dreamed of the beach, she dreamed of a home and family.

Common vision, we had none. By day eight we had to talk. While Johanna was anticipating a month in Hawaii and then we settle down, I wasn't so sure. She gave me an ultimatum. She said I needed to commit to building a life together or breaking up. Good for her, I thought. It wasn't committing to building a life with someone that scared me, what bothered me was that we each had different ideas as to what that life would be. And if we wanted different lifestyles, why was I afraid to committing to breaking up? Why do we sometimes cling to people or situations for security? Why do we settle for less than we deserve and want? Was I afraid to hurt her? Was I afraid to be alone? Were we not killing each other's spirits? Were we not killing each other's dreams? Yes, relationships teach us about ourselves, but they also teach us what we want and what we don't want. It's a process of discovery. Yet, sometimes we ignore what we discover. Sometimes old patterns and behaviors resurface. We can't help ourselves. We know there is a new way, but we struggle. Is this all part of the lessons?

We talked and we talked. We agreed to separate. We didn't break up. We separated. On day ten in Hawaii, two days before the marathon, Johanna flew back to Los Angeles alone. The ball was in my court. Johanna left and I was to decide did I love her enough to come off the road, settle down, get married and have a family. As she said, "I needed to commit to a life together or commit to breaking up."

I was alone. At times relieved, at times scared. I was reading *Zen and the Art of Motorcycle* and there was a line that struck me. It read, "sometimes truth knocks at the door and we tell it to go away." In June at Johanna's home in southern California, truth knocked. In August when she arrived scared and penniless in New England, truth knocked. In Florida, as we house-sat for Jamie and Charlene, truth knocked. In California, at her parents' house before flying to Hawaii, truth knocked. Yet, each time I told it to go away. Now, alone in Hawaii, truth was knocking again.

I ran the marathon and finished in 3 hours 50 minutes; the same time I ran in Boston back in April. It was a rainy, misty day and the race started at seven a.m. in the dark. The starting line fireworks were inspirational and the downtown Honolulu Christmas lights were beautiful. At mile thirteen the sun came up. I ran twenty miles at an eight minute mile pace; on target for a 3:30 marathon. Then, the wall. The last six miles were a challenge. My sanity was again questioned. Finally, the finish line. Another dream realized.

As I ran the race my thoughts were of Johanna and some of the travelers I had met. John from Toronto who said, "Let her go. She is young and you are both at different stages of life." Phil from Vancouver would say, "If you have the travel bug and try to settle down, you will be unhappy, because it won't just go away and has to be lived away." Dianna's words of "Sugar Daddy" would echo in my mind. Jimmy Day's statement, "When the flesh is joined, it must be torn apart," would sting as I thought of Johanna back in California. Lyle's reason for breaking up with Johanna for being emotionally unavailable would continue to haunt me.

In my mind, I would re-read the letter she left under my pillow:

12/10/99

My darling little blue-eyed Prince,

Remember when I used to leave you notes like this? It seems like that was so long ago. I don't know if what we're doing is right or wrong, but it seems like the best possible thing in order to get our relationship back on track.

We just need to have faith that our love will survive. I have that faith. Do you?

I love you more Napoleon than I ever thought I could love someone. I give you my heart and pray you come for me.

I'm so scared, but our love is strong: we proved that today by doing this. I'll think of you every moment of every day. I'll see you in my dreams.

I love you forever,
Your Beautiful Flower

Did she really love me? Was I just afraid? Did I really have different dreams? And if I do have different dreams, why do I neglect them? Why do I settle for less? Can we make it work? I began to wonder, would our relationship be different off the road, in an apartment, both working, both feeling as partners?

It seems like our whole relationship was a pattern of losing myself in a pattern of care taking and then empowering myself, by practicing self-care and the discovery of self. In the beginning the voices encouraged me to check it out. Discover if we were compatible. Then, red flags ignored. Was I looking at our potential compatibility and not our actual compatibility? Was I lost in a world of illusion? I realized it's okay to want love, to be loved, to be needed, to be comforted. It's okay to have emotional needs. But, what of a common vision? What makes me happy? What makes Johanna happy? I must identify my needs and wants. I must express my needs and wants. No one will know me as well as I can know myself. Self care. No one is going to brush my teeth, feed my soul, or live my dreams. I must actively participate in my life. I must identify what I want and co-create it with the universe. Which is the greater crime, someone stealing your dreams, or you giving your dreams away?

Johanna was not at the finish line. She was in California. That was real. I would spend a few more days alone wondering if my dreams were real or if I should I go to Johanna?

On the 16th, Sean and Dianna from Maryland arrived. They had planned to spend Christmas and New Year's Eve in Hawaii. It was good to see them. I had called and told them about the Banana Bungalow and they had made reservations. They loved the beach and we would hang out all day. Eventually, on New Year's Eve Sean planned to ask Dianna to marry him. As for me, I felt like I was in "relationship limbo". We separated. We didn't break up. Johanna and I talked on the phone and missed each other. I was torn in several directions. Johanna knows what she wants. She doesn't like the road, she wants to settle down, she wants to be married, and she wants a family. Deep within I know I love the road and am not ready to settle down. But, would I ever get married? Would I ever have kids? Perhaps someday, or is that a lie? Am I in love with Johanna and just afraid to do the work? Or am I afraid to be alone?

Over the next week I hang with Dianna and Sean. We go to the beach. We play tourist. My body is still sore from the race and I rest. I miss running. I recognize that I can't grieve the relationship because we didn't end it. We just separated. To make matters worse everywhere I look I see happy couples in love. Christmas and New Year's Eve will be lonely. Shouldn't I be with Johanna?

My heart knows what I want. But, my mind tells me I should be with Johanna. On December 24th, 1999 I leave Hawaii two weeks early and fly into Los Angeles on Christmas morning. Another window of opportunity to break away bypassed.

CHAPTER THIRTY-FIVE
RAGGED AND DIRTY
"BACK IN COLORADO"

Dylan and I left Foss Lake and Okalahoma, drove to Amarillo, Texas, and headed northwest to New Mexico and north on Route 25 to Denver. It was good to have a run and a swim. I love running in the heat and then cooling off in the water. The best is on a beach, where it is so hot one doesn't even stop to take the sneakers off. Run and dive. Plus, the added bonus is a quick wash when there are no showers.

I'm on the road again, with the mind thoughts drifting in and out. I love to just drive, have a cigar and just think, letting my mind wander. Is it a dream state? Is it my subconscious mind making an appearance? Today's thought, "Men hug to have sex, woman have sex to be hugged." I read that somewhere. It seems true. Men feel loved when having sex. Why? Women feel loved when being hugged. Why? Can you balance the two? Are we just different?

The Denver crew, who normally have their campout in July, were hosting it the weekend before the New Mexico Labor Day 2000 bash this year. Seems no one could make it in July, so they had to reschedule. I met Jimmy Walker at his home and was able to clean up after several days on the road. Jimmy had a ten month old half lab, half rottweiler dog named Stella and a fenced in back yard. She and Dylan would play for hours together. Jimmy's life had changed somewhat also. Amy from Detroit had recently moved to Colorado and she and Jimmy were building a life together. Another happy couple.

I arrived on Thursday and on Friday morning drove to Breckinridge for the campout. It was like I was going back to reclaim my soul. Last year Johanna and I attended together. This year I would go alone. Riding in The Dub in shotgun position to the campout was my friend, Ed Gunner. We call him G for short. G flew in from Detroit for the weekend. He is in his mid-thirties and presently single. We had a great talk and our friendship deepened. We talked about the power of sex and how it blinds us and distracts us from what we really want. We agreed we had spent most of our lives having sex and then trying to figure out if the woman we slept with was a compatible mate and that this pattern was no longer working. I told him about Josephine from Atlanta and how we met back in May while I was visiting Atlanta. We talked all weekend and only kissed. We spent the next seven weeks talking on the phone and getting to know each other. No sex, just intimate sharing. We were building a foundation and were not blinded by sex. We could discover things about each other and be honest with what we found. A new path for me.

The campout was a lot of fun and once again the highlight was when Teddy Reilly took me trout fishing. He and his brother, Steve and I fished all day on Sunday after everyone left. It was great to see Teddy with his brother. Teddy is a big, tough kid who grew up on the streets. His brother Steve, who's now twenty, was in a bad car accident when he was seven. Apparently, he went through the windshield and in addition to suffering many scars was partially brain damaged, which left him a little slow. Teddy was so patient with him baiting the hooks and taking the fish off his line for him. Steve caught the biggest fish of the day and I would brag to everyone about it, calling him the master. Later I would share with Teddy that the tough guy image in my mind was ruined. The love and tenderness he showed towards his brother showed me who he really was. It showed his inner, true self.

Dylan had a ball all weekend. He, Stella and four other dogs ran in a wild pack the entire weekend looking for fallen hotdogs and hamburgers.

Sunday night I was back in Denver and on Monday Jimmy and I would drive The Dub to New Mexico for the Labor Day 2000 party. I couldn't wait to see Josephine. I went to bed dreaming of the upcoming weekend with Dylan on the floor, I thought heard him singing, *"You angel, you, you're as fine as anything fine. The way you walk and the way you talk, it sure plays on my mind."*

CHAPTER THIRTY-SIX
WHEN HE RETURNS
"THE BREAK UP"

Johanna picked me up at five a.m. Christmas morning at the airport in Los Angeles. I had returned and she was overjoyed. I was happy, too. It was good to hold her, good to see her, and good to be with her. Perhaps we could have a new start. We spent Christmas Day with her family and I slept at their home for one night. Her old roommate was hosting a New Year's Eve party. I decided to get a motel room for a week and then after the party we would leave for the road. While in the motel I would have some repairs to The Big W made.

I shared with Johanna that I loved the road, but thought that I loved her, and couldn't just walk away wondering. I told her that if she stayed in California and I stayed on the road, I would always wonder, could it have been different if we had a home, each had jobs, and created a true partnership together? I told her I would like to travel for the month of January and then if my old boss would take me, go to work from February to August. After that we would have to move to the beach. New England wasn't where I wanted to settle and start a new life. We could each work, save some money and then find a place to build a life together. I could live near the beach and she could work and go to school. I could make enough money to fly home and see the kids once a month. We could live together and see if things were different. I didn't want to talk about marriage or kids until September. For now I just didn't want to be left wondering, "Could we have made it work off the road?"

She was game. The next week would offer many reasons that I should never have left Hawaii, but again I ignored the Red Flags.

First, I found a newspaper with the advertisements for "strippers wanted" in bikini clubs circled. I questioned her and she said it was fast cash to get her life back on track. She didn't want to do it, but if it was over between us, then she had no choice. I couldn't let this happen, could I?

Next, it turns out the chiropractor check bounced. Her parents were pissed and she just kept changing the subject.

Lastly, while I was in Hawaii and she was back in California she had dinner with three past lovers. All friends of course, but my trust issues were making an appearance. I couldn't believe how jealous I was. Was it a control thing? Was I afraid? Was it real? Was it all in my head? There was no trust and there never was. Not a good foundation.

I had always envisioned New Year's Eve 2000 on the beach somewhere making love. Now I found myself at a party with people I didn't even know. At midnight Johanna gave me a peck on the cheek. I knew at that moment I had made a mistake. I never should have left Hawaii. Was I afraid to be alone? Did I really wonder if we could make it off the road? Was I just rescuing her from the bikini clubs?

Looking back I know this relationship taught me a great deal. My heart was always trying to point me in the right direction. My heart knew my dreams and always tried to lead me in that direction. The biggest lesson I learned was that being aware of your heart and listening to your heart is just a start. Learning to trust your heart and express your heart's intentions is how you begin to live by the heart. I had many opportunities and looked the other way. If it doesn't feel right, it probably isn't. How could I trust another when I hadn't learned to trust myself? How could I love another when I hadn't learned to love myself? I could honor another, when I hadn't learned to honor myself?

In early January, 2000, Johanna and I left California and drove Route 10 across the United States to Florida. We stopped in New Orleans, Louisanna and Biloxi, Mississippi. We visited a casino for dinner and some ladyluck. I loaned Johanna $50 and she won $70 playing Blackjack. She wanted to go to Disney World. She had money and felt good. We stopped in Orlando and spent a day with Mickey. I missed the kids. We spent a week in Key West. I was grieving the loss of the road. Heading north we visited with Jamie and Charlene. Continuing north we stopped in North Carolina and rented a motel for the Super Bowl. The St. Louis Rams beat the Tennessee Titans. A year ago I watched Johanna as she watched the game with Reggie in Florida. I remember saying to myself, "I want that." Well, now I had it. We arrived in New England and it was snowing.

I had called my old boss before leaving California and told him I would take the job February first. He also had an apartment I could rent. No lease, no first month's rent, no last month's rent. Just move in and start working and paying rent. We had no furniture and had to buy everything. With each new purchase a little piece of me died. The clincher was a vacuum cleaner. I just couldn't believe I bought a vacuum cleaner. Was I just going through the motion of a life off the road?

Johanna got a job at a local restaurant and I was working at my old job. I justified that I was learning the computer system and programs that were new to the appraisal industry, was making good money, could spend time with Joey and Sara, and eventually would move to the beach.

Talking on the phone with friends in California, Johanna learned that her old roommate split with her boyfriend. Seems the roommate wanted to be engaged, but the boyfriend didn't. The marriage talk began. Not only did she want to get engaged, she didn't want to leave New England. She didn't want to dig in at work, in the home or even school over the summer, if it meant leaving at the end of August. This and all the snow was about all could take. I knew in my heart it was over. We were killing each other. Neither one of us honored the dreams of the other. We couldn't see past our own individual visions. We were not compatible. The truth could no longer be denied and the knocking was unbearable.

We lasted six weeks together off the road in an apartment. I would never have to worry about always wondering "if we could have made it work off the road". We couldn't make it work. Our differences were too strong. Our time together in New England was no different than before. All of our problems followed us off the road. Everything I had been journaling about since last June was the same. It wasn't just about getting married and having kids. That was big, but it was also all the little things. Johanna had romanticized the road and found out that she didn't like it. I had romanticized life off the road and found out that I didn't like it. Now off the road and trying to live together we fought all the time. I didn't meet her expectations and she didn't meet mine. On March 14, 2000 we broke-up in anger. It was ugly and we each said things that hurt the other. The kind of things you can never take back. We were like two wounded seven year olds, both wanting to be right. Looking back I wasn't mad at her, I was mad at myself. Time and time again I ignored my heart.

I now realize that part of the journey is recognizing that we often lose touch with our center. We become distracted. What are the tools we use, who are the people who help us and where are the places that help us reconnect with our center, our heart voice?

I was reading a book by Kevin J. Todeschi called *Edgar Cayce on Soul mates*. In it I read that soul mate connections exist to help each other, to challenge each other to learn lessons and develop spiritually. It was a bond in which dreams are realized and one's selfhood is encouraged to blossom and grow.

What had I learned from Johanna?

Previously, I thought that I had mastered lessons with Lily, Corrina, and Jane. Lily showed me that I could love again and when two people have different visions for their futures, it's okay to part. No one is right, no one is wrong. I had thanked Lily for our love and we each went our separate ways. I ignored this time and time again with Johanna. Corrina showed me that couples could enjoy a season of love together and when it was over they could let go in love. They could honor each other best by letting go in love. With Johanna I recognized our season was over many times, but refused to let go. Jane showed me the lesson of self-care. With Johanna I practiced self-neglect. Time after time my needs were not met and I stayed anyway. I took care of her and neglected myself. Why didn't I trust my heart? Why did I believe others and not my heart? My heart would speak to me, I would run it by another, they would tell me my heart was wrong, and I would believe them and not my heart.

Was Johanna in my life to smash home these lessons I previously thought I had mastered? Did the power of sex blind me? Was I learning that it wasn't enough to be aware and listen to one's heart voice, that one needed to trust and express this voice in order to live by the heart? Were we working out something from a past life? Was I now at a higher level of awareness? Did I need to bottom out with Johanna to be true to my path? Was I simply addicted to the sex and care-taking? Would I find my path again? Did I learn lessons about money and partnership? Would I love again? What were my dreams? Would I betray myself or stay true to my heart? Johanna had given up her life in California and I had given up my life on the road; neither worked. We killed each other's spirits and dreams. We failed to honor each other's visions and dreams. We would each cling too long and crush our love. Ironically, now apart, we were free to soar and become the people we fell in love with. Holding on had become more painful than letting go.

I was single again. Hurt, angry and stuck in the snow of New England. What do I do now? I had committed to work until August. The money would be needed for more road time. I would give up the apartment on the first of May and park The Dub at my friend Gill's apartment for a month. I would move into the campground in Barre, Mass. after July first. A summer with the kids would benefit us all. I thought of my time with Johanna from last May until now. I learned a great deal about myself from her. To thine own self be true. Be still and listen, the truth will set you free.

Thanks Johanna.

CHAPTER THIRTY-SEVEN
ANGELINA
"REGROUPING FOR THE ROAD"

Four days. That's all it took and I was dating Angelina by the following Saturday night. Each ending makes way for a new beginning. While I grieved the loss of Johanna, I enjoyed the discovering of Angelina. My thoughts create my reality, and I tried to focus not on the loss of a relationship, but the infinite possibilities of the future. What would I now create? My dreams were alive again. Not the dreams of a relationship, but the road. Angelina was a playful distraction from the sorrow of loss. We played while I regrouped for the road.

It was St. Patrick's Day weekend 2000 and I was at a party with some friends. Dianna and Sean were back from Hawaii and visiting Boston for the weekend gathering. They just returned from dinner with Lily, who they remained friends with. They filled her in on my recent breakup with Johanna and brought her to the party. She looked great and was excited to see me; thinking I was off the road and single, perhaps we could rekindle our relationship. She was even so bold as to suggest we sneak off and make love. I surprised myself. Instead of jumping at the chance for a quick roll, I asked her if she was still looking for a husband. Has what she wanted changed in the past two years? I explained that while I was single, I was still not finished with the road. We could make love, but then what? Nothing has changed between us. While she wants a family man, I want something else. We still held different visions. Discouraged, she left the party shortly after that. I was beaming. Perhaps a lesson was mastered. I didn't go down a wornout path. I took the higher road. Dianna wanted all the details. I simply told her, Lily and I chose not to go backward, but forward. Within three hours I would be challenged again.

Angelina walked by me at the party and our eyes locked. Recognition.

Angelina had just broken up with her boyfriend three weeks earlier. I told her Johanna and I had broken up four days ago. She was from Miami, but presently a second year law student at Boston University. We talked the night away consoling each other. Neither of us had any interest in a new relationship. Perhaps some fun times, but we both acknowledged that we were still getting over our last lovers. Sharing about our past and our dreams was fun. We both loved the beach and had a passion for travelling. However, when she told me she someday wanted to get married and have four children, I responded, "I'm getting a vasectomy and a dog." We laughed and from that moment on, Angelina and I always lived in the truth, and reaped the rewards for doing so. We would constantly joke, "Let's stay real."

The vasectomy was Dianna and Sean's idea as I had a habit of dating woman who wanted to some day have children. They said this would send a clear message to any future woman who had hopes of having children with me, even in the face of my declarations, that I was not only not interested in having children, but not capable. I haven't actually had the procedure yet, but my time with Johanna made it clear; I didn't want anymore children. I was happy with the two I had and I needed to smash that home to any future mates.

The post-Johanna period was a season of rediscovery of my self and my dreams. Looking back, I could see that I had become very sick over the past 10 months and had lost myself. At times it felt like I had created in ten months with Johanna what it had taken me ten years to create with my ex-wife. The same feelings and dynamics I had in the marriage were present with Johanna. It was as though I had recreated the same relationship. Fortunately, there were no children and no lawyers this time. I had lost myself and ignored my inner heart voice over the past months. Why do I choose to believe another and not myself? Why did I give up my dreams for another's dreams? Single again, I felt free to be me and would guard this freedom. Not that others were trying to snatch it away, but I now knew that I was susceptible to throwing it away. I realized that with Johanna, at some point I went from victim to volunteer. Boundaries were ignored and dreams disappeared.

With Angelina I felt alive. We played in Boston and eventually after about three weeks we played in bed. I wasn't moving in and she wasn't coming on the road. We were friends and could openly talk about our pasts and our futures without ever feeling threatened. She was always telling me how handsome, funny and awesome I was. It felt nice to be loved and appreciated. It felt nice to have some emotional needs met. Give, give, give doesn't work. A relationship needs to be give and take. Not just take, take, take. This leads to victimization and resentment. The bruises heal slowly, but they do heal.

We dated from mid-March until around the first of May. I call it the season of laughter. She had this great laugh, and it was so easy to make her laugh. I was open about my road plans in August and she had plans to summer in Greece starting in late June. I would joke that it was a relationship with a built in termination clause. We would comfort each other during the grieving period of our past lovers. I believe the Universe sent us to each other as a friendly distraction, so that neither of us would return to our past partners, a pattern we both exhibited.

Only the truth will set you free. I had learned from Johanna that the false comfort of illusion eventually is shattered by the reality of truth.

Angelina and I lived in the truth. Sometimes I would stay at her place and sometimes she came to mine. However, most times we stayed in our own beds. I had learned that sex was very powerful and often sabotaged my dreams. Often we would just hold each other and sleep. Comfort arms to ease the transition. We knew this was not a life-long match. We knew that we were just having a season: a season of laughter.

Angelina came from a very wealthy family from Miami.

Sometimes the Universe has a sense of humor, I went from dating Johanna with no money, to Angelina with no concerns of money. At times I felt like I had an Aladdin complex. She was Princess Jasmine slumming with the homeless Aladdin. I went with her when she picked up her brand new BMW automobile. When she was sixteen, she and her dad drew up a contract, that if she could quit smoking for six months, he would purchase the car of her choice. April first was six months of smokeless time for Angelina. Phone calls were made and the contract was executed as she purchased a $35,000 set of wheels. She came from a world of money, cars, clothes, and credit cards. We would joke, that I was "Napoleon in Rags" and that she always wore the latest fashions. The external trappings didn't impress me that much and Angelina wasn't used to that. She came from a world where how you looked was everything. Her last boyfriend owned several Boston restaurants and was a prime candidate for marriage in her parents' eyes. She feared that someday she would marry for money and not for love. As we played, her eyes were opening. She could see how unhappy she was in her past relationship, yet she felt she had to stay. It was a financially secure future. Now she was wondering if perhaps money wasn't where it was at. Often, she would say how happy she was with me and how she was discovering how to play and laugh. She told me that she would take this with her and always remember that she loved to play. Perhaps I came into a woman's life for a reason, just as they came into mine.

I called her my Miami Brown Sugar. She was always tanned. Being from Miami helped, but so did the salons. Our season of laughs lasted about six weeks. We stayed real. We lived in the truth. By May 1st, 2000 she was busy with final exams and our time as lovers was at an end. Friendship. We would now be the best of friends. Living in the truth, honoring each other, and playing was a great foundation for our friendship.

As I wrote in my journal I asked myself what I had learned from the "season of laughter?"

I had honored the truth. Angelina and I weren't a compatible life long match. We knew from the beginning that we were simply distracting each other from the pain and grief of our past lovers. We honored each other's different visions and dreams. We kept our expectations of each other real. We were an "in the meantime" relationship, and we honored that truth. I love her most for never trying to steal my dreams. I remember sharing with her my dream of writing, and she simply responded, "I can't wait to walk into a bookstore and see it on the shelf." We never got lost in the power of sex. Sometimes we were intimate physically and sometimes we were intimate emotionally. We each knew sex wasn't the connection we were looking for. Staying real. We chose to talk openly and honestly. The truth will set you free. I was aware of my heart, I listened to my heart, I trusted my heart, I expressed my heart, and was living by my heart.

Thanks Angelina.

CHAPTER THIRTY-EIGHT
I SHALL BE FREE
"SUMMER SESSION II"

Upon my arrival in New England in February, 2000 with Johanna, the kids were very excited to have me home. While Johanna and I shared the apartment for six weeks, I kept it for another six weeks through the end of April. For three months from February through April I felt trapped and snowbound away from The Big W. There were days I would just go out and sit in The Dub in the rear parking lot, smelling the memories and examining the photos on the walls. I could spend hours reliving the moments in the photos. Like the bumper stickers on the rear of The Big W, the interior was plastered with photos of friends and places visited. A tribute to Soul School– Playground Earth.

On May 1, 2000 I moved The Big W to my friend Gill's driveway and Summer Session II was officially beginning. It was two years since I had moved into The Dub back in May 1998. I would spend a month in Gill's driveway and then the summer at the Coldbrook Campground in the kids' hometown of Barre, Mass..

Johanna was planning on returning to California, but chose to stay and build a life in New England. Perhaps she couldn't return. Either way I try to send loving thoughts and hope she is chasing her dreams of school and a family. Over time we would both heal and grow.

One of the first gifts of our breakup occurred when I shared with my ex-wife that Johanna and I had broken up and

I needed to tell the kids. Both Joey and Sara had grown fond of her and I knew they would be sad that we were no longer together. Surprisingly, it opened a door of communication with my ex-wife that had not previously existed. While we had always strived to put the kids needs first, we were now openly talking about each other's lives, our marriage, our divorce, and our dreams. We don't go out for coffee everyday, but I have sat down to dinner with her and the kids in their home. The healing continues.

Ex-wife. I hate that term "ex". It seems so negative. Perhaps I could just say the woman I was formerly married to, or the mother of my children, my former wife, my first wife, or the woman who I once lived the script with. Just a thought.

While I had dated Angelina for six weeks our decision to just be friends instead of lovers coincided with my move to Gill's driveway in The Big W. I do not regret my time with her, nor would I have done things differently. I still cherish our friendship. I'm still amazed that we met and began dating only four days after my breakup with Johanna. While everyone couldn't believe I was dating someone new after only four days; I knew when our eyes met that something special was happening between us. There was a real connection at a soul level. Others would only focus on our recent breakups and say, "you need to be alone" or "you're always in a relationship". But we knew that we shared something special.

How much time between relationships is appropriate? My divorce was in 1994 from the woman I was formerly married to. I met Lily in the fall of 1997. There were three years of alone time there. Lily and I separated in the summer of 1998 while I was beginning my life in The Dub. Three months later I met Corrina in November, 1998. Three months of alone time there. Corrina and I separated in late January, 1999 and I began dating Jane on March 1, 1999. Five weeks of alone time there. Jane and I separated on April 1, 1999 and Johanna and I began dating in mid-May, 1999. Six weeks of alone time there. Johanna and I parted in mid-March. Angelina and I started dating four days later. Looking back, I would often wonder, were they great relationships that I messed up, or were they messed up relationships that I tried to make great? Either way, they all served a purpose and taught me lessons.

Who makes the "in between relationship" rules anyway? Seems everyone is an expert when it comes to others. Time alone, time in a relationship. I still believe teachers appear when the student is ready. We are all souls at different levels of awareness. Our paths cross and lessons are presented; to be mastered or ignored. While Lily, Corrina, Jane, Johanna, and Angelina all came into my life for a reason, I must believe I came into theirs for a reason too. Each of our journey's has been unfolding. In each season we discover more about love, more about our dreams, more about our true natures. Sometimes we sleep through the challenge, other times we grasp the lesson. I was to learn that each moment contains the potential for a lesson to affect us for a lifetime. There is no right or wrong path, only my path.

Two years in The Big W and five relationships later, I am ready for some alone time. Time to reflect, time to plan for my junior term on the road, time to enjoy the kids, time to dream, and time to live.

Summer Session II had begun.

CHAPTER THIRTY-NINE
PRECIOUS ANGEL
"HEADING TO ALBUQUERQUE"

Jimmy and I left Denver in The Big W at around eleven p.m.
Monday night. It was about 400 miles to Albuquerque, New
Mexico, along Route 25 South. At fifty miles per hour, that was
eight hours Dub Time. Jimmy made the coffee and we hit the
road. Jimmy only drank Starbucks Coffee. After hanging with
him for over a week, I was starting to lose my taste for gas
station coffee and slowly becoming addicted to the gourmet
brands he was so fond of. I drove the first 200 miles and he
drove the second 200 miles. Most of our friends would be flying
in on Thursday and we would all be staying at the downtown
Hyatt for the weekend party.

Some would say, "Dub Time was not real time." To me it
was better. As I travelled the country, I was be amazed at how
often I had no idea what time it was or what day it was. Twice,
I actually forgot the month. I love Dub Time. Everyday is
special. Mondays are like Fridays, Wednesdays can be Sundays,
and Thursdays can be Saturdays. Everyday is a holiday, everyday
is special, and everyday has the potential to create your dreams.
Why do Mondays have to be depressing? Why do you have to
have special plans on Saturday night? Everyday in Dub Time is
sacred.

Jimmy and I arrived Tuesday morning and would have a
couple of days to explore. Tim from Atlanta came in early and
so did a few others. I would stay in Tim's room for two nights
and on Thursday, when Josephine flew into town, she and I

would share a room with John and Melinda who were also flying in from Atlanta. Jimmy's girlfriend, Amy, would be driving from Denver on Thursday. Tipping the Valet Captain, I was able to park The Big W directly in front of the hotel in the area reserved for buses and oversized vehicles. It worked out well, as each day friends who left their pets at home would jump at the chance to take Dylan for a walk.

Sometimes it's amazing what one can see while observing others. I wonder, can we actually learn lessons from others' experiences or do we only recognize the lessons that we have been through? Amy and Jimmy reminded me of Johanna and me. Amy had dreams of a family, while Jimmy never even entertained the idea of children. They both talked about and knew that each had different visions, yet remained together, hoping that the other would change. Amy had given up everything in Detroit and had moved to Denver to build a life and create a family with a man who never wanted any children. This would haunt them like it haunted Johanna and me. Why was it so easy to see it in them, yet so murky in my own case?

Later as Dylan and I went for an inner city concrete run I would think about relationships. I called it my "opening the door theory". When do we start taking each other for granted in a relationship? Why do we try to change each other? When do we stop treating each other like we did on the first date? If I treated you on the first date like I treat you now, would there have been a second date? When do we stop opening the door for our lovers? Why do we treat strangers with more courtesy than the ones we hold dear? I vowed I would always remember to open the door. Little acts of love. Little acts of respect. Little acts to show I didn't take you for granted and that you were precious to me.

Then of course there was my "baby theory". Why do our parents stop treating us like the baby they were so in awe of? When does childhood become a living hell of programming? When do we stop cherishing the journey of the soul? We damage each other, judge, hurt, and condemn each other. We lose sight of the journey of the soul. We look at babies and see beauty. We look at adults and judge. When do we stop looking at each other in awe? Why can't we believe in each other, support each other, teach each other, care for each other, work for each other, play with each other, and laugh with each other as we share the journey?

Two days and Josephine would be in town. We would spend Thursday to Tuesday together. On our run I thought I could her Dylan singing, *"Precious angel under the sun, how was I to know you'd be the one, to show me I was blinded, to show me I was gone, how weak was the foundation I was standing upon?"*

CHAPTER FORTY
PATHS OF VICTORY
"PLAY, WORK, REFLECT, AND DREAM"

On May 3, 2000, Joey turned ten years old and pitched two innings in his team's baseball game. One year ago I was on the road on his birthday with my friend, Jimmy Walker. I swore this year we would be together. We had a magical day and a magical game as Joey struck out six. The summer was fantastic and the kids and I spent many days together. We played baseball, went to Red Sox games, went to movies, went shopping, went bowling, went roller-skating, went swimming almost daily in the campground pool, had campfires at night, and just laughed and played. Some nights they slept over in The Dub, we played games and cooked breakfast in the morning. We celebrated Sara's birthday and Father's Day in June. In August we celebrated my 39th birthday. It was a magical summer with the kids.

Working back at my old job offered new challenges. While I started in February, I had made it clear it would not be permanent. My goal was to make some money for the road and spend time with the kids. Originally my plan was to be back in New England in May to be with the kids for the summer, so a couple of extra months was no big deal. I worked about 25 hours per week, which left lots of time for the kids. Besides the extra money would come in handy on the road. I had spent more money than I had anticipated over the past year and it was time to replenish the kitty. Working a professional job and living in The Dub was not an ideal match. Dub time and The Dub lifestyle do not easily fit in a 9-5 schedule. Fortunately for me,

I didn't work 9-5. I would often go into the office late at night, where alone, I could do in 4 hours what it took a day-worker 8 hours to do. My work habits were unorthodox but I produced results and my boss was pleased. The biggest challenge was not getting caught in the world of illusion. A world, which to me, was full of distractions from my soul journey. It would be necessary to stay focused on Soul School–Playground Earth. The job was a means to an end. I felt like I had two years previously when I moved into The Dub and was preparing for my freshman term on the road. I was only in New England for the kids and to earn some money. I felt like I was repeating my past, only this time I knew what the road held for me.

My mornings were a time for reflection. I would continue my routine of coffee, journal time, followed by a run. If I had any inspections I would try to get them completed in the afternoon. At night I would go into the office and prepare appraisal reports. I learned the new computer systems and the programs of Microsoft Word and Excel. After working for a few hours on business, I began writing some personal stuff. I was now organizing my journals and thoughts. The writing process was beginning. The dream was real. I was saving money for the road and a laptop personal computer. My present life in New England was not what I wanted to create forever, but it was enabling me to achieve my true desires; time with the kids, and money to travel and write.

Daily I would continue to journal and reflect on my freshman and sophomore terms. Two years ago I had left Lily and New England in The Big W not knowing why, just honoring the tugging on my soul. I traveled the entire country and dated Corrina from South Carolina, Jane from Florida, Johanna from California, and Angelina from Boston. What had I learned? What mistakes did I make? What made me happy? What were my dreams? What was my plan?

I entered the following in my journal:

What had I learned? I left for the road to spend time alone, yet many teachers appeared along my path. Honoring my heart voice hasn't always been easy. When I initially took time for the road, my sanity was questioned. I truly believe the past two years unfolded as they were supposed to. Each friend, each port, each lover, each lesson was presented by the Universe for my schooling to unfold. People and places come in and out of my life in order for me to experience what I need to experience. The journey of my soul is much bigger than my time on this planet. Over the past two years I became aware of the bigger picture. It's not about cars, suits, houses and credit cards, its about the journey to oneself. My mind is concerned with the ways of the world; my heart the ways of the spirit. While my mind lives in fear, my heart believes in the Universe. My lovers taught me about love and the journey of my soul. By living in the world and participating in relationships, we are challenged to grow. Distractions are all around, but if we can be still the heart will speak.

What mistakes have I made? Are there really any mistakes? Didn't I learn from each action? Was it right or wrong? Could I have learned the same lessons by staying in one place? Did I need to travel? I think so. My heart led me to the road. Time out from the distractions of the day-to-day grind. But even the road offered distractions. There were times I didn't trust and didn't express my heart voice. I obeyed the irrational fears and limiting thoughts of the mind. Other times when my heart would speak to me I would express it and be told by another I was mistaken. Why did I believe them and not my heart? Why was I swayed so easily?

What makes me happy? I love the beach. I love to run in the sun. Slow mornings with coffee and time to write. Simple meals prepared at home. Time to read. Time to play. I love to travel and see new places. Visits with friends. Good music. Time alone. Quiet places. Companionship. Love.

What are my dreams? I know my time in The Big W and on the road is not finished yet, but someday I will stop. What will I create? I see me living in a small beach community in a simple home. In the mornings I arise and have coffee overlooking the surf. Some journal time and then a run. In the driveway an RV for random trips. To earn an income, I write the stories in my head. Once a month I visit the kids for 5-7 days in New England? Perhaps someday they come live with me? Lastly, I share this with the love of my life. Not a lover for a reason, not a lover for a season, but a lover for a lifetime. Is that too much to ask? I don't think so. It's my dream and I'll co-create it with the Universe.

What is my plan? I'll finish the summer in New England with the kids. Work will provide some money to travel in The Big W. I'll venture to the road for another year with my dreams close to my heart and my heart leading towards my dreams. I'll continue to study in Soul School–Playground Earth. I know what I value. Now I must examine and discard the limiting beliefs I cling to. The heart must reprogram the mind.

It's time to love, learn, play and dream.

CHAPTER FORTY-ONE
WHEN DID YOU LEAVE HEAVEN?
"JOSEPHINE"

I was single, seeing the kids every chance I got, and working for the time being. Angelina and I had taken a trip to Erie, Pennsylvania in April, and in early May I had taken a trip to Burlington, Vermont to see Dylan. He was born on April 17th and was only a couple of weeks old when I first saw him. He was one of eight in the litter and one of two males. Even though I was based in The Dub in Barre, Mass., I still had a little travel bug during summer session II. My friend Tim was hosting a Memorial Day 2000 Weekend getaway in Atlanta and I decided to attend.

Originally Angelina and I were supposed to go together, but since our recent separation the Atlanta plans were up in the air. However, her best friend Don, whom she grew up with in Miami, was living in Atlanta and at the last minute she called and suggested we still go together. No problem I said. And it was no problem. We are still great friends.

She told me as we were boarding the plane that she was happy we could go as friends but that she just couldn't handle it if I ended up flirting with anyone over the weekend. I assured her my flirting days were over. Weekend romances didn't work for me. I reminded her how when we met back in March, and how our eyes locked and there was this sense of knowing we should be together. That, I told her is the only way I would be with anyone. There had to be some soul connection. I wasn't looking for a physical connection. I was tired of that distraction. So rest assured, there would be no flirting and I didn't foresee any soul romances either.

How wrong I was.

Over the weekend in Atlanta while out to dinner, Josephine entered the restaurant and our eyes met. Time was still. I had been here before. I glanced at Angelina and I knew I was in trouble. It was as if my entire journey on the road, my entire journey of my life, led up to this moment with Josephine.

Soul recognition. Deep within I knew we'd been through this before. How long had it been? Where have you been? Has all the work, all the lessons, all the decisions, all the experiences, been for you?

My mind answered, "No. Not Josephine. It couldn't be. Could it?"

My heart was at peace. Relax. Let it unfold. We were drawn together.

Many times I would read how destiny assures the meeting of soul mates or individuals within the same soul group, but the level of awareness and the decisions we make determine whether they stay together for a reason, a season, or a lifetime.

Josephine was 31 years old, divorced three years, working in the medical field, and lived alone in her apartment just outside of Atlanta in Tucker, Georgia. We had known each other since the early nineties. She was married and I was married when we first met. We both eventually got divorced, but each time our paths crossed we were dating others.

Now the attraction was mutual and deep. We would spend the weekend talking, laughing, and sharing about our past and future dreams. She was amused that I was travelling with my ex-girlfriend. Tim had told her I was coming for the weekend and she was hoping to see me, ex-girlfriend or not.

Coincidently, we had each had several relationships since our divorces and were both at a point were sex first just didn't work. It was too powerful and too blinding. We both knew it was time to walk a different path. A higher path.

I shared of my past two years in The Big W on the road and how I had plans to travel again in August. There was no urge to invite her on the road, nor a desire to abandon my plans and move to Georgia. However, I was excited to stay in touch as I traveled and get to know her better from a distance, safe from the entanglements of physical contact. She would later share similar thoughts.

On Sunday night a gang of us all went to the movies and saw *Mission Impossible II*. This would be our theme. As Josephine and I began the process of discovering each other, no one approved. People would talk to us each separately and say, "What are you doing? You two are not a match. Don't go down that road." The important thing is, we knew. We were the only ones who believed.

To our mutual friends, Josephine and I on the surface didn't appear to be a match. They would point out that while I wanted to travel, she enjoyed the comforts of her home. I was a runner, she had a hip replacement and her idea of athletics was watching a Braves game at Turner Field. While I was outgoing and spoke to everyone, she called herself the Ice Princess. She had boundaries and many people mistook this for snobbery. She also spoke her mind and had an opinion. Why do men call a woman with an opinion a Bitch? I think many of my male friends felt threatened.

Ironically, we had many of the same mutual friends, but rarely interacted with them at the same time. As the news spread around the country amongst our friends that Josephine and Napoleon were romantically linked, skepticism was the word of the day. Mission Impossible, perhaps not. Spiritually something was happening to each of us. On a soul level we had connected. We believed.

I flew back to New England after a late night kiss on the morning of May 29, 2000. Looking back we would consider this our anniversary date, the morning of our first kiss. We were both excited to get to know each other from a distance without the possibility of being blinded by sex. There was no pressure, no need to rush. Our paths were running parallel and it was if we had forever.

CHAPTER FORTY-TWO
DON'T KNOW WHY THEY KICK MY DOG
"JUNE, 2000"

On June 10, 2000, I traveled to Burlington, Vermont, and Dylan and I became family. We drove the 235 miles back to Barre. Our first four hours together was on the road. He was eight weeks old and all puppy. Joey and Sara loved him. While everyone agreed he was a beautiful dog, once again, everyone questioned why I was getting a dog. No support, just, "Don't you think an RV is too much for a dog?", "Shouldn't you settle down before you get a dog?", and "You travel too much for a dog.". I was thinking just the opposite, what a great life for a dog. Dylan would see more of the country then most Americans do. Besides, we would spend all of our days together, running and exploring. I ignored the dream snatchers.

On June 12th we celebrated Sara's eighth birthday. That day she participated in a dance show at her school. She was thrilled to have me in the audience. The next week Sara made her First Communion. It was also Father's Day. It was nice to be able to share it with her. She was so beautiful and so excited to be the center of attention.

Being in the church felt strange. My early exposure to God and spiritual principles was through my parents' church. I said my rosary's and knew by the age of twenty I had racked up at least a million years in purgatory just for the things I was thinking of doing. My parents were devout church-goers and ever since my divorce would encourage me to attend Mass and all would be well in the world. It's not my intention to bash organized religion. I have to believe many people have their spiritual needs met with the religions of their choices. However, for me it seemed pretty shamed-based and I couldn't comprehend a God who needed to punish me for all of eternity. I now believed in a God that placed no conditions upon me. His or her love was constant, regardless of my behavior. I could create my own hell on earth by choosing to ignore the lessons presented to love, or create my own heaven on earth through the mastering of lessons and attainment of greater awareness of the God within each of us. Additionally, it made no sense that only those blessed to be born in a certain religion would be saved. One would think that an all-knowing and all-loving God would be kind enough and smart enough to create a religion available for all souls on the planet. Then again, was religion a man-made concept? Was the shame I felt a human creation? As I traveled, reading and experiencing life, Soul School–Play Ground Earth, made more and more sense. Reincarnation and the journey of my soul, soul mates attracted as teachers, master guides, life after death, karma, and many eastern philosophies were more realistic and believable for me. One shot on this planet to evolve didn't seem like enough time. At least for me. No, many lives, many lessons, to be aware of our hearts and the journey to our higher self, seemed to register with me. We were powerful spiritual beings having a human experience. The further I walked this path, the further I was isolated from those that resisted my Truth. But I knew that only the truth would set me free. The journey would continue with or without the consent of others. We each must walk our paths and find our individual truths.

Josephine and I stayed in touch by phone, cards and letters. We would correspond this way for seven weeks before seeing each other again. Talking on the phone and sharing our innermost selves without the threat of physical contact, we were able to build a foundation based upon truth. On our first phone call after my visit to Atlanta she asked what I was doing and I responded, "Reading."

"Reading what?" she asked.

Hesitating, I replied, *"Camino"* by Shirley MacLaine.

I guess I was slightly embarrassed. Perhaps I didn't seem like the typical MacLaine fan. Or perhaps it was all the ribbing and attacks on Ms. MacLaine's experiences and her public sharing that made me hesitate. However, no longer needing validation from others and committed to my path, I shared what I was reading.

It was the best answer I ever had. Actually in this case it was the only answer. What happened next surprised me. It seems one of the major problems Josephine had experienced in past relationships was spiritual compatibility. Josephine was well aware of Shirley MacLaine's books and so much more. My honesty opened the door for us to share about our spiritual lives. We spent the next four hours talking. Many of the spiritual things I was experiencing and becoming aware of over the past two years were part of her everyday life. She didn't share a lot of her beliefs as she was often made fun of and considered weird. She kept her circle of intimate friends intentionally small. Many times this was interpreted as snobbery or bitchiness.

As I shared of Soul School–Playground Earth, she shared of some of her spiritual experiences. As a child, at the age of six, she had a near-death experience after being struck in the head with a golf club. She talked of chakras, aura, and energy leaking. She shared of psychics, channeling and mediums. She meditated, burned incense and candles. She often felt other's energy and needed to be aware of the company she kept. She said she was intuitive and at times she would see things as if channeling herself. I was dumbfounded. I finally met a woman who not only shared my enthusiasm for spiritual knowledge, but seemed further along in her development and awareness than I was. Was the student ready? Had a new teacher appeared? These were my feelings. Later I was to find out, Josephine felt the same.

Our talks continued and we grew closer. I shared my dream to travel over the next year with Dylan and write about my journey on the road and my inner journey from head to heart and the lessons of my life. She offered nothing but encouragement. As we grew closer emotionally, the yearning to be together physically was growing. The distance between New England and Atlanta was doing for us what we probably wouldn't have done had we been in the same city. Each day my thoughts were more and more of her, as hers were of me. However, I knew my time on the road wasn't finished and I needed to travel alone. I half expected her to try to change my mind. Instead she shared that she had no desire to take me from my path. The last thing in the world she wanted was a man in her arms with his eyes staring at the road. While the road was not something she desired or a lifestyle she understood, she did understand my need to complete it on my own terms and not prematurely abort it and always be second guessing myself. Our time would come when it was right.

CHAPTER FORTY-THREE
NO MORE AUCTION BLOCK
"JULY, 2000"

July fourth weekend I had friends gathering in Minnesota.
Josephine would like to have come but had used all her sick
time at work and financially it was not a sound decision for her
to go. Over the weekend, I was harassed by a few friends about
our relationship. How could I explain our spiritual connection,
our soul recognition? No, I just told them that it was nice
getting to know someone without jumping in the sack. Besides,
I still had my road plans. How did everyone become an expert
on Josephine and me? Did anyone really know us? We were
enjoying the process of discovery and we were not distracted by
sex. We were living in the truth. We were becoming more and
more aware of the big picture.

While in Minnesota I met several women who found me
attractive. Offers were made and offers were declined. I patted
myself on the back. Why? Technically, I still considered myself
single and available. Josephine and I were not dating. How
could we be, we hadn't had sex yet. So I patted myself on the
back thinking I chose the higher road and didn't just reach out
for some immediate gratification. Later, back in New England, I
realized it wasn't about me not acting out because I recognized
that sex just for sex didn't work for me. Rather, it was about the
fact that I was in a relationship. I had begun an emotionally
intimate phone relationship with Josephine and didn't even
realize it. Now for some this may seem shocking, but for me it
was a huge lesson. I thought the relationship started with sex.

Not so. Emotionally I was becoming entwined with Josephine. By not acting out in Minnesota I was honoring the connection we had begun. Some souls are more aware than others. While at times I feel like a spiritual giant, more often than not I feel spiritually retarded.

My friend Paul Almay from New York City was in town and talking of his past relationship. I had known Paul for years and he was always bragging about the women he had sex with. For about ten years it was, "I slept with this one, I slept with that one." At times it was nauseating. Anyway in the past year he too was learning sex first wasn't leading him to the woman of his dreams. He was trying to walk a different path. We talked on and off all weekend. He was sharing about his past girlfriend and he made the comment, "I didn't need two daughters"; referring to the dynamics of their relationship. In that moment my problems with my relationship with Johanna made sense. I had two children. I didn't need three. We met and fell in love and somehow I became her father, or at least father figure. Why? I don't know. But as father and daughter it would never work. It was doomed from the start. We were never partners. It was a toxic relationship early on, but denial is powerful. I'm not blaming her. I'll own fifty percent. But the reality was, I didn't need three children, I already had two.

Returning home from Minnesota, the summer rolled on. The kids were busy with baseball and Girl Scout camp. We played and I worked.

One weekend I worked Friday, Saturday, and Sunday, day and night. People thought I was nuts working on the weekend, but I really didn't live by a 'days of the week' calendar. I found a great freedom in this. Work when there's work. Play when there's not. Anyway this particular weekend I worked straight through and billed for $4,800. My wages would be 50% or $2,400 for the weekend. That Monday I slept all day until three in the afternoon. Upon awakening I felt guilty. I wasted the day. I'm a bum. Deep within there was still this limiting tape from my past, "If you don't get up before eight a.m. you're a bum." Intellectually I knew that I worked all weekend and deserved to sleep. But the tapes are relentless. My head and heart would often battle over this. With the mind constantly pushing for a 9-5 lifestyle and the heart trying to live each moment in the moment, the battled raged. Deep within I knew that I could make my own rules. Perhaps, that was what the road offered, a chance to make the rules, to define success, to create my life on my own terms with my own understanding of a higher power.

Sleep. I love sleep. While my mind is cluttered during the day, my spirit sores with unlimited potential as the subconscious plays during sleep. It cracks me up when you call someone and you know you woke them up and they pretend, "Huh, what? Oh, no. No, I'm not sleeping. I'm awake." Like it's some kind of crime to sleep. I try to enjoy it now when someone calls and wakes me up at ten in the morning, "Yes, I was out like a light. What time is it, ten? Call me back at ten-thirty, that's when I like to get up." Just a game, I guess.

In the third week of July, after seven weeks of talking on the phone, I flew to Atlanta to visit Josephine. On my trip the previous May I had gotten bumped on my flight from New England to Atlanta and received a $300 voucher on Delta for my rerouting to Chicago en route to Atlanta. A three hour delay for $300, I'll take that deal any day. Our original plan was to meet in Virginia Beach the weekend of the 22nd, but we rationalized that we would be at a beach party with all our friends. Thus, the week before Virginia Beach I flew to Atlanta for a weekend together without the distractions of our friends and the party.

We were both excited about seeing each other after seven weeks of sharing on the phone. She told me that over the seven weeks she had revealed more of herself than she normally does in a relationship. She was taking risks and so was I. On the phone we held nothing back and shared our true selves. Was it safe? Was it the fact that we weren't having sex? We shared openly and honestly. For me, speaking my truth was a challenge. So often I would hold back or lose sight of my dreams because I was blinded by sex or I was afraid to offend or hurt the other person. On the phone I shared openly my plans for the road and my desire to someday live at the beach. Josephine asked where I was on my journey and what I was available for. I shared honestly that a long-distance relationship was the best I could do. I wouldn't be available for at least one year. I was not willing to lose my self or my dreams. She made it clear she was available to discover who I was and what we had. Neither of us was in a rush. There was no panic, no grabbing, and no neediness. Eventually we spoke of sex on the phone. We agreed that at some point we would like to have sex. We spoke openly about what we enjoyed and didn't enjoy. We even had HIV Tests completed over the summer. In mid-July, seven weeks after we met back in May, I arrived in Atlanta.

The weekend had its share of ups and downs. Literally. We had a great time just hanging out talking and laughing, sharing and dreaming. She cooked and also we went out for dinner. We hugged and we kissed. Eventually, we slept together.

It was one of the weirdest bedroom encounters I've ever had. While making love to her, her face changed. It literally became a different face. It was a face from my past. I knew that face. It was a comfortable face from somewhere in my past. Then blinding colors, blues, greens and yellows. Distracted, I lost my erection. This had never happened to me. Struggling with what was happening as far as her face and these colors in my mind, combined with the bullshit manhood tapes of sexual performance, I became withdrawn. I had once heard a friend say, "My relationship sucks, but I stay because the sex is great." I could identify with that. But now I found myself thinking, "My relationship is great, but the sex sucks." And to make matters worse it was my fault. Regaining my erection and trying to win an Olympic medal we consummated the relationship. Afterwards Josephine asked me where I went. She said that she enjoyed the love making, but then I disappeared, I went away. She was right. I was lost in trying to be a real man. Please her, show her I got the goods, I'm the man. It was open and honest talk. I wanted to run, but stayed. I shared about her face changing and my recognizing the face on some soul level. I shared about the bright colors and my getting distracted.

Something was happening and I wasn't sure what it was. Over the course of our relationship this would happen often, not just during sex, but during other intimate moments as well. Now looking back, I know it has to do with past lives and her channeling abilities. However, on that weekend visit in July it just took the wind out of my sails.

The following weekend, as planned, Dylan and I drove The Big W to Virginia Beach and Josephine flew in from Atlanta. Our friends were staying at the Holiday Inn. We spent Thursday night in The Dub and Friday and Saturday nights in the hotel. We enjoyed a magical weekend of talking, laughing and lovemaking.

Josephine was schooling me not only spiritually, but also in bed. She showed me how to stay in the moment, stay present. Olympic, prove-your-worth sex, was not what she was longing for. Slow, tender lovemaking was a new world for me. We had what I call, soul sex.

As the weekend progressed several of our friends approached us and said they had heard we were together and couldn't picture it, but now after seeing us together, they would share that we were perfect for each other. We believed. Now others believed. My friend Paul was calling us, "The Princess and The Pauper". He would joke with Josephine, "Napoleon teaches you to play, and you teach him to grow up." Of course only a child would travel the country in an RV claiming to be in Soul School–Playground Earth.

The highlight of the weekend was exploring the Association for Research and Enlightenment founded by Edgar Cayce, and located on 67th Street in Virginia Beach. After spending hours in the library, I got a massage at the Health Center. It was a real thrill to actually see Mr. Cayce's pictures on the wall, the foundation he dreamed of, and the records of thousands of readings he conducted over his lifetime. Naturally, I stopped at the bookstore on the way out. I picked up a copy of Brian Weiss's *Messages from the Masters,* and Richard Bach's *Out of My Mind.* In his book, Mr. Bach travels to another time, a parallel universe, where he encounters individuals who, through the decisions they made split away to an alternate time, an alternate reality. Dr. Weiss shares in his book the wisdom of the Masters, the spirit guides who shape our destinies. He talks of the tapping into the power of love and that love is all there really is. I read both at the beach in the sun and the journey continued.

On Sunday night I took Josephine to the Virginia Beach airport. Her flight was delayed two hours, from eight to ten. We would hang in The Dub, laughing and singing. Josephine has a wonderful voice and is always singing something. As a child she performed, but now it was more of a private pleasure. At one point, while listening to a CD, she began singing Marvin Gaye's song *Let's Get It On*, as the music played. When she reached the verse in the song where it goes, *"What's wrong with me loving you?"*, it dawned on me that I still fear love. Those words just struck me and I knew I was still afraid of love. Those words cut through me and gave me permission to let go. There is nothing wrong with me loving you. I could tap into the power of love. I have no need to fear love. I am love. Was my need for solitude a reaction to my fear of companionship? Later I would journal:

> I'm different, yet the same.
> I'm complex, yet simple.
> I'm separate, yet part of.
> I'm a man, yet a god.
> I fear love, yet I am Love.

As she flew back to Atlanta, Dylan and I drove through the night to New England reflecting on another weekend of love shared.

The last weekend in July Sara was in the local production of the musical *Oliver*. When she marched out singing on stage, I just melted in my tears. She was awesome. I wouldn't have missed it for the world. I brought her flowers and after the show we took pictures. She was beaming.

CHAPTER FORTY-FOUR
I DON'T HURT ANYMORE
"AUGUST 2000"

My 39th birthday was August 1, 2000. I moved into The Big W at the age of 36 just before my 37th birthday, back in May of 1998. Time was marching on. For my birthday I started Dylan running. A mile and half was all he could handle. That was good because since the marathon last December I was in pretty bad shape. I had two months recovery before I could run again. The rain in Hawaii on race day didn't help my knees. Perhaps I have a touch of arthritis in the right knee. It was sore for two months. After that it was the snow of New England in February and March. Pretty much four months of no running. May through July I only managed to run about three days per week at only two or three miles per run. I was 15 pounds heavier than I liked to be. Too many pizzas. On my 39th birthday I recommitted to my training and Dylan and I would start at ground one. We would progress together.

I had read Oprah's book, *Make the Connection*, years earlier. What a power of example she is. I wish I could have been there when she finished the Chicago Marathon. I always liked that title and would say to myself when I was out of shape, "Napoleon, make the connection. It's what you put in your mouth and what you do with your feet." Swearing off Pizza and committed to Dylan, our training began that August.

On the first weekend of August, Dylan and I traveled to Maryland to visit with Sean and Dianna. Sean had tickets to a Bob Dylan show in Columbia, Maryland again. The plan was for

Sean and I to go to the show and for Dianna to watch the dogs. She had two of her own, Zak and Tonka and was dog- sitting both Willie and Abby for friends. Dylan made five. Dianna loved it as they all rented the movie *My Dog Skip*. Sean and I were in the eigth row for the show. It was awesome. The next day we headed back to New England.

The second weekend I used the remaining credit on my Delta flight voucher and returned to Atlanta. Josephine celebrated my birthday with gifts and love. It's funny. I'm much better at giving gifts than receiving. Friday night we attended a Braves game at Turner Field with our friends, Melinda and John. Saturday night we all went to an old fashioned southern restaurant called Miss Pitty Pat's Porch. The food was fantastic and the setting was right out of the movie, *Gone with the Wind*. Furniture from the movie was on location in the restaurant.

On Sunday night as we laid in bed, Josephine asked me if I would let her love me. It dawned on me that though I was letting her in, I still needed to learn how to receive love. Like receiving presents, receiving love was awkward. I told her that I would let her love me.

Monday on the flight home I reflected on our love. We lived in the truth. I shared my dreams and my goal of the road. We had compatibility on many levels. Spiritually we shared many of the same beliefs. Sexually, I was learning to make love. Our connection was a soul connection. Financially, she was not looking for a Sugar Daddy. She was self-supporting. Travel; while I longed for the road, she liked a home base. She did enjoy travelling, but liked to return to the comforts of her home. Climate; she loved the south. She wasn't looking to move to New England. She grew up in Texas, and spent the last ten years in Atlanta. As far as the beach was concerned, she would be willing to move there someday, but not in an RV, she would need a home. Children; since her divorce she had given this much thought. Her conclusion was that she didn't want children. She liked kids, but at this point in her life, she had decided she didn't want to begin that journey. She had grieved this fact and accepted she would never have children. She wanted a lifetime mate. She was not looking short term, but long term. She wanted to share her life with another. She was not willing to settle for less.

We were in love. It was not a needy, desperate, cling on for dear life love, but an accepting, patient, let's see where this love goes. At times it was awkward for both of us. We were both on new ground, new territory. We challenged each other to love differently. It began with seven weeks of emotionall intimacy, emotional vulnerability, eventually progressing to physical intimacy. We shared several weekends in Atlanta and one in Virginia Beach. We both honored the truth. We both practiced self-care and boundary expression. We both were willing to love and be loved. We both expressed our needs. We both had dreams and were willing to see if they would be compatible over time. Neither of us felt pressured, rushed, or forced to make it work now. We had time, and time would unfold, revealing our paths. It was okay to love and it was okay to chase your dreams.

We believed while others doubted. We would walk our paths. We were both strong personalities and I nicknamed our relationship, "Two Stars". Sometimes she would shine, at other times I would shine. There was no dominant partner. I was dating an equal. At times she would be the teacher and I would be the student, and other times I would be the teacher and she would be the student. I called her "Sweet Tea" and she called me her "boy". I was in love, and I didn't hurt anymore.

CHAPTER FORTY-FIVE
CHIMES OF FREEDOM
"JUNIOR TERM WITH DYLAN"

On August 16, 2000 Dylan and I said goodbye to the campground, goodbye to the kids, and goodbye to New England. We were heading to New Mexico for the Labor Day 2000 gathering of my friends. As we drove through the night I felt free. Free to reflect, free to dream, and free to live.

Life changes quickly. I've tried to enjoy the cycles and seasons. People and places come and go. I remain the constant, yet I am constantly changed. I began contemplating my two month review or "Two Month" theory. Life changes substantially ever two months.

It was August 2000, and we were on the road again. In June, I was working, staying in The Dub in Barre, Mass., and talking to Josephine on the telephone. In April, I was stuck in an apartment with The Dub in the rear parking lot as I enjoyed the season of laughter with Angelina. In February, Johanna and I had come off the road, my running was nonexistent, the kids were excited, and my old job was a new reality. In December there was the Honolulu Marathon, the beaches of Hawaii and the separation from Johanna. In October, house-sitting at Jamie and Charlene's, the trip north to New England from Florida and Halloween with the kids. One year ago in August 1999, Johanna flew in from California and we hit the road together. In June, the warning times ignored at Johanna's in southern California. In April there was the breakup with Jane in Chicago and the running of the Boston Marathon. In February, time alone between Corrina and Jane while exploring the beaches of Florida. In December I shared 24 days with Corrina. In November, hitting the road freshman term. In September I was making my final preparations for the road. Two years ago in August 1998, living, working and saving, alone in The Dub after breaking up with Lily. In May 1998, the purchase and move into The Dub while dating Lily. Yes, every couple of months life changes. Do we?

The journey of the soul in this lifetime will experience a few bumps, a few challenges. Do we rise to the occasion? Do we learn the lessons? Do we walk through the painful days? Do we grasp the fact that each moment leads us to the next moment? Each moment contains the potential for a lesson to affect us for a lifetime. Do we understand that the Universe sends us teachers to assist us? Nothing is wasted, it's all Soul School–Playground Earth. Where will I be in October? December? February? April? June? Next August? One day at a time, one lesson at a time, it will be revealed. Often I reflect on how painful my divorce was and questioned why. Now, it is so clear. It was the crisis that turned my eyes from the external journey to the internal journey. The tragic blessing ripped my world apart and put an end to the great numbing. The awareness began and there was no turning back. We can look back, but it is forward we march as we try our best to live in the now.

As I reflected over the past several years, I was also dreaming of the upcoming times on the road and life ahead. Over the past couple of years I had traveled to many places for short periods of time. Now I was entertaining the notion of travelling to fewer places for longer periods of time. Was it the beginning of my needs for community? Maybe. Living in The Dub for over two years now and considering The Dub my home, I still felt somewhat homeless. Or was it just a lack of community? Often while visiting friends I would envy the strong bonds of daily friendship in the lives of my friends. It wasn't really envy, but rather more of a craving. Solitude and companionship. The balancing act continued. Not the need for a female companion, but the desire to hang with the boys.

To have a weekly get together, to have men in my life on a daily basis to share, talk and laugh with. For now I was happy with my long-distance relationship with Josephine. While I was on the road, she would be in Atlanta. It was three months since we met and I was enjoying the slow process of discovery. I enjoyed having a girlfriend and I was okay with the distance apart. But, another form of companionship was starting to come to my attention. Yes, I often saw my friends around the country, but that was over weekends and for short time periods. What I was beginning to crave was more of a daily community of male friends. It wasn't strong enough to make me permanently settle down, but it was growing stronger. While I was in New England for six months, the cold and my lack of desire to be there, kept me mostly working and playing with the kids, with no time or desire to create this male community of friends. As I traveled, my desire to settle in a beach community grew stronger and stronger. I would dream of a beach home, a companion, a community, daily runs, writing, time with the kids, and a luxury RV in the driveway.

So we drove through the night, content to be discovering Josephine from a distance, dreaming of hanging with the boys, and excited to be free and on the road again.

The last two weeks of August, 2000 were busy as Dylan had his first swim at Lake Hartwell in South Carolina, we spent a weekend in Atlanta, Georgia, with Josephine talking, laughing, and coffee on the couch; we traveled north to Vikki in Nashville, Tennessee, west to Graceland in Memphis, we explored Tecumseh, Oklahoma, and enjoyed weekend camping with the Denver crew in Breckinridge, Colorado.

It was Tuesday, August 29, 2000. We were in Albuquerque, New Mexico, and Josephine would be arriving on Thursday.

CHAPTER FORTY-SIX
MILLION DOLLAR BASH
"LABOR DAY 2000 WEEKEND"

Waking up in the downtown Hyatt in Albuquerque, we had the room to ourselves on Friday morning, September 1, 2000. Josephine flew in from Atlanta the previous day with Melinda and John. They were up early and out of the room by eight. Tomorrow, Josephine and I would return the favor and would have to make the early departure from the bedroom we were sharing. It was agreed that we would get the room the first morning, as we don't see each other as regularly as Melinda and John do.

Eggs Benedict, waffles, coffee and fruit. Eating room service naked in bed is not a luxury I experience often in The Dub. We had made love earlier and would repeat the intimacy on a full stomach after cigars and bubbles in the tub. Not The Dub, the tub. Taking a bath, bubbles, Josephine and a cigar, with Marvin Gaye singing in the background, that was my magic memory from the weekend. We didn't leave the room until sometime after twelve.

It was three months ago that we kissed back in Atlanta in May on Memorial Day Weekend. We spent seven weeks talking on the phone. In July I had flown to Atlanta and she had flown to Virginia Beach. In August I flew to Atlanta and I had stopped in Atlanta in The Dub on my journey west. Now, here in New Mexico we would have our fifth weekend together. I love the Thursday to Tuesday weekends.

We spent the weekend with time alone and time with

others. The weather was 80 degrees and sunny. Afternoons by the pool were very festive. Someone took this great picture of Josephine and me dunking each other under the water. Later, I would have it framed. It was fun getting to know our mutual friends at the same time. While some still scoffed, most were being swayed. Not that we needed anyone's approval. But we were even starting to hear things like, "You two look great together", "Who would have thought how cute you two are", and "Here comes the happy couple". It was nice. More challenging was when we heard things like, "So when is Josephine moving into The Dub?" or "When's the move to Atlanta?". After the restaurants, after the pool time, after the general hanging out with friends, alone in the privacy of our room, we would talk.

Josephine would often say that she didn't understand my lifestyle on the road in The Dub, but would never try to talk me out of it. She had her home, and was well aware of the inner journey she had embarked upon. For me, somehow the inner journey was related to my travels. Perhaps in my life off the road I was just distracted and caught on a treadmill. I needed to make a physical break from the script, a walk-about for the soul. What I realized most is that there is no need to explain it, I must just honor it. My journey is my journey. Your journey is your journey.

We were growing closer and closer. Our emotional and spiritual relationship was now also physical. Our time on the phone and weekends together were always magical and it was getting more and more difficult to part when the time came to say goodbye. Our souls were entwining and separation was painful. Yet, for me this was a great challenge. I knew in my heart that it was not time to stop and move to Atlanta, nor was it time to invite another companion on the road. I was honoring my truth and this pleasure was greater than the pain of separation. We would talk of the big picture versus the little picture. The journey of each of our souls was eternal. We didn't need to reach out for immediate comfort and gratification. Our inner journeys would continue while we were apart, with Josephine in Atlanta and me on the road. This was new territory for both of us. Neither one would cling. Neither one would give up their path for the other. We would walk separately, until the time to walk together was revealed.

Throughout the weekend people who had grown accustomed to my travels would ask where I was off to next. I would respond, "Thinking of going to Sedona and maybe Zion National Park and Bryce Canyon. After that I may check out Denver for a month or so. Hang with the boys." While I enjoyed the excitement of the unknown, Josephine needed a little more. She would ask, "Where do I fit in?" She wasn't demanding, she was just looking for a little clarity. I assured her she fit in. Atlanta was only a flight away.

I was actually really enjoying our long distance relationship. It was neat having someone special in my life, yet at the same time being able to continue my journey. Also, as I traveled, I was already spoken for. Romantic road distractions, which were a part of my past travels, were now eliminated. It's as if I could spend time in solitude, and my need for female companionship was partially being met. Free of the longing to be with another, I could focus on my other needs.

Josephine was special. I knew from the moment our eyes met in Atlanta three months ago that soul recognition had occurred. It was if each relationship prior to meeting her was preparing me for our encounter. The road too was special and now based upon my lessons, I could honor them both. I could travel my path and also enjoy the process of discovery and the challenge of entwinement with Josephine. Our time apart wasn't a desperate, needy, "I miss you time". But rather a looking forward to seeing you, I wonder where this is going, "I miss you time".

On Sunday night a gang of forty of us road the Sandia Peak Tramway to the top of the Sandia Mountain. While atop the Peak an electrical storm hit, shutting the Tramway down and leaving us stranded for several hours. We all rushed to the restaurant and the chaos began. While everyone rushed to order food at once, Josephine and I silently slipped to a side table for two and had a romantic dinner away from the chatter of the group. She would joke it was our first real date. Prior to this we had always been out with a group or another couple. We toasted to our time together, our love, and our future.

We enjoyed our long weekend in New Mexico. Six days, our longest time together. On Tuesday I drove Josephine to the airport in The Big W and we said our goodbyes. Over the next few days, I would reflect on our many moments together. I could hear her laugh and would think of her beautiful face as I fell asleep.

Dylan and I pulled out of the airport and watched the planes taking off. I was thinking about what my friend Amy once said, "I pray for rocks and God wants to give me diamonds." With his head out the window and staring at the sky I could swear he was singing, *"Oh, babe it ain't no lie, this life I lead is mighty high."*

CHAPTER FORTY-SEVEN
SANTA-FEE
"TIME ON THE ROAD"

Labor Day 2000 weekend in New Mexico had come and gone.
Josephine and I enjoyed our time together and time with our
friends. She had returned to Atlanta and I was on the road. My
plans were to go to Sedona, Arizona. But as usual, I headed east
to Santa Fe, before going west to Sedona.

I spent several days exploring Santa Fe. My friend, Zeke
Dreward, who now lived in Boston, was originally from Santa
Fe. He was visiting family and friends after the weekend bash.
We were able to spend some time just talking and catching up.
After my breakup with Johanna, he was one of the men I would
talk with along with Jimmy Walker from Denver and Jimmy Day
from Vermont. Another friend, Nate Catcher, who had moved
from Michigan, was now living in Santa Fe. I had stopped for
a visit two years earlier with Jimmy when Slinky joined our
travels. Teddy Reilly had since moved to Denver. Nate and
his girlfriend, Lee, and I went to lunch and talked about the
dynamics of relationships. I admitted I had made my fair share
of mistakes, but each relationship was valuable and taught me
more about love and myself. Nate was a kick boxer and very
good at it. After they began dating, Lee became interested in
the sport and was also becoming very accomplished. They had
found a common interest.

Many times friends would say to me that I needed to date
a runner. It was one of my great passions and why shouldn't I
share it with another? Over the years I would often evaluate

my compatibility with a woman based on the fact; did she run? I have finally concluded that it isn't so much about finding a woman who runs, but rather finding someone who understands what running means to me. Someone who would encourage me to run. Someone who would recognize that it makes me happy and that makes them happy. Not someone who would complain about my running, but someone who would embrace it as part of who I am.

From Santa Fe, Dylan and I headed west back towards Albuquerque, across the continental divide, into Arizona to spend the night in a Wal-Mart parking lot in the Flagstaff area. In the morning we drove south along Route 89A to Sedona. What a ride. The drop in elevation was about 4,000 feet. Down, down, and down we went. Hanging on the side of the road enjoying the U-turns. Traffic behind The Dub was at a crawl. Every now and then I would pull over and let those in a rush, rush by.

We spent the first night in a small campground called Hawkeye RV located in downtown Sedona. In the morning we went swimming in Oak Creek. The water was cold, but felt fantastic after our two mile run. We had our weekend of companionship and now it was time for some solitude. With no agenda, we explored and researched Sedona.

Reading a copy of Mary Lou Keller's book *Echoes of Sedona Past*, Dylan and I were beginning to experience the energy of this sacred area. Sedona has long been considered a holy place attracting many with a spiritual thirst. As Mary Keller would describe, "Some people claim that all of Sedona is a vortex, a power place of spiraling energy turning either clockwise or counterclockwise. Many claims have been made about meditations, healings, visions, sightings and channelings of psychic nature and other unusual experiences due to vortex energies. The Native Americans, who knew about the vortex energies in this area, came here for healing and spiritual experiences. They called Sedona the Land of Fire."

Between runs we played tourist. We explored Bell Rock, the Chapel of the Holy Cross, Courthouse Rock, Cathedral Rock and Oak Creek Canyon. On our second day we were invited to the Sedona Pines RV time-share resort. For sitting through a ninety-minute sales presentation, our reward was two free nights at the resort. The pool and jacuzzi were our motivation. The presentation somewhat disturbed me. For $10,000 you got one week a year at the resort. Was Sedona becoming a financial vortex? A ten minute sales pitch movie said we all deserved one week a year to relax, after all we endured the stress and neglect 51 weeks a year. Buy now. You deserve one good week. Why don't we deserve 52 good weeks?

What I remember most is our runs. We went for a three miler followed by a hike in the West Fork in the Red Rock Mountains. Ideas were flowing in my head. Following the hike, I journaled the following thinking of my relationship with Josephine:

My whole life I bought into the belief of "together forever", for better or worse. As I hiked I thought of my running example. I'm not looking for a runner to date, but rather someone who understands what running means to me, what running does for my spirit. Likewise I realize I'm looking for a companion who supports my spirit. Yes, common interest and sexual compatibility are important. But I need someone who nurtures my spirit. My fear of commitment is a fear of getting stuck in a relationship where my spirit is dying. I remember our talk in New Mexico. We agreed that neither of us wanted to recreate the marriages we had. The marriages which had caged our spirits. What I realize is that as long as my spirit feels alive I will stay in a relationship. Together forever in a dying spirit relationship doesn't work. I need to recognize whether my spirit is soaring or being crushed. If soaring I can love and grow. If dying I must practice self-care and remove myself from a relationship that is killing me. You nurture, accept and love me. I need not fear you. My spirit is challenged to soar, to grow, to be alive. You have not tried to steal my dreams or cage my soul. So what am I getting at? What is my clarity? Together forever, for better or worse doesn't work. I'm not talking about bumps or growing pains. I'm talking about spiritual support, nurturing, caring. Is one's soul alive or dead? What leads to the dampening of a spirit? Old beliefs. Old patterns. It seems like a whole set of shit kicks in when people get in a relationship. Everyone brings baggage. The challenge is to create something new. I am love. I have no need to fear love. I am responsible to recognize if people are toxic to my spirit or support my spirit, my journey. I am free to stay or go, not be stuck for better or worse. My yardstick is my spirit. Am I alive or dying? My ideal – a soul supporter, a dream believer. Combine this with common interests, sexual compatibility, shared vision, laughter and love. I need to feel alive, not dead. Past relationships were crushing me and I didn't know how to practice self-care. Now I know. You help me. You show me how to be present. You say you are not going anywhere. Neither am I. It is a spiritual journey this time on earth. What I know now is it's okay to eliminate blocks to my spiritual evolvement. When the spirit is crushed, the season is over, it's time to move on. Yet at the same time we must embrace that which nurtures the soul. We need not fear love. I embrace you. So it's not, together forever, for better or worse. It's together today, supporting each other's spirits.

Perhaps it was the energy or perhaps the time alone? Either way I had some new insight into my self and relationships. The belief of together forever, for better or worse, was deeply engrained in my mind. My heart would whisper, "It's okay to follow your path. It's okay to practice self-care. It's okay to have dreams. It's okay to love. It's okay to move on. It's all part of the lessons." If I was to be successful in building a relationship with another, of sharing a life, I would have to create something new. Recreating and reliving the past no longer worked.

Another day. Dylan and I ran four miles in and around Oak Creek. We ran in the water, on its banks, and through the woods. We discovered trails and swimming holes. At one point it was as if time stood still and I was an Indian running the trails. I could have run all day. I was free.

Later at night I would write:

"Remember Me, Remember You"

Time has shifted
The veil has been lifted.
Years ago I heard her speak
Never thinking she would be the one I seek
Through the crowd I saw her face
Just quick hellos, no heart embrace
Always with another
No moments to discover
We once shared a dance
Fate or Chance

On our final day, I splurged and spent $35 on a 15 minute plane ride touring Sedona from above. It was exciting to see the places we had explored from the air. After four days it was back to The Dub, the road, and heading west. I could barely him hear, but Dylan was singing, *"When you're standing at the crossroads that you cannot comprehend, just remember, death is not the end."*

CHAPTER FORTY-EIGHT
DESOLATION ROW
"LAS VEGAS"

We climbed out of Sedona and returned to Route 40 West in Flafstaff. Heading west we drove until Kingman, Arizona and started to the north along Route 93 with visions of the Hoover Dam and Las Vegas.

Wow. What an energy shift from Sedona, Arizona to Las Vegas, Nevada. We arrived at around ten p.m. and the lights were flashing. The city of excess: bars, gambling, strippers, all you can eat buffets, hotel resort shopping, and neon lights shining bright. Did anyone feel in Vegas? Eat, drink and be merry. Excess. Excess. Excess. Indulge. Indulge. Indulge. Escape. Escape. Escape. What kind of a vortex was Las Vegas?

I had been to Las Vegas several times. But for some reason coming here after four days in Sedona, the place just seemed really negative. Was I become more aware? Was I becoming more sensitive? I thought of the energy in Key West, New Orleans and San Fransico. While some would consider these places party places, I always felt just below the surface there was a level of tolerance, a spirit of acceptance.

The next day I found a parking place and spent the day tanning at the Flamingo Hilton Pool. Sex, booze and gambling was thick in the air. We managed a concrete run along the boulevard, but by five in the afternoon it was time to leave. The energy of Sedona and the energy of Las Vegas couldn't co-exist in my system.

So less than 24 hours later we found ourselves heading

north along Route 15 we were off for the solitude of Zion National Park in Utah. As I was leaving Las Vegas I had the strangest feeling. It was a feeling like I was travelling and retrieving pieces of my soul. I was vaguely aware of this when I returned to Breckinridge without Johanna. I was travelling alone and reclaiming part of myself as I roamed. Pieces from the past, a past on the road with Johanna.

The sun had set and Dylan had a look in his eye, as if to sing, *"All the people we used to know they're an illusion to me now."*

CHATER FORTY-NINE
HAD A DREAM ABOUT YOU BABY
"MOVING ON"

We rented a campsite in Zion National Park in Utah at $14 per night for a couple of nights. Fortunately, they had one trail that they allowed dogs on. Dylan and I went for several runs followed by a swim in the icy mountain streams. We played fetch for hours and Dylan was too exhausted to even play with the deer, who would wander to our campsite. Later, he would chase the lizards and I would call him the "Lizard Dog".

Safely away from Las Vegas, we relaxed in the mountains of Zion. On our first day exploring we met a young couple, around twenty years old, from Maine. The two of them and their dog, Shady, were driving to Santa Barbara, California to start a new life together. She had just graduated from school and would find a teaching position. He would do whatever he could find. They were in love and excited about their dreams. I thought of Josephine.

As I slept that night I dreamt of her. We were walking the beach while Dylan chased the birds.

In the morning I wrote:

"Mornings without you"
Morning coffee in your bed
So many thoughts fill my head
My angel so far away
Yet always with me

To play at the beach
Away from the cold
A soul mate shining star

I would hike in Zion on our second day. I alone amongst the tourist couples. Once again I was aware of battle between solitude and companionship. Wouldn't it be nice to hike with a lover? Perhaps another time. For now I was somewhere in Utah, she was in Atlanta. Nothing happened by mistake in the Universe. The plan would unfold. Our inner journeys would lead us each to our higher selves. Would our external journeys reunite us? I would think of our times together and the strong connection beyond the physical plane. Did we know each other from another lifetime? Was our time apart in this lifetime, similar to lifetimes apart? In the evening we had a campfire and I wrote of my lover, Josephine:

"Remember"

We are sure to remember
Christmas always comes in December.
But what of lives and lovers gone before?
Can we be certain, will we be sure?
I often wonder who you are,
 my eyes just can't see back that far.
Feeling you sleep within my arms,
 did I once protect you from harm?
Time apart and your memory does not fade away.
My heart, my soul long to travel your way.
Wiping tears from your cheek,
 are we the lovers that we always seek?
Were we once queen and king?
What I'd give to hear you sing.
Do you remember me?
True love is free.
We are sure to remember
Christmas always comes in December.

The next day we drove to Bryce Canyon National Park. Again we secured a campsite. At night the temperature dropped. Mornings were chilly. Coffee and a walk with Dylan just to warm up. During the day I hiked alone down into the canyon along the Navajo Trail. I liked Zion better. It was dog friendly and had a nice river to swim in. We spent only one night in Bryce and decided to head north towards Denver.

While in New Mexico, Jimmy was trying to convince me to come to Denver and work for his roofing company as a salesman. If I had been looking for a place to settle down and work it was a great opportunity. But realistically it wasn't what I was searching for. I did agree to come to Denver. Not to work, but to hang with the boys.

Heading north along Route 12 and 24 we drove through the Dixie National Forest. Reaching elevations over 10,000 feet, The Dub was crawling. Birch trees surrounded us. Later, telling the story, no one would believe that I saw all these birch trees in Utah. We eventually drove 70 East and stopped in Green River, Utah. It was Friday and we were tempted to stay the weekend as the annual Melon Festival was coming up. Tempted, we continued on. We had been on the road for twelve days and figured we could make Denver by midnight.

Alternating between sleeping and having his head out the window, Dylan would stare at me, reading my thoughts and repeatedly sing, *"When did you leave heaven, angel of mine?"*

CHAPTER FIFTY
GOTTA SERVE SOMEBODY
"MONEY FOR YOUR SOUL"

We arrived in Denver late at night and woke up Saturday, September 16, 2000 in front of Jimmy's Sherman Street apartment. Dylan was happy to be reunited with Stella. They would play for hours in the fenced-in rear yard.

The plan was to stay for a month parked at Jimmy's. On the weekend of September 30th my friend, Chris Wheelman, and I planned to drive to southern California for our second men's weekend retreat in Catalina hosted by Dean Lewis. Chris had a new mini-van and he was anxious to take it on a long distance trip. I told him I would leave The Dub at Jimmy's and make the ride with him. The following weekend, Jimmy and Amy, along with Teddy Reilly, Reggie, and I would fly to Detroit to visit E, who was hosting a little get together. So with two trips planned, Denver would be my base for a month. Jimmy wanted me to work, but I told him I would only commit to one month in town. The plan was to head to the beaches of Florida on October 16, with a trip to Atlanta on the way.

Teddy worked for Jimmy and was doing extremely well. While I was there he purchased a new pickup truck for $35,000, putting over $18,000 down as a deposit. It worked out well for me as he loaned me his old truck while I was in town. I felt right at home. Every third vehicle is a pickup truck in Colorado. Pretending to work, I would hang with Teddy most days. I say pretending because I really wasn't planning on staying more than a month and it took about one month to learn the language and business of roofing sales. Most jobs were insurance jobs and the selling was pretty straight forward, "Would you like a free roof?" Wind and hale damage was very common in the area and it was all covered by insurance. Both Jimmy and Teddy were bankrolling a small fortune and living rather large for a couple of boys from Michigan. The money was tempting. My mind would insist, "Travel later, make money now." But my heart knew, "Don't forget Soul School-Playground Earth. There will be more job opportunities. What about your dream to travel and write?"

It was nice hanging with the boys. Whether it was the movies, dinner, a little poker, or catching a Bronco's or Rockies game, my need for male companionship was getting met. I missed having a community of friends and felt part of the Denver crew. We caught the last home baseball game of the Rockies and sat along the first base line. Jimmy would reach down and scoop a little of the field gravel for Joey. Another day Jared Moon and I went to a Bronco's game against the Kansas City Chiefs. The Bronco's lost and Jared cried. I picked Joey up a Terrell Davis shirt and put it in the mail. Eventually he would get six shirts; one from Nashville, Denver, Minnesota, Atlanta, St. Louis, and Detroit.

On Wednesday the 27th Chris Wheelman, Stuart Burnside and I hit the road in Chris's mini-van heading south to Catalina. Chris's life had changed a little since a year ago when I parked The Dub at his bachelor pad while I was dating Johanna. Reggie had moved out and in with his new girlfriend Samantha, or as Reggie called her, Sammy, while Chris's girlfriend, Tina, and her two girls moved from Texas and in with Chris. The transition from bachelor to family man was something Chris loved, but at the same time he was looking forward to this road trip and hanging with the boys in Catalina.

We drove through the night and arrived in Pomona, California, at my friend Rick Wood's home. Paul from New York and Sean from D.C. had each flown in earlier the night before and we all went out for breakfast. The southern California sun felt good on my shoulders. In the ten days I had been in Denver it had snowed once. While it lasted only a day or two, The Dub didn't look good covered in snow.

On Friday we all drove to the dock in Newport Beach and went to our assigned boats for the weekend trip to Catalina. It was hard to believe that it was one year ago that Johanna had picked me up at the docks. Once again collecting fragments of my soul, I enjoyed the weekend with the boys. We fished all day on Saturday and I believe I had the record with twelve catches. Sunday night Chris, Stuart and I drove through the night and headed back to Denver. While Stuart slept, Chris and I shared about our lives and our loves. Engaged to be married, Chris was planning a life with Tina. He asked about Josephine. He knew her well. I told him I wasn't sure about our future. I was in love, but for now she was in Atlanta and I was on the road. I enjoyed having someone special in my life, but wasn't ready to abandoned my dreams of travel and writing. I had betrayed myself too often in the past. Could I someday have both? Time would tell. For now we each walked our paths.

While we were in Catalina, Jimmy had moved out of his home in Denver and into a home in nearby Littleton. The two bedroom house had a fully finished basement, which Jimmy would use as an office and the rear yard was three times as large as the Sherman Street apartment. Dylan and Stella played all day and were exhausted most nights.

The following weekend, as planned, we all flew to Detroit. Dylan and Stella stayed at the Shiloh Country Resort for dogs. I went on line and found this resort kennel. The photos included an in ground swimming pool. I figured Dylan would find his way into it somehow.

Staying at Hotel G (Ed G's house), we played all weekend in Detroit. Jimmy, Amy, Teddy, and Reggie were all from Michigan and were excited to visit with friends and family. Teddy took me to his mom's for a corn beef and cabbage dinner. It was good to see his brother, Steve, again. I still call him The Master. Naturally, there was a deer hanging in the garage. His dad shot it with a bow the previous day in their back yard. Teddy wanted to take The Dub someday up into Montana and hunt for a week.

Perhaps if it was summer we would have gone, but the weather was getting too cold for me and I was dreaming of the beach.

After returning to Denver, Jimmy was putting the pressure on me to work selling roofs. I hadn't really done anything over the past month as I was just hanging with the boys and observing. On Thursday night, as I was preparing to leave on Monday October 16th, Jimmy made me an offer I couldn't refuse, "Stay one more month. Work the leads we have. You have seen the business for a month and you know how it works. I need you to lock-in some work for the winter months. If you stay, I'll buy you a plane ticket to New England to visit the kids and one for Atlanta to visit Josephine." I knew what he was thinking. If I get a taste of the money, I'll never leave. But for me it was an opportunity to help him out, stay with the Denver crew another month, and get a visit with the kids and Josephine. I agreed and began selling roofs.

Overall it was a productive month. The cold weather was moving in fast, so Dylan and I moved into Jimmy's basement for four weeks with The Dub parked out front in Littleton. Amy and Jimmy were setting up their new house and at times I would wonder if I would do this ever again. I was involved with ten roofing jobs and made about $5,300 for the month. The money would come in handy on the road and visiting the kids and Josephine. If making money was my goal, I would have stayed and built a life in Denver. But that wasn't my goal, and my dreams stayed alive. My soul wasn't for sale. In the past relationships were distracting. Now money would be the test.

CHAPTER FIFTY-ONE
ON A NIGHT LIKE THIS
"JONO'S CHAPTER"

We called him Jono. His real name was J. Owen Skeats.
Originally from New York City, he had moved to Colorado
several years earlier. He owned a condo, which eventually was
like a flop house for visiting friends to Denver. I had an open
invite, but never stayed.

Jono was a computer person. Not a geek, but he knew his
stuff. One of my goals while in Denver was to purchase a laptop
computer. Jono was my mentor. He researched a few companies
on line after I told him what my needs were. Eventually, we
went to Circuit City and purchased a Compaq Presario with
a four year warranty and leather case for $1,700. I had $2,000
allocated for the expenditure and put the savings into my gas
account. Jono set it up and I was up and writing. Up until now
I would journal in my notebooks. Now I would slowly start to
write this narrative on my new laptop.

Jono worked strange hours. He was a setup man for
conventions and shows in the Denver area. His boss was always
looking for extra guys to work and Jono asked if I was interested
one weekend. It would be a Saturday, so you earned time and
half. Eight hours at $18 per hour. I never would turn down the
extra money, but really I was just looking forward to working
and hanging out with him for the day.

We worked a computer show at the Colorado Civic Center
in downtown Denver. He picked me up and we spent the day
setting up show booths. I did what I was told and managed not

to break anything. I left at six p.m. while Jono stayed until after ten. They needed me for Sunday, too. Jono planned to pick me up early. When we arrived ten minutes late and the crew was full I was told I could go home. Jono gave me his wheels and told me to call later and he would let me know when to pick him up. It worked out well for me, because when I returned to Jimmy's house there were two tickets to the Bronco's game against the Chief's. Later around nine at night I called Jono on the phone and we agreed that I was to pick him up at ten.

I hadn't seen Dylan all day so I brought him for the ride. The plan was to call Jono on his cell phone when I was out in front of the Civic Center waiting for him. I pulled up, made the call, and decided to move from the drivers seat to the passengers seat before he came out. With the car running I hopped out, shut the door of the Jeep Cherokee and proceeded to walk around to the other side. When I got there the door was locked. Going back to the driver's, I was surprised that it was locked too. Apparently, when I got out of the car, Dylan jumped and hit the power lock button. I stared at him and he at me. The radio was blasting and the engine was running. Dylan was locked in and I was locked out. As he barked at me, I hit the ground, laughing hysterically. By the time Jono arrived I was out of control. One of those laughs you just can't stop.

Jono asked "What's so funny?"

I just pointed at Dylan.

He said, "What?"

"Dylan locked me out."

He couldn't hold back. It was too unreal. We both laughed uncontrollably.

Eventually, Jono walked two blocks to the fire department. One truck, eight fireman and a half an hour later we were still locked out. There was nothing they could do. Dylan was running from window to window as the fireman were trying to get him to hit the button again. Jono and I stopped laughing.

Jono told me to stay with the jeep. He went inside and returned with a thin, metal yardstick. Somehow he managed to get in the window and pop the power lock button. Dylan was free and we could have the Jeep back.

Later on the ride home I mentioned this would be a funny chapter about my times in Denver. Jono just said, "Cool. I get my own chapter."

CHAPTER FIFTY-TWO
TIME PASSES SLOWLY
"WORKING AND DREAMING"

On October 19th, after working for four days selling roofs, I flew to Atlanta to visit Josephine. I had been away for 44 days. Over that time we had stayed in touch on the phone. Sundays was our date night. I had mailed her cards and letters and she had sent a few to me in Denver in care of Jimmy.

It was great to be back in her arms. The subway series, Mets versus Yankees was taking place and we boycotted it together. She was a Braves fan and I was a Red Sox fan. It was a lose-lose situation for us.

We spent our days sleeping late, coffee on the couch, making love, and getting reconnected. While we had been dating going on five months I still had the feeling we were only scratching the surface. We pretty much stayed at her home, though on Sunday we did take a trip to nearby Stone Mountain. Mostly we just talked.

Fortyfour days was a long time to be apart. Josephine didn't mind me travelling, but she did suggest it would be nice if I could make it to Atlanta a little more frequently. I missed her and we decided to make plans for Thanksgiving Day, Christmas and New Year's Eve.

I was to return to Denver and work until November 16th and then drive The Dub to Atlanta for Thanksgiving weekend. From there I hoped to be back in the southeast part of the country and within a days ride to Atlanta.

Monday morning Josephine awoke and went to work.

My friend, Tim Hogan, picked me up and drove me to the airport. We had lunch and caught up with each other. Awaiting my return at the airport in Denver was Jimmy. I would work Tuesday to Friday and then it was off again.

Halloween weekend I flew to New England and had a visit with the kids. Joey had his last football game of the season on Saturday and I was able to share in the joy of his several tackles and fumble recovery. The name of his team was the Bull Dogs and each time they scored the team would dance as the P.A. system played, "Who Let the Dogs Out?" The Bull Dogs beat the Indians and Sara and I were the number one cheerleaders. Later, we would go bowling and get pumpkins for Halloween.

That night in my hotel room I would watch the movie *Rudy*. I loved it. Everyone believed and told him he would never play football for Notre Dame. Only problem was Rudy didn't believe it. Again I asked the question, "Why do people refuse to support our dreams?"

Sara planned Sunday. We would shop at the mall, go to Chucky Cheese, and do some ice skating. Unfortunately, I flew home on Monday and missed the trick-or-treating on Tuesday night.

On the flight home I read Lance Armstrong's book *Its Not About The Bike*. What a great story. Mr. Armstrong talked about a concept he called "survivorship". To him, he went through a period after beating cancer where he wanted to go on a permanent vacation. He felt entitled to it after what he had been through. He had trouble adjusting to ordinary life. My mind began questioning my whole journey. I wondered, was I going through survivorship after my divorce? Was I on a permanent vacation? The answer from my heart was no. I wasn't on a permanent trip. The road, The Dub, would end someday. This was not forever. This was time to connect to myself. It wasn't about being separate and isolated from the world forever. It was about solitude and connecting to my true self. It was time for a journey from the world of my head to the world of my heart. It's also interesting to note that Mr. Armstrong didn't go on a permanent vacation, but rather made one of the greatest comebacks in sports history by winning the Tour de France.

Upon my return to Denver I discovered that Teddy had just returned from elk hunting in northern Colorado. Teddy shot a 1,200 pound elk. It took him two days to get it off the mountain and out of the woods. In the morning we had elk and eggs. He was a hunter. I had read that true hunters, those that kill for the meat and not the sport, take the powers of the animal they sacrificed. I believe Teddy was one of those men.

Back in Denver, I worked on selling a few roofs. Like the month before, I enjoyed hanging with the boys. I had learned the business and was creating a few projects for the company. In the meantime we played.

My friend PJ Moore is a professional comedian and I was able to catch a show at the local comedy club. PJ gave me a bumper sticker for The Dub. It read, PJ MOORE SUCKS! Later as I would travel the country people were always asking, "Who's P.J. Moore?"

Jimmy and Teddy liked to play poker. They were out of my league. I enjoyed a nice friendly two dollar game. They, on the other hand, played a little more seriously. We went to a few underground poker games. Sometimes I lost and sometimes I won. I left Denver pretty much even. One thing I was aware of was the energy at the poker table. It reminded me a lot of Las Vegas. Nobody seemed happy. For me I was aware that it didn't matter if I won or lost, I was still affected by the gambling energy at the table.

One of my favorite times in Denver was when Amy and I would just hang on the couch and watch a movie and talk. Sometimes she would second guess her decision to move from Detroit to Denver. Her desire to have children only seemed to be growing, while Jimmy's position of never having children was unchanged. I never told her what to do, but shared that the voice of her heart, her true voice, would always speak. At least that was my experience. As I spoke of Josephine, I shared that while I knew we were compatible, the real test would be if we shared a common vision for a future together. Fortunately for me, having children would not be an issue for us. We both knew that we didn't want to have any. I was happy with the two I had and Josephine had made her decision. One thing Josephine did have to consider was the fact that my children may live with me someday. She has told me she has thought of this and really had no problem with it. Time will tell.

One night Annie and I watched the movie *Capitan Hook* with Robin Williams. Peter Pan was trying to fly again. He had forgot how. They encouraged him to think one happy thought and then he could fly. The power of our thoughts. The power of our minds to create our reality. Be careful what you think, it just might come true. The reprogramming would continue. Think loss and lose, think love and love.

The first two weeks in November, my last two in Denver went by slowly. I couldn't wait to hit the road in The Dub. I made a commitment to stay and help Jimmy until November 16th and would honor it. But it was tough. Some days the temperature would drop down into the teens. I wasn't running much and was eating entirely too much. I longed for the road and for some time with Josephine. We were both aware of the big picture, but at times the little picture was a bitch.

On one of my last nights I went to the movie *The Legend of Bagger Vance*. In the movie the caddy, played by Will Smith said something like, "We all have our own swing. We all have our own path to walk, which no one else can walk." I knew it was time to leave Denver. It was time to walk my path.

All in all I spent two months in Denver from September 16th to November 16th. When the day came to leave, I was ready. I had accomplished what I set out to do. I had bought a laptop computer with Jono's help, was able to hang with the boys, took a few trips, experienced staying in one part of country for an extended time, and made a little money. I valued my time with friends and love the Denver crew. But for now it was cold and I was dreaming about my visit with Josephine and dreaming about the beach as I watched the weather channel and the only orange color on the map was in the southeast.

CHAPTER FIFTY-THREE
CAN'T WAIT
"OUR FIRST MAJOR HOLIDAY"

Dylan and I left Denver on Friday, November 17th, almost exactly two months from the day we arrived. I wondered if Dylan would miss Stella. It had been three months since we left New England. We headed east on Route 70 out of Denver, across Kansas, into Missouri, Illinois, Kentucky, and across Tennessee, to my destination in Georgia; Atlanta and Josephine. It was about 1,200 miles and we did it in two days of hard driving.

We arrived on Sunday November 19th and I planned to celebrate Thanksgiving in Atlanta and then head to Florida on November 30th, as I wanted to be near the beach for the first week in December. I would visit for twelve days, twice as long as any visit we had previously had together.

We spent Sunday in each other's arms. It was great to see her again and it was great to have the cold weather of Denver behind me. Monday morning required Josephine's early departure for work. I slept in after getting up and feeding Dylan. He was good this way. If I arose between seven and eight to feed him he was good for an hour outside by himself. Then I would arise again and bring him in. Back to bed and we both rested. Finally waking around ten or ten-thirty, it was if the whole morning was some kind of dream. I called it Dylan's "dream feeding".

I spent the remainder of the morning writing in my journal and reflecting on my time in Denver. I had stayed a month longer than I had planned to. While Dylan enjoyed his time with Stella, the cold weather had gotten to me. I did make a little extra money and I did get to hang with the Denver crew. But my running suffered terribly. Once again I found myself heavier than I like to be. Dylan and I began our training once again. We went for a three miler in the afternoon. He was bigger and stronger than he was last August. I was bigger and weaker. Later we would go stock the refrigerator. Oatmeal in the morning, salads for lunch and some kind of rice and beans for dinner would be our routine.

Monday, Tuesday and Wednesday were all similar with Josephine working during the day and Dylan and I enjoying our quiet time. While it was great seeing each other, our relationship was facing a new challenge. Unlike our times together before, we were now faced with the clash of our different lifestyles. She worked nine to five, Monday to Friday. It reminded me of the challenge I faced with Johanna. This time I knew better than keeping it inside. On Wednesday night we talked. Josephine admitted that while she was overjoyed to have me with her, she was a little overwhelmed having me in her space and having her routine disrupted. She didn't try to pretend it wasn't real and she didn't insist it would magically go away with our Thanksgiving plans. No, she just acknowledged its realness and that it would be something we would need to work through. I was walking a new path. She had a long week and that night I washed her hair and massaged her feet.

Thursday was Thanksgiving Day and as Josephine would say, it was our "first major holiday" together. We spent the day at her friends, David and Beth's. She had moved to Atlanta ten years earlier from Houston, Texas. She went through a divorce three years ago and decided to stay. David and Beth were her best friends. She would call them her true father and mother.

What a spread. While I ran in the morning, Josephine baked pies; apple and pumpkin. She never ceases to amaze me in the kitchen. We had the traditional turkey and football. I met all the visitors and we had a magical day.

Friday we drove to Tybee Island just outside of Savannah,

Georgia; about 250 miles east of Atlanta. We had planned this trip prior to my departure from Denver. I was aching to see the ocean. We left at around noon and I was somewhat agitated. The plan was to leave at ten. I finally realized it's not just about me. Sure I travel most of the time on my own time schedule. But now I am in a relationship with another. With that came small hurdles and delays. How important is it, I asked myself? Ten or noon, does it really matter? Relax. Enjoy the day. There are two of you now.

We stayed at a small bed and breakfast, called The Fort Screven Inn, a few blocks from the beach. Josephine loved it and I have to admit it was very romantic. I would have been okay at a cheap motel, but she really wanted the bed and breakfast. I wondered if is this one of those things that means something to women, while men don't really care? That night we had dinner at the Crab Shack Restaurant with her friends, Adam and Veronica, who were spending Thanksgiving in Savannah. It was my first low country boil. Adam was Beth and Davids's oldest son and Veronica was his wife. In the morning I was able to run on the beach. I was the only one who went for a swim. Later we spent the day walking around Savannah and shopping. I was starting to get that "obligation to buy something" feeling when Josephine surprised me by handing the clerk $20 for the ring I was debating on buying. She completely caught me off guard. Was she a Sugar Mama? No. She was just someone with the potential to be a true partner.

Saturday night on the 250 mile ride back to her place in Atlanta we got into a heated discussion. We had had such a pleasant weekend. How did we get here? I think we were in a power struggle. We are both very strong-willed and love to be right. Sex wasn't our issue. We seemed to be very compatible. Money wasn't our issue. No Sugar Daddy. No Sugar Mama. I think power or control may be our issue. We both relish equally the illusion of control. Had we each met our match? About an hour from her home things had settled down and we stopped at a toy store at a local outlet shopping mall. I told her to pick out any game she wanted. She chose LIFE. We stopped at a nearby

Denny's Restaurant for burgers, shakes and a game of LIFE. We played and had a blast for well over an hour. We didn't run from the conversation. We talked our way through it. We both spoke our minds. Then Josephine said something, which would come up time and time again in our relationship, "I guess we will just have to agree to disagree." Can you do that? I guess you can. It seems to work for us. Is it about honor? Is it about equality? Is it about respect?

Sunday we went to a friend of Josephine's baby Christening and party. I was on display. Those who had heard about me over the past six months could finally meet and see me. Naturally everyone approved. Or at least they kept their negative comments to themselves.

Monday, Tuesday, and Wednesday Josephine worked during the day and we played at night. Thursday was November 30th and as she went to work, I went for a run before my departure for the southeast beaches of Florida as planned. We had shared twelve days together since my arrival from Denver. I had started a new journal a few days before. I was now in the habit of giving each journal a name. My present journal was dated 11/28/00 and called "Key West Calling". Our first major holiday had many magic moments and some interesting challenges. Pulling out of her apartment complex driveway, I was sad. I planned to be on the road for twelve days and then return, as I would be flying to New England out of Atlanta on December 15th to spend some Christmas time with the kids. But for now, it was getting harder and harder to part from this beautiful soul. I could hear Dylan singing, barely above a whisper, *"And though our separation, it pierced me to the heart, she still lives inside of me, we've never been apart."*

CHAPTER FIFTY-FOUR
RESTLESS FAREWELL
"KEY WEST CALLING"

I left Josephine's home and headed out of the Atlanta area driving south on Route 75 to the sunshine of Florida. I had no real agenda other than finding the beach and running in the sun. As I traveled ,I reflected on my visit with Josephine.

We had been dating six months now. We shared special times and we worked through a few relationship squabbles. I missed her, but knew I wasn't ready to give up the road. There was still a tugging on my soul to travel in The Dub. Thinking of her, I realized that she challenged me to be present in the relationship. There was no room for illusion or fantasy. She was direct and spoke her mind. If I were going to survive I would have to follow her lead. She was a power of example to me. Direct communication beat mind-reading any day. We enjoyed our Thanksgiving time and I was now looking forward to spending Christmas with her. It was the first Christmas in a long time I was really looking forward to. As a matter of fact, we had Christmas cards made up with a photo of Dylan, Josephine and me at my suggestion. We mailed them out just prior to my departure south.

We drove 500 miles and slept at a rest area on Interstate 75. In the morning we drove another 150 miles and found ourselves in Naples, Florida. It was 80 degrees and we had a thirty minute run on the beach with two dolphins just off shore. After spending the day at the beach, we drove to the Florida City Wal-Mart, just south of Miami, and spent the night preparing for the drive to The Keys the next morning.

Stopping at mile marker 48, we went for a forty minute run at Pigeon Key, had some lunch, and continued on Route 1 to

Key West just in time for the sunset at mile marker number one on Route One. I love the sunset over the Gulf of Mexico.

It was December 3rd and we woke up in Key West. We slipped easily into one of my favorite routines of all my travels. Each morning we would awake in the Publix Shopping Plaza, drive to the beach, go for our morning run and swim, have a little oatmeal, and then read all day in the sun. The cold weather of Denver seemed so far away. I had been here with Corrina and Johanna. Was I collecting more pieces of my soul? Had I left a piece of me here? Either way it felt great showing Dylan the ropes of relaxation of Key West.

Later in the day I found a coffee shop where I could have a coffee, check my Hotmail e-mail account and do a little typing. I received the following email from Josephine:

My dearest Napoleon,

I dream about us. Dreams so real I can touch them. We have done this before. True love knows no boundaries. Time and space do not exist. A deep knowing has taken hold and will not let go. Your touch so familiar. Kisses that reach down and command me to remember. Our bodies fit like missing pieces. Your laugh rings through my ears like a favorite song. I know you. I have known you. I want to know you once again. I called out for you to come; yet I did not know it was Napoleon Zimmerman. What joy I felt that you were so close, not worlds or lifetimes away. We will love again. What a gift this is. Sometimes we do not come back in our concept of the "same" time. We search and never find our one love. We discover others; love, create wonderful experiences, but it is still not them. We are together, living and loving each other. I hold it sacred. I know obstacles will fall. They have and will continue. Soon my love; soon. It was meant; we were meant to be.

There is you and only you.

Love,
Josephine

Needless to say it made my day. It was strange being in Key

West. I was really enjoying my road time with Dylan, but was equally missing Josephine. I had longed for the beach for many months, but the ache of loneliness and the absence of Josephine were both growing stronger. I was growing restless. My values were in conflict. While the tugging on my soul to experience the road was still strong, there was a feeling just below the surface that many lessons and experiences still awaited me in Atlanta with Josephine.

I met my friend, Bob, who I had seen the past two winters. I called him New Foundland Bob. He was from Canada and spent six months a year in Key West living out of his Dodge Caravan. He painted pictures on pieces of wood in front of the Hemingway House to earn some money.

I met two kinds of guys on the road in Key West. First, there were the men in their fifties, divorced, living out of automobiles and hardened from the challenges of their lives. Most would drink heavily at night. Second, there were guys in their thirties, living in RVs, and feeling a little lost and disillusioned, while searching for something.

Bob was a free spirit. However, this year he had a female travelling companion with him. Pulling me to the side, he complained to me that often he would have to stay in hotels and go out to dinner more than he liked. I thought of Johanna and was grateful to have that season behind me.

While in Key West I began working on Josephine's Christmas present. I would eventually buy her a few gifts, like a DVD player, but I really wanted to create something special. I decided to make her a card. I had many pictures of the two of us and created a book/card of our relationship. Some pages would have photos and others would have little sayings from times we shared. I even had the post card from Sandia Peak, the ticket stub from the Braves game we went to and the room key from our stay in New Mexico. The card ended with a love story I wrote just for her. I worked on it over a three-day period in Key West and also when I returned to Atlanta. It would be the first story I ever completed and the first of I shared with others. I called it "Two Stars" and it reads like this:

TWO STARS

A long time ago, as far back as anyone can remember, perhaps for all eternity, there was LOVE. The Forever Beings, or "Lovers" as they were originally created, knew nothing but love, embraced love and never lived in fear, for they were love itself. They lived in innocence and never knew loneliness. All was "ONE" in the Land of Bliss.

Then something happened no one could explain: each Being divided into two spirits. The Being creatures who lived in a state of bliss for all time would now descend upon the plant earth as spirits, assume human form, and try to remember as they would search for the Love they once knew so well. One theory was that through incarnating into the flesh the Beings could grasp and experience an even greater sensation of love than their present existence permitted. Another theory put forth was that this was simply the design from the beginning of time. Love evolves continually and knows no limits. Lastly, some just believed that love was mostly just taken for granted and by knowing the absence of love, a deeper respect and appreciation for love could be gained through the human condition. For whatever the reasons, the "Lessons of Love" would be learned in the human form, enhancing the love of the spirit world of the Beings of Bliss.

Before the incarnation period began, the Beings split. Each newly split half would be a whole called a "spirit". One spirit would be called the female energy or yin and one spirit would be the male energy or yang. This energy would dominate the essence of the newly created spirit. The spirits would then choose to incarnate into flesh called human beings, alternating between female or male form in various lifetimes. While the dominating energy, yin or yang, was always present, there were different lessons of love to learn as a flesh woman (female) and as a flesh man (male).

Each Being, or Lover, would choose a name as it split into two spirits. This name was for all eternity and the newly divided spirits or souls would be the only two to recognize this name. It was there soul name and as the spirits incarnated and reincarnated into human form there would be a longing to find the other soul who recognized this name, for that soul would be their soul mate from their original existence in the realm of Bliss when they were simply Beings of love.

Our story begins at the dividing time. TWO STARS was the name our Love Being chose for its spirit travelers. Each soul incarnated into the flesh with a vague memory of the other and the time they were "ONE". Destiny would see to it that each soul would meet its mate, but based upon love development, human circumstances, and the many negative traits of the human form, these mates would come together for only a reason, a season, or a lifetime. There would always be recognition at a soul level, but many times no recognition would exist at a human level. When the two levels of recognition were combined the bliss known only previously in the Being world of eternity could be experienced in the human world.

Two Stars divided and began a series of incarnations over many centuries. The soul mate paths of each spirit crossed many times over many lifetimes. The union took different forms and lasted varying lengths during each lifetime. Sometimes the yin was a man and sometimes the yang was a woman. In one life the yin was a child while the yang was a parent. In another the yang was a child and the yin was the parent. There were times as brother and sister and times as sister and brother. Each lifetime permitted the souls to experience their soul mate and to love from a new perspective while gaining a greater understanding and appreciation of Love.

As Two Stars spirits developed over various lifetimes each soul grew at a different pace. Each had lifetimes full of memories and each, through lessons mastered, received special gifts as they developed. Yet throughout their journeys both had a special remembering as their time as "ONE".

Our tale progresses to the present incarnation. Two Stars spirits or souls have taken human form once again and are identified by the human names of Josephine and Napoleon.

Josephine in the female form has the dominating energy

of the yin or female. Napoleon in the male form has the dominating energy of the yang or male. In this lifetime their dominating energy has matched their chosen human form. However, traces of characteristics of both male and female have been developed in each as a result of alternating between male and female lifetimes over many centuries. This is in accordance with the law of balance and the lessons of love.

In this incarnation their paths have crossed several times. While there was always a vague recognition at a soul level, there was never any recognition at a human level until recently. Both were busy interacting with other souls. Not soul mates, but perhaps some spirit in their soul group from their world of Bliss. These souls assisted in love development, which was often necessary for soul mates to meet on similar fertile love ground. As destiny would bring the mates together, no recognition would occur if the love lessons were not of an equal schooling. As it happened, both chose similar paths this lifetime; struggling with addictions, dysfunctional childhoods, marrying abusive partners, surviving betrayal and divorce, overcoming material wealth, and remaining true to one's inner self on their individual spiritual journey in a world of chaos. Both had known limited loves and were searching for something greater. Throughout this incarnation both had learned the value of solitude and self-care but longed for the companionship of a partner with no limits, no conditions, and no fears. Someone they could be themselves with, no masks, no games, no make believe. Someone they could live in the truth with. Someone with whom they could not only be in love, but someone they could also love. Deep within, they both remembered there existed someone with whom they could share a common vision of how life could be enjoyed in a world of love. Many lessons were mastered and each grew to a higher level of awareness and love in this present incarnation.

In linear time, a time frame for the human mind, the simultaneous recognition at both a soul level and human level of the two searching souls of Two Stars took place in May 2000 in Atlanta. Two Stars souls had found their mates in yet another lifetime. A deep remembering began to surface. Other lifetimes and lessons were recalled.

There was the life when Josephine was a queen and Napoleon was a peasant and a life where Napoleon was a rich nobleman and Josephine only an entertainer who would sing for him. While the longing of the two was real, the times of each life would permit no such love. Denied their love, this mismatch in the eyes of society would be a barrier that in some lifetime would have to be ignored if their union were to succeed.

Some lifetimes they took turns as the parent and learned to love, nurture and instruct the soul of the child mate. This parental love would be an obstacle in this life union, as each would bring to the relationship a knowing that the other lacked. As lovers they would have to learn to teach by example in a loving way as well as to be students of the other.

In other shared incarnations and even in the present life there were lovers who betrayed or hurt people and made the souls fear love. This distrust of love and of opening up to the possibility of love was another barrier to surmount. Could they love again and more importantly, could they master the lesson of this lifetime: COULD THEY ALLOW ANOTHER TO LOVE THEM? Could they open their hearts, be vulnerable, and let another glimpse their deepest desires, fears and needs? Could they remove the barriers of love they had used to survive in this lifetime? This fear of love was a great challenge and if conquered the rewards would be great.

There were many lives full of passion and lovemaking, an art form Josephine would recall in depth and Napoleon could barely recall at all. One prominent life was their times on the outskirts of Paris. Napoleon vividly remembers forcing himself upon Josephine. Now he would learn to be present during their lovemaking and experience passion beyond a mere physical sensation. He would need to learn the tenderness of the world of sexual love expression of the soul through the physical body. Olympic sex, while gratifying to the ego, did not serve as a soul connection.

Throughout time the two had progressed and as the soul mate recognition of Two Stars deepened during this lifetime each brought gifts and lessons for the other. Each would be a teacher and each would be a student.

What they shared in common proved to be fertile love ground for the two souls. Each had a spiritual thirst, a desire to love as the Being they once were. Each knew the pitfalls of a hasty romantic plunge. While geography of the human condition played a role with Napoleon in Boston and Josephine in Atlanta, the souls decided to explore and investigate the other before joining their flesh. In other words, they would get to know each other before human sex. They spent seven weeks talking on the human invention called a telephone. While not physically in each other's presence, they could begin to bond emotionally. Valuing truth, they proceeded to divulge the essence of their spirits from afar. Through letters, cards, and phone calls they began to share bits and pieces of themselves. Each day they began to think more and more of the other. Could this be the one? Could this be real? Do I remember you? Slowly they revealed their inner secrets, thoughts, beliefs, ideas, values and dreams. The process of discovery was underway.

As they grew more intimate and familiar, the distance apart was a hurdle to overcome. The times apart were painful to each, like the echo of separation over the centuries. Additionally, there were other challenges as each soul was told by other hurt humans, "This is not a match." While many doubted that the union was possible, the souls believed in each other. Literally the souls had the opportunity to master the lesson of being true to one's heart and not the voices of the doubting masses.

It was agreed. In July they spent two weekends together. Napoleon flew to Atlanta and visited with Josephine at her home. The remembering became stronger. As Josephine allowed Napoleon in her sacred space and during their first hours of lovemaking strange things were taking place within Napoleon. Flashes of bright colors and other lifetimes dominated his thoughts. New physical sensations were occurring. This lifetime consisted primarily of what he called man sex, prove your worth sex. Now he was being schooled in the art of lovemaking by a soul he knew he recognized. Josephine, on the other hand, was entertaining a sense of "knowing" with deeper and deeper levels of conviction. Later in the month they spent a weekend at

Virginia Beach. The souls were falling deeper in love and living in the truth. While in past relationships each soul would betray their own sense of self, they both knew this repeated pattern would not work. Each soul had to be true to its own awareness or suffer the consequences. While the scoffers scoffed, those who witnessed the souls together firsthand were in awe of the new human match. One friend observed that while Josephine was teaching Napoleon how to grow, Napoleon was showing Josephine how to play. The student and teacher, alternating lesson plans, loved, laughed and cried together.

August consisted of another flight to Atlanta, a drive to Atlanta and a week together in New Mexico.

Like the letters and phone calls, physical contact opened the door to a deeper yearning to know more, experience more, to touch more, to love more. Each soul was venturing into unknown territory and taking risks of expression as it attempted not to repeat behaviors from their pasts. Each knew that living in the truth would lead to long-term happiness. By stating one's true needs and intentions, each was learning this was the pathway to having those needs met. In this way the soul mates could hope to find out whether or not they shared a common vision for this lifetime. As promised, destiny assured their meeting in this incarnation, but they themselves, based upon their spiritual development, would have to provide the nurturing environment for a successful life of love together. Could they overcome the obstacles and challenges presented by this human incarnation? Could they hold onto their reunited love from the time as "ONE"? The baggage accumulated in this lifetime would have to be examined and eliminated from their new union if happiness was to prevail. The human condition is full of spiritual disease that would need to be conquered. Egotism, fear, selfishness, grandiosity, greed, self-will, and the taking of each other for granted were challenges to all lovers. Avoiding the repeating of limiting, destructive relationship patterns would require constant vigilance.

After three months together as a couple, they unknowingly entered what they now refer to as the "REIGN OF TERROR".

Napoleon travelling the country on both an inner and outer journey of awareness, a walk-about for reflection, stopped in Denver for two months. While both souls recognized that the individual journey of love lessons was of high importance, the common journey of love lessons could be of a similar priority. However, the first journey was needed if the latter journey was to have any chance of succeeding. Napoleon and Josephine began to talk of this as "the big picture". Each had private lessons and revelations to understand. So while Napoleon traveled and Josephine stayed in Atlanta, both walked their personal journey of love and the big picture was being slowly revealed.

The problem was the little picture. Physical longing for each other was intense. Forty-four days apart was difficult. The letters, gifts, cards and phone call dates were losing their ability to satisfy the deep ache of the eternal souls for one another. Finally, in mid-October and early November, flights from Denver to Atlanta were coordinated and the lovers were reunited.

Passion, lovemaking, coffee in bed, long talks on the couch, dinner dates, and private baths provided the time together to fall deeper in love. Each soul could live the common journey of love again. Not as a fantasy of the mind, but as a reality of the heart. The images in their heads were real, not made of dreams.

Finally, Napoleon departed the Denver area, headed east, and the lovers spent twelve days together in Atlanta. As Josephine named it, "Their first major holiday together".

While the extended visit allowed the two souls to enjoy and relish each other's presence it also offered new challenges to surmount conflicts common to most human love relationships. Both the joys of companionship and the bumps of entwinement were equally treasured by each soul as a blessing of the lessons of love.

Josephine and Napoleon enjoyed their first major holiday together. Partaking in Josephine's homemade pies and feasting on a turkey dinner, both were truly grateful for the other on this Thanksgiving weekend in Atlanta. A trip to Tybee Island and

Savannah provided a setting for romance and time away from the hectic pace of the world of noise in which they lived.

One major challenge the souls encountered was the blending and balancing of their two different lifestyles. While Napoleon had literally dropped out of the daily routine and pressures of everyday life, Josephine was in the thick of it. Several mornings required her leaving the warmth of their entangled slumber and venturing to her workplace. Often she would return tired and drained of energy. This was a new dynamic for the couple that would normally arise from bed at their leisure around mid-day, spend hours on the couch with coffee and conversation, and avoid the distractions of the outer world. The lovers were offered the chance to be considerate, kind, loving, thoughtful and unselfish in the face of this new challenge. Surprise massages and pizza deliveries combined with sweet kisses and kind words helped create and maintain their atmosphere of love.

Other challenges included learning to express disagreement when a personal boundary was threatened or overstepped. Could the two souls be true to their individual selves and inner essence in a graceful manner or would they resort to pouting and manipulation? This union of Two Stars offered the souls the opportunity of taking the higher road and avoiding the limited patterns of mistakes in past love relationships.

Finally, could the reunited souls separate once again after their extended visitation and days of love? Napoleon was off to the beaches and sunshine of Florida, as his travel journey was not completed. While his inner self-journey took him out of Atlanta, Josephine's inner self-journey required her to stay in Atlanta. Could the two souls hold on to their ideals and beliefs of the big picture and survive the little picture?

The answer was yes!

The time apart while Napoleon was in Florida and Josephine was in Atlanta proved to be a valuable period of solitude for each soul. Both would have private time for reflection, for appreciation, for dreaming, and for remembering. Each unknowingly was lighting the way for the other to a deeper understanding of love. Each was the lover they prayed and hoped for. Each provided the other with unconditional love, acceptance, and the freedom to just be who they were. Each was a teacher and a student. Both were mastering challenges and lessons of love.

As Napoleon drove out of Atlanta he felt as if he was leaving a piece of is heart behind. After months in the Midwest he knew he needed sunshine to replenish his soul. While he ran the beaches of Florida rejuvenating his spirit, there was an undercurrent of loneliness just beneath the surface. Day after day he wrote in his journal and inventoried his life. Who was he, where was he going, what was his destiny? It was if he was between worlds. Lost between dreams with no compass to navigate, no maps leading home.

Out of this period of confusion two truths emerged. First, he knew he needed the beach. This value of living in a warm climate rippled and affected so much within him. Second, he knew he needed Josephine. This revelation startled, him to say the least. He had spent the past three years creating a life where he needed no one. A life on the road with no place and every place called home. Now what? Slowly, as he watched each day's sunset, he surrendered. Armed with these two facts of his existence, he simple made the decision to stop making decisions. He would return to Josephine knowing only that he needed her and the beach. How this would play out was none of his concern. He acknowledged his needs and released them to the universe.

Josephine's experience was similar. While she stayed in Atlanta, a piece of her heart traveled with Napoleon. Deep within she ached with the knowing they were to be together, yet he was out in the world living a life without her. How could this be? On one level she recognized and honored that Napoleon needed the uplifting of his spirit that the sunshine of Florida would provide. She was also aware that he still was working things out within his own inner private journey. However, there were times when she was despondent, called in sick and was ready to put all her things in storage and join Napoleon in the south. Of course she didn't and the days of separation only further strengthened her knowing. Napoleon was her soul mate and their time together would come soon. While she did have moments of inner intense struggles, she ultimately released their love to the universe and awaited Napoleon's return to Atlanta.

At this point in our story the two soul mates have been reunited. As we end this narrative both are anxiously anticipating their upcoming second major holiday together and envisioning a life of love.

Their first major holiday was of gratitude over Thanksgiving weekend. Their second would be Christmas – the season of love and giving. Historically this was a holiday Napoleon avoided due to excessive commercialism and painful memories. Destiny sometimes plays tricks and is full of ironies. Sometimes roles reverse and the question now is, "Can Josephine teach Napoleon to play this Christmas and does Napoleon have anything to teach Josephine to help her grow?"

Some would say that Two Stars souls were running parallel in this lifetime. I would simply say they mirror each other.

Is the past the future? Is the future the past? Is it all the present? When apart are they really together? Is it just a dream, this return to self and have they always been "ONE" as the Forever Being in the eternity of the Land of Bliss? Perhaps Love is really all there is and all there ever was and all else is just an illusion.

EPILOGUE

He calls her "Sweet Tea" and she calls him "My Little Boy". Yet, you and I know they really are **"TWO STARS"**.

CHAPTER FIFTY-FIVE
TO BE ALONE WITH YOU
"MISSING ATLANTA"

Sitting at the beach I was reviewing my journals. I found the following poem I had written while in Sedona.

Destiny slowly unfolds
Sometimes one must be bold.
Soul Recognition
New Definitions.
Long distance calls and emotions shared
How could these two possibly be paired
We simply start to date
Others argue about our fate
Ignore the crowd
Truth must be spoken out loud.
Weekends of play
Where are you today?
Miles apart
Your're in my heart
Remember me, remember you.

It was time to head north. Leaving Key West, we drove from six at night until two in the morning. Covering 400 miles in the eight hour drive, we awoke somewhere just north of Daytona on Route 95 within 100 miles of St. Augustine, Florida. We drove to St. Augustine and the beach. Dylan and I had run in Naples, Pigeon Key and Key West. Now we would complete my four favorite beach runs in Florida with a run in St. Augustine. I let Dylan run free and I never felt so much love for him watching him hopelessly chase the seagulls up the beach and then turn heading straight into the waves and daring the gulls to play. I was considering a run in Hilton Head, but was missing Atlanta. They say time is an illusion. With Josephine time flew. On the road time usually was irrelevant, but now it seemed to crawl. So I headed northwest to be alone with Josephine considering once again the battle of solitude and companionship. Maybe it was the holidays? Maybe it was love? Whatever it was, I had had my beach fix, my run fix, my sun fix, my Dub fix and my road fix. Maybe it was the tugging of the incomplete lessons awaiting my soul? Looking back, my time in Key West and on the road was like being lost between two worlds – the solitude of the road and the comfort of a lover's companionship. I remember when I left Atlanta how I felt sad, like I was leaving a piece of my soul behind. But on the road, travelling to Naples, Key West and St. Augustine, I felt like I was retrieving pieces of my soul. Was I now free to return with no ghosts haunting me from my past?

My trip lasted only eight days instead of twelve. I returned to Atlanta on December 8th around nine at night and surprised Josephine. She began to cry, she was so excited. We would share another week together before my week trip to New England.

I shared with her that while I was on the road this time I realized three things were important to me. First, I loved my children, Joey and Sara. They would always be in my life and someday I hoped they would live with me. Second, I loved her like I never loved another. She challenged me to actively participate in the relationship. I enjoyed our compatibility and hoped we would someday live and share a common vision for a life together. And third, I loved the beach. Being near the ocean and in the sun nurtured my spirit, my emotions, and my body. How these three things would come together I did not know. My awareness was enough and I would release the outcome to the Universe. For now we shared a week together and grew deeper in love.

Before departing for New England we purchased a

Christmas tree. I was childlike in my anticipation of spending Christmas with Josephine. She loved the holidays and it was contagious. I would try to play up the commercialism, but her love for me and for the season disarmed me. She was teaching me to play. I would pontificate about the "Retail Drug Dealers" and their lore of easy credit and discount prices trying to hook new clients and she would simply ask me what I wanted in my stocking.

As planned, I flew from Atlanta to Boston on December 15th for my visit with Joey and Sara. Dylan would go to the local kennel and wasn't too pleased. I promised extra large bones for Christmas. Last year I was in Hawaii and missed Christmas with the kids. While they enjoyed the presents from Hawaii, they were now looking forward to having me home. The year before we celebrated the days following Christmas. This year we would celebrate just before the holiday. Their mom had given me a list of the things she thought Santa would be bringing and a list of the things the kids said they wanted that Santa might not be aware of. My job would be to steer them in the right direction. My gift was $150 each to spend at the mall. This would be a daylong adventure. It's interesting to watch, as they decide how to spend their own money. They behave slightly different when it's their budget and not Mom or Dad's pocket. Sara's big purchase was a leather jacket from The Gap.

I was flying on Air Tran Airways and the airports were jammed and full of delays. Naturally I volunteered to get bumped to another flight if it was needed. As luck would have it they needed my assistance and for a three hour delay I received a roundtrip flight voucher to anywhere Air Tran flew. Money in the bank.

We spent our days shopping, skating, bowling, eating out and going to the movies. At night I was sleeping at a local Super Eight Motel. Calling Josephine, she would tease me saying, "It's too bad you're all alone in a cheap, sleazy motel. Oh, the things we could do."

The real highlight of the visit was Sara's performance as an elf in the Christmas play *Santa and Mrs. Klause.* I brought flowers for her and Joey brought some for his new girlfriend. Ten years old and he had a girlfriend. I wish I could tell him all I knew, but I realized I was still figuring it out myself. While I wished I could spare him the heartache of romance, I knew his lessons would unfold as surely as mine were. I would never deny his soul these lessons, I could only be there for him.

I kept my Honda Civic registered and insured for my trips home to visit the kids. Usually, I would keep it at my dad's while travelling in The Dub. However, on this trip I purchased a one way ticket to Boston and planned to drive the Honda to Atlanta and keep it at Josephine's.

Leaving New England and reflecting on my time with the kids, I drove to Germantown, Maryland and had a visit with Dianna and Sean. To my surprise, our Christmas card was hanging on the wall. It was as cold in Maryland as it was in Massachusetts. At least in Atlanta it was in the fifties. Little did I know it would soon drop to the thirties and The Dub would be covered in snow.

The next day I drove straight through to Atlanta, 600 miles away, and was ready to celebrate Christmas with Josephine. We had been apart for a week and I hadn't run in a week. It was December 22nd and it felt good to be in her arms and feel the warmth of her bed.

CHAPTER FIFTY-SIX
YOU CHANGED MY LIFE
"THE GIFT OF LOVE"

It was a magical Christmas. I was in love and with my lover and my friend. Often we would look at each other and just stare in disbelief.

"Who would have thought I would be so in love with you, Napoleon Zimmerman."

"No, who would have thought that I would be so in love with you, Josephine."

"I love you."

"I love you, too."

"Merry Christmas"

"Happy Christmas and a Merry New Year," I would respond.

We were both amazed. We were both happy. We were both believers. We were both present for the unfolding and the remembering. Deep within we knew. At a soul level we were in love.

That morning I wrote in my journal:

Day before Christmas
Dylan tours Petsmart
Gingerbread cookies to be made
Breakfast with love
Ave Maria in the air
Coffee on the couch

Lovers in Bed
Remnants of snow outside
Big W in the cold
New pajamas for Napoleon
Josephine's voice sings
Presents under the tree
Angels behind the scenes
Day before Christmas

On Christmas Eve she opened the gift I made for her. I was so nervous. Would she like her card? Would she like our story? Would she think I was a sap? My mind was still feeding me self-doubt. My heart just whispered, "love."

As she read, the tears streamed down her face. "Yes," I shouted inside. She liked it. Later she would tell me it was the best gift she had ever received.

Christmas Day was a repeat of Thanksgiving at Beth and David's home. Our second major holiday was as outstanding as our first. At night we made love and held each other throughout the night.

Between Christmas and New Year's Eve Josephine had to work. We slipped into our routine of her arising early and coming home at five. While she was away Dylan and I would journal and get our run in. Snow in Atlanta is unusual, but we did get a little, enough to make a snowman. The Dub doesn't look good covered in the white stuff. Sometimes Dylan and I would just sit inside and smoke a cigar listening to music. I was content knowing the beaches were less than 300 miles to the east.

We had plans to fly to San Francisco for New Year's Eve weekend. Dylan would be in the kennel and again wasn't pleased. After our return, I planned to spend a few months in Key West at the beach. My conflicting longing for the ocean and to be with Josephine would haunt me during my days alone. I wanted to run in the sun, but was so at home in her arms. Perhaps she could fly south or I could make weekend trips to Atlanta. But for now we would explore San Fran together.

Prior to our departure we did a little clothes shopping. My road look, which was commonly referred to as "Napoleon in Rags", was not something Josephine was too thrilled with. While practical for the road, she felt it was a little sloppy. She had bought a few items for Christmas for me, but really wanted to pick out a New Year's Eve outfit for me. Not a suit and tie, just something a little more presentable, a little more respectable. Mostly I wore either Gap cargo shorts or jeans with holes in them. She said I was stuck in the eighties. For shoes I wore Timberland boots with the laces cut and untied. On top I usually had a T-shirt with a Polo button shirt over it, and of coursed unbuttoned. "Napoleon in Rags".

I have this theory about clothes. I think we should only own the clothes we love to wear. Each item we consider ourselves to look great in. Never reaching that point in our wardrobe where we have to wear something because everything else is dirty. Throw away those clothes we only wear because they are the last clean things we have available. I call it my "Cool Clothes Theory".

We bought some Timberland shoes, new jeans (no holes) and some dress shirts. Nothing fancy, but a little dressy. Throughout the weekend in California I received nothing but positive feedback and really did enjoy looking good in the company of this beautiful woman. While some exclaim, "Hey where are your work boots?", others would claim Josephine was trying to change me. But I knew in my heart I wore nothing that made me uncomfortable. I was just taking advantage of her fashion knowledge. We would repeat the whole scene again in March as we attended a wedding together.

New Year's Eve was a Sunday and we arrived in California on Friday. It was our first flight together. I had flown several times to Atlanta and she had flown to Virginia Beach and New Mexico. I remember we had a little fight on the plane. The details escape me, but I'm sure it was pretty important at the time. I started to withdraw. She asked how long I was going to pout. "Fifteen minutes," I responded. In that moment of joking my pouting disappeared. She had disarmed me again.

Many of our friends were in town for the weekend and Marilynn Wilke was hosting a party to usher in the New Year. Saturday we went for dinner in Chinatown and on Sunday afternoon had burritos in a local Mexican restaurant on Haight Street. I love the burritos in San Fran. Nothing even close in New England. They are so big you can only eat one. They wrap them to go and you need two hands to eat them. Sunday night we danced in each other's arms and at midnight kissed for a good five minutes before anyone else could wish us a happy new year. It was the complete opposite of last year with Johanna. I knew I was in the right place with the right soul. It was a good feeling from deep within.

While in San Francisco I did my annual review of my values.

I knew I still valued a warm climate. Living in a beach community would satisfy that value. I would be near the ocean and in the sun. I knew I valued my fitness. Living in a beach community would allow more opportunities for running. It's cold and difficult to train most of the year in the north. I knew I valued my spiritual self. Living in a beach community in the sun and running would help me stay not only physically fit, but would also ripple into my emotional and spiritual well-being. I can offer no proof of this, but know it's true. I knew I valued my financial independence. My funds were starting to get low and living in a beach community, would allow me to write and work when necessary. I knew I valued my children. Living in a beach community and having a home would allow trips to the north and perhaps even the possibility of them visiting me at my home. I knew I valued travel. Having a home base in a beach community I would still be able to take trips whenever necessary as I planned to always have an RV in the driveway with a full tank of gas. I knew I valued self-improvement. Living in a beach community with a home would allow me to set up my own library and writing room and also give me the opportunity to participate in community activities and local educational courses. I knew that I valued friendship and my friends seemed to be scattered throughout the country. Living in a beach community, perhaps I could create some local friendships. I knew I valued companionship. My lover lived in the Atlanta area. Would she move to a beach community? I wrote in my journal the following conclusions after two and half years of living in The Dub and on the road:

I know my time on the road is not completed. However, I am getting ready to settle down. I will someday live in a beach community near the ocean and near the sun. I will have a small home to run from, to read in, and to create a writing room. I will be involved in a spiritual community and enjoy friendships, participate in activities, and be able to work, to have fun, to improve myself. I will have an abundance of money to visit the kids with and to be able to have them visit with me. I will run, read, write, eat properly, cook, have friends, travel at will and share all of this with a partner who has a similar vision. I know the time is not now, but I'm getting close.

While I knew my time on the road and in The Dub was not finished yet, I also knew I was getting close and a beach community was where I would eventually stop. I had traveled almost 50,000 miles over the past couple of years. I was becoming aware of who I was and what I hoped to create. I had seen the desert, been to the mountains, but knew in my heart it was the ocean that fed my soul. Someday I would live in a beach community and share my life with another. It wasn't time yet, but I was getting close.

We returned to Atlanta on January 2, 2001 with my plans to leave on the 8th.

CHAPTER FIFTY-SEVEN
YOU' RE GOING TO MAKE ME
LONESOME WHEN YOU GO
"STAYING"

Over the course of the next week as the time for me to leave was drawing closer, I didn't want to leave. My time with Josephine and my lessons felt incomplete. Could I wait a little longer for the beach? Perhaps Springtime in the Carolina's would satisfy my needs?

Josephine and I started to visit a local new age center called "The Inner Space" just outside of Atlanta. It was once an old steakhouse and had since been converted to retail and office space. I called it the "Dinner Place". I would browse the used book section and Josephine would shop for candles and incense. Each month the center put out a magazine called The Oracle, which advertised the classes they offered at the center. On Sundays they held a free Manifesting Meditation at eleven thirty in the morning. Josephine and I began attending. The group leader, Mr. Jack Frederickson, was starting an eight week class on January 17th entitled, "The Chakras". As I was getting The Dub in shape for the road, I couldn't get this class out of my mind. I was slowing becoming aware of my own energy levels and those of the people around me. I often thought of the differences between Sedona, Arizona, and Las Vegas, Nevada.

My heart was guiding me and encouraging me to enroll. I ran it by Josephine and we decided I would stay at her home while attending the class. Sundays we would go to the Meditation together and on Wednesday I would go to class.

The class ended on March 14th and the wedding we planned to attend was on March 17th. The beach would have to wait. For now we would spend the next twelve weeks together and then the road. I would plan to leave for the beach starting April first.

I knew I loved Josephine and I knew I loved the beach. The course on the Chakras would be fun but I wasn't sure I could handle being in one place for so long. When I first arrived in the Atlanta area Josephine suggested that I use her home as a base for my travels, returning every couple weeks to her. We decided that we would take a few weekend trips to the beach and to satisfy my desires we planned three trips. These trips were planned with Josephine's home as a base for the two of us. The trips were: one to Hilton Head in January, one to Tybee Island in February, and one to Jekyll Island in March. Later when I was back in The Dub and on the road, she would meet me on Edisto Island, South Carolina in April and Cocoa Beach, Florida in May.

By now Josephine and I were talking about a future together. I wasn't content with relocating to Atlanta and she wasn't jumping at any prospects of living in The Big W. When we met last May I had shared that it would be at least one year before I would be done in The Dub. Josephine knew she loved me and would indeed move to a beach community, but she needed time to put closure on her life in Atlanta. I had shared my "value review" thoughts from San Francisco with Josephine. She was well aware of my beach community desires and said she shared a similar vision, but again restated she would need at least a year before she could move. So, in addition to satisfying my need to run at the beach, our beach trips were designed to see if we could find a beach to relocate to.

On January 8, 2001 I recommitted again to my running with Dylan and decided to spend the next 12 weeks in Josephine's home. The plan was to spend a few months together. I could run, read, write, take a class, create some friendships and share it all with Josephine. Then the road, the beach and The Dub once again.

I was reviewing my journals and found the following poem I wrote for Josephine:

Entwined

Two lovers, one love
Two paths, one destination
Two voices, one truth
Two languages, one story
Two schools, one lesson
Two lives, one vision
Two fears, one god
Two questions, one solution
Two minds, one dream
Two bodies, one passion
Two souls, one hope
Two historys, one future
Two hearts, one emotion
Two stars, one sky
Two, one.

Josephine and I were both happy and we thought the twelve weeks would last forever.

CHAPTER FIFTY-EIGHT
WINTERLUDE
"SUMMER SESSION III: RUNNING, WRITING, WORKING & CLASS"

I did indeed stay twelve weeks with Josephine. We had many more ups than downs. My running and Dylan's running climbed from thirty minutes to sixty between January and March. I was reading and I was writing. I made some friends and even started a business. Some days it was warm and some days it was cold. I was nowhere near the beach, but was learning to trust myself and learning of love.

One of the first things I did was stock the refrigerator. Josephine and I loved coffee in the morning. While I enjoy some oatmeal and some fresh fruit, she rarely eats anything in the morning. She makes sandwiches or brings soup to work for lunch. I enjoy a good salad. Dinnertime I like rice and beans, some tuna, or Josephine's nachos. She is usually tired and will go for fast food take-out or whip up something. She loves meat. She claims it has to do with growing up in Texas.

My "food availability" theory applies specifically to my eating goals. I believe we eat what's available. If I have healthy food available I'll eat it, if not it's pizza, burgers or Chinese. If I hang around junk food long enough, I'm going to put it in my mouth. So one of the first things I did was stock the refrigerator.

Dylan and I had been running periodically. Between the cold in Denver, the travelling we were doing and the December cold snap in Atlanta, we really had no routine. Now we had twelve weeks to dedicate to getting in shape for our beach runs in the spring. We started at a base of thirty minutes. Just under four miles, I estimate. Each week we added a few minutes. Gradually building up to 60 minutes. Actually, our last run in Atlanta on April 1, 2001 was 73 minutes. Between my consistent eating habits and our training routine I easily lost 10-15 pounds and felt in good shape. Good enough shape to sign up for the Peach Tree Road Race coming up over the July 4th weekend and to send away for an application for the Atlanta Marathon which would be run on Thanksgiving Day in November.

Mornings consisted of a "dream feeding" of Dylan and eventually getting up around ten. First thing up, I would make the bed. The "woman who I used to be married to" had taught me this habit. It wasn't much work, just line up the pillows and shake out the comforter. I love climbing into a made bed at night. While making coffee I would collect the dishes from around the apartment and either empty or fill the dishwasher depending upon what needed to be done. Putting my coffee in the living room, I would bring all clothes and shoes into the bedroom, gather up some laundry, and throw in a load. I was pretending to be a "house boy". Josephine loved it. At night I had a completely different routine, if you know what I mean.

During the day I usually spent an hour or two reading and writing in my journal. By then Dylan was ready for a run and the sun was shining bright. After a post-run salad, we would type a little of this narrative on the laptop Jono helped me purchased back in Denver.

Josephine returned around five and while she was exhausted, I was ready to play. Many nights we would talk and often rented videos or read. She liked to go to bed around ten because it always took us two hours to get to sleep.

After a couple of weeks I decided to start a business. It wasn't anything fancy. I had some business cards made up for $23 and bought a rake and gloves for $8. My cards looked something like this:

ODD JOBS COMPLETED

Moving, need a hand -call for help
Painting, need a hand -call for help
Yard work, need a hand -call for help
Napoleon Zimmerman, 770-555-5555

Josephine was little skeptical as to what I was up to, but had learned to humor me with many of my ideas. After I spent the money on the business cards I was a little unsure myself. My mind began to question the whole process. "Hey, no one wants to hire you", "What kind of work can you do?" My heart simply encouraged me to hand out a few cards. The first card I handed out was to one of Josephine's neighbors, Mrs. Craig. She asked how much to rake her yard. I hadn't thought about quotes. I suggested we just work on an hourly rate. For $10.00 per hour I got the job. It took 17 hours. I would have quoted $100 for the job. I'm glad we went with the hourly rate. I kept busy for about seven weeks and grossed about $2,000. Dylan and I did mostly yard work and a little painting. One day we even hung some gutters. It was for fun and only part time. The extra money came in handy on our beach weekends.

My classes met on Wednesday nights. As I mentioned, Jack Frederickson was the instructor. There were two of us in the class. Myself and another man named Andrew. The first class was an introduction to the seven Chakras. Each following week was dedicated to one of the seven Chakras. The first week Mr. Frederickson explained that the opening of the Chakras goes hand in hand with spiritual growth or advancement. Knowledge of the Chakras, however, does not guarantee advancement, but allows the opportunity for one to experience a new level of internal power. He explained that the word Chakra was Sanskrit, part of the language of India, and meant wheel. The Chakras spin, each at a different speed. He talked of the subtle energies of the body and said it was debated that there could be tens of thousands of Chakras throughout the body, but that we would focus on the seven major Chakras over the next seven weeks. We would end each class with a meditation session trying to open and clear the Chakras seeking balance in each one. I was most fascinated with the concept of "leaking our energy" and how we give our power away. Past relationships with family, friends and lovers were all making sense in light of some of the following ideas that Mr. Frederickson had about the Chakras.

The first Chakra is called the Root Chakra. This is where our survival instincts are centered. Also, the first Chakra is about our tribal belief systems, our sense of community, and our relationship to the group. I had been seeking balance in this Chakra when I ventured into the unknown in The Dub and revolted against the limiting beliefs of my programmed mind.

The second Chakra is called the Sacral Chakra. Even though this Chakra relates primarily to sex, it relates more to sexual love and intimacy. The first Chakra is about lust and raw sex while the second is making love and feeling intimacy. When leaking energy from this Chakra you are leaking over things about sex, power, and money. Mr. Frederickson explained that while the first Chakra dealt with the tribe, this Chakra was more about one on one relationships. My relationship with Johanna sure seemed like I was leaking energy or power in these areas.

The third Chakra is called the Solar Plexus Chakra. While the first Chakra is how you survive in a group or community and the second Chakra is how you survive one on one, the third Chakra is about how you work with yourself with power. The third Chakra is about self-esteem; how you feel about yourself. It's your center of confidence and honor. This Chakra is where you make strong personal boundaries. It's about self-validation rather than seeking approval from others. This was a challenge I was well aware of. I had to validate my own dreams because almost no one encouraged me to walk my path.

The fourth Chakra is called the Heart Chakra. Ideally, the Heart Chakra should radiate from a strong, solid center of self-acceptance with compassion towards others. Mr. Frederickson said it is the abode of mercy, the center of universal love, not limited to loved ones or those who return love. It is the compassion for the stranger, the purely altruistic love. This love is non-manipulative, impersonal and seeks nothing in return. The fourth Chakra is your emotional zone, your internal reality. We are aware others are on their spiritual paths and who are we to judge another? We have compassion. In this Chakra we lose power by dwelling on the past. Something I did for almost two years after my divorce. He later talked about how at first we followed the tribe's heart, then one day we decide to follow our own hearts. This I could certainly identify with. My mind and heart battled often.

The fifth Chakra is called the Throat Chakra and sometimes called the voice of creative expression. He talked of how this Chakra focused on learning to accept your own originality and expressing this. In the first Chakra we detached from the tribe and everyone else's view of who we are. Once you do this, you can find your own uniqueness through self-acceptance. Finding your inner voice will make you question all your core beliefs. I remembered how years before I was first becoming aware of the tugging on my soul and the voice within encouraging me to leave for the road. With the fifth Chakra creativity usually comes with flashes, spurts and explosions. He talked about looking at this Chakra as getting out of your own way to let your talents shine through. You don't work it, you just let it flow on its own. When this Chakra is shut down we get a fear of expressing our truth. Was my journey in The Dub and my desire to write and share part of this Chakra? Part of my truth? I could certainly identify with the fear of expressing it. While my head (tribal beliefs) constantly tried to get me to give up, my heart (my inner voice) consistently encouraged me to keep at it. Keep walking my path regardless of the masses.

The sixth Chakra is called the Third Eye Chakra. Here the ability to transcend the logical thought process that requires deduction before conclusion is located. There is a direct knowing in this Chakra and a recognition of spiritual realities. When awakened, this Chakra brings magic to life; a meaning deeper than the everyday humdrum view of a mundane existence into inspiration and bliss. I was thinking of my past life recognitions with Corrina, Jane and Josephine and my experience with Dr. Weiss and Tecumseh. He talked of transcending into altered states and opening your intuition. Lastly he stated that maturity of this Chakra is the dismantling of the rational mind to allow the irrational – angels, time travel, miracles, bi-location, and manifestation of the Divine instantly to come in and happen. Each week we would end with a meditation and on Sundays Josephine and I were attending the Manifestation Meditation. Each week I was finding it easier and easier to enter into an altered state. I was told as you continue to work with this energy, your intuition will sharpen and you will learn to trust it. Yes, trusting the heart voice and not the voice of another. I knew this lesson well.

The seventh Chakra is called the Crown Chakra. Sitting on the crown of the head, this Chakra represents thought, consciousness and information; the knowing. The seventh Chakra awakens us to a full perspective and the purpose of the soul. This Chakra represents the experience of the Divine. Completely open, this Chakra brings Divine guidance, the will to merge with the Divine and have all our actions guided by the merger. We receive a flood of sacred awareness. We are connected. We are one. When we get beyond our fears, we come to freedom. The ego surrenders to the Divine. All of life is a spiritual path. The journey of the soul never ends. We are here to love, to learn and to play. Lastly, Mr. Frederickson said blind faith in the leading of God would keep you from losing energy through the Crown Chakra.

I was grateful to have the opportunity to have taken the class. What I recall most is that we are on a spiritual journey from selfishness to self-fulfillment. Somehow I also knew this was related to my relationship with Josephine.

Mr. Frederickson said he studied seven different texts to prepare for the class. One was Caroline Myss's book *Anatomy of the Spirit*. She talked of these energy centers as being regulators of the flow of life energy. We become zapped of our energy by our attachments and by other people's negative energy. One's purpose is to live in a manner that is consistent with one's spiritual ideals. We are meant to discover both our personal power and our shared purpose for being alive within a spiritual context. She further believed that all physical disease began with the spirit and emotions of the individual. Every attitude we hold is a positive or negative power for which we are accountable. It is her hope that we care for our spirits as consciously as we care for our physical bodies. I found this so true. We would often brush our teeth, comb our hair and put on pretty clothes, but would neglect our spiritual and emotional well-being. I began to mediate on the Chakras and the sacred truths she believed each Chakra contained. Their areas:

First Chakra:	All is one.
Second Chakra:	Honor one another.
Third Chakra:	Honor oneself.
Fourth Chakra:	Love is Divine Power.
Fifth Chakra:	Surrender Personal Will to Divine Will.
Sixth Chakra:	Seek only the Truth.
Seventh Chakra:	Live in the Present Moment.

Where had I surrendered my power? Which relationships from my past and present were draining my power? Where did I need to reclaim my power?

I reflected upon my divorce back in 1994. I was the first to get divorced in my family. As a matter of fact, I am still the only one divorced. The tribe stuck together no matter what. Was I losing power on a first Chakra level? My relationship with my wife was over. Later I would seek out others in society who had experienced a divorce. Was I looking for a new tribe? I was not alone. Was I reclaiming power?

Betrayal, loss of trust, anger, confusion, bitterness and aloneness. Was I losing power on a second level Chakra? My primary one-on-one relationship over the past ten years was over. My identity as a husband meant nothing. Eventually I would be in and out of several one on one relationships. Was I reclaiming power as each one ended with my needs unfulfilled?

As for my relationship with myself, I played the victim and was full of self-pity in the initial stages of my divorce. The divorce and things we accused each other of would later turn into a blessing. I alone knew my truth and could turn to no others for validation. It was only myself who could validate my truth. I knew what I did and didn't do. Let the accusations fly, I knew the truth. I could hold my head high. Was I reclaiming power?

Eventually the gift of forgiveness and compassion for my former wife was felt. Had I reached a level of acceptance? Had my heart been opened? Had I started to let the past be the past? Was I reclaiming power?

Creativity. Was my venture in The Big W a creation of my need for space, for time, for reflection, for discoveries, for a journey to self? Was the external journey in The Dub and my efforts at writing a reclaiming of my power? Was I setting boundaries and expressing my uniqueness? Was I letting my talents shine? Was I discovering my higher self?

Third eye intuition seemed a little remote for me. Yet, I indeed was becoming open to spiritual realities I had never encountered; past lives, meditative states, channeling, manifesting and co-creating with the Universe. Was I reclaiming powers from my birthright?

I was becoming aware that all paths are spiritual paths. At moments I was aware of the sacredness of all life. We are all connected. All is one. There is a god within each of us. We are love and need not fear love. The external journey in The Dub was just the setting for my internal journey. We all walk the same path. The journey of the soul is for eternity. We need not fear death of the body as the soul lives on.

I was realizing that the opening and closing of my energy centers we all related. The journey I embarked upon after the pain of my divorce was a journey of spiritual discovery. It was a battle between the limiting programmed voices of my tribal mind and the inner, knowing, higher self expressing itself via my heart. My life and my journey was a process of claiming the infinite power of the creative universe within each of us. As I claimed my power I could co-create with the Universe, with God. As I leaked my power I could drift in indecision and wallow in victimization. The choice was always mine to make.

I parted with Lily and knew I was capable of love again. We knew neither of us was right or wrong. We had different visions of what we intended to create. We each claimed our power as we separated.

Corrina was free to follow her heart, as I was mine. I had enough love and power to accept her for herself and me for myself. I could enjoy the memories of our time together and I could release her in love, wishing her the best. I would journey on and claim my power.

Jane taught me self-care. I was worthy of my own self-love and self-care. Our season was short, but I realized I alone could practice self-care. I alone could claim the power of self-worth and practice self-care.

Johanna taught me a great deal about the leaking of my energy, my power. Deep within I knew the truth and as it knocked at the door and I told it to go away. I was aware of my heart voice, I listened to my heart voice, but upon expressing it, I didn't trust it nor live by it. I now realized that once the journey of self-awareness begins it is difficult to turn one's back on it. The voice can be temporarily ignored, but it will never go away. I had leaked so much energy with Johanna that it was offensive and ugly when I finally reclaimed my power.

Angelina and I lived in the truth. We ignored the tribe and began dating after only four days. We had a season of laughter. We each were true to our own selves. Our hearts were open and full of acceptance of the other's dreams. We were aware that we were had embarked upon a different dream, a different vision for our futures. We loved, learned and played. Perhaps with lived within the power.

My time with Josephine was equally rewarding, yet very challenging. She was teaching me to be present and live in the moment, to practice self-care expressing boundaries and honoring hers, and to cultivate and nurture love. We would school each other over the next twelve weeks. I would love like never before and deep within I knew our souls had been reunited.

For now both my external and inner journey would continue.

CHAPTER FIFTY-NINE
TRUST YOURSELF
"A CRASH COURSE IN LOVE –MORE
BASIC TRAINING"

We spent twelve weeks together at Josephine's home from January 8th until April 1st. She had her Monday through Friday routine of working and enjoyed playing on the weekends. I had many routines: my dream feeding Dylan routine in the morning, my running routine, my writing routine, and some days my working routine at Odd Jobs Completed. I also had to adjust to her nine-to-five lifestyle. Really it was an eight-to-four lifestyle. Staying up all night didn't really fit her lifestyle. Josephine liked to get to bed around ten. Usually we stayed up to midnight while in her bed: sometimes laughing, sometimes playing, sometimes talking or sometimes making love. Some nights we did all four. I was aware of the days of the week and had to remind myself that you played on weekends when you worked Monday through Friday. I was used to playing and creating each day as any other day. But now I was in a relationship with another, not just by myself.

I started on a new journal on 1/9/2001 and entitled it "Looking for a Lighthouse". Over my morning coffee I randomly wrote:

Looking for a lighthouse.
Somewhere in between.
Learn how to play.
East, West.

Beach run.
Ideas, theories, notes.
Someone tell me the road to travel,
I need a lighthouse, I need a guide.
Do I settledown?
Do I build a life?
Which beach is write – oops!
Dreaming still.
Is that wrong?
Self knowledge, self care, self neglect, self love.
Do we all have guides?
Is there a soul contract?
What of ghosts from the past?
Was it all in the plan to reach this moment?
Am I recreating or creating?
Does anyone remember me?

The weather had broken and it was mostly in the mid to high fifties during the day in Metro-Atlanta. Usually I tried to run between twelve and two. It was in the twenties and thirties in New England. Thank God I wasn't there. Naturally I would also check southern Florida: seventies. Ouch. I still had the beach in my dreams. I told myself come April I would take a trip along the coast of South Carolina and North Carolina. Get off the pity pot and enjoy your time with Josephine, get your running on track, and start writing. My mind lived in fear and hinted I would never see the beach again. My heart knew better and that it was time for a season at Josephine's home.

Each morning I had my cleaning routine. Josephine and her housemate, Linda used to like to play "Jenga Trash". The object was to see how high you could stack the trash on top of the already full bag before it toppled to the floor and would have to be put in two or three bags and brought to the dumpster. I didn't play and just brought the garbage out each morning. It would be one of the first things they missed when I left for the road. I also got the biggest kick out of doing Josephine's laundry. I had come full circle on the domestic front. She appreciated all I did and it made me feel like I was contributing.

I love to be there when she came home from work around five. She was always exhausted from the day's activities and the heavy traffic. I tried to time her arrival home and have coffee ready. Occasionally dinner would be ready, but most days she liked to eat later in the evening. She was a great cook. Of course I was used to eating a lot of canned food in The Dub. My favorite was her nachos. Many evenings around seven she would make a batch and we would lie on the couch eating nachos and watching a movie rental. Then it was off to bed and a few hours in each other's arms. Some mornings, while up feeding Dylan, I would make her coffee and try to sit with her before she left at seven-thirty for work. But most mornings she would dress while I was fast asleep under the covers. She would wake me up with kisses and tell me she loved me. And then it was goodbye until she returned again at five. These would be some of the little things I missed when I was back in The Dub and living on the road with Dylan.

I was slowly beginning to learn a few lessons about love. Often while out for a run with Dylan I would contemplate the lessons Josephine was helping me master.

The first lesson was that I needed to put the magnifying glass away and pull out the mirror. If I focused on any negative traits of Josephine I would become depressed and scared. I also learned that mostly what you accuse others of is what you are most guilty of. This isn't just about me. I find it's also true when others are accusing me of something. Listen when others complain about you, they will tell you a great deal about themselves.

I truly believe that our thoughts create our reality and if I chose to dwell in the negative aspects of a situation, my reality was full of negativity. No. I would choose the positive. What's good about my partner? What are her assets? I was learning once again that what you focus on grows. Our thoughts manifest our reality.

Another lesson I learned was that I needed to embrace the whole of who Josephine was. I needed to embrace the whole package. Love her faults as well as her virtues. I realized I wasn't looking for a woman who was a "constant woman". I wasn't looking for someone who was always the same. No. I chose to honor our differences and all of her. We each brought different skills, attitudes, and dreams to the relationship. How could we nurture each other? How could we support each other? How could we help each other grow in our spiritual development? I began to recognize the playful Josephine, the sexy Josephine, the responsible Josephine, the creative Josephine, the bossy Josephine, the messy Josephine, the tired Josephine, the caring Josephine, the needy Josephine, the trusting Josephine, the scared Josephine, the need to be right Josephine and the loving Josephine. She was a dynamic person with varied moods and personalities and so was I. There was the playful Napoleon, the sexy Napoleon, the responsible Napoleon, the creative Napoleon, the bossy Napoleon, the messy Napoleon, the tired Napoleon, the caring Napoleon, the needy Napoleon, the trusting Napoleon, the scared Napoleon, the need to be right Napoleon, and the loving Napoleon. Who was I to limit her? No. I would embrace the entire woman. I would love the entire woman.

I was also learning that it's not my job to fix Josephine. Care taking never worked for me. When Josephine had a problem or a down day, I didn't have to offer a solution. I didn't have to assume the burden of solving the situation. I was learning to listen, to comfort, and to love. I could support her without losing myself. I could be her friend and her lover. Playing the martyr didn't work. It became a lose/lose situation. At times it was difficult, as it was easy to swing to the other extreme and become selfish. Walking the line between self-care and selfishness sometimes became blurred. Fine tuning the vision is part of the journey from selfishness to self-fulfillment. On the road I was learning to live alone. In Atlanta I was learning to live with another.

One lesson that would resurface time and time again was learning to live in the present. At times Josephine would do or say something and I would feel wounded. My feelings would be hurt. I learned that at these times I would lose my power if I chose to retaliate in anger or if I chose to withdraw and pout. More often than not I would start to shut down, to withdraw. Josephine would challenge me to express my hurt, to explore the situation, to resolve the conflict when it occurred, not three days or a week later. I was learning to be present in the relationship, to honor us both, and to live and love in the moment.

I was learning to trust myself in our relationship. I needed to voice my dreams, my thoughts, my concerns, my hurts and my love. Self-care began with self-awareness. I was the only one who could identify my needs and my wants. I needed to trust my heart and express my heart. Sometimes we just agreed to disagree. We were both strong willed and had strong personalities. Sometimes we had to acknowledge that we were both right.

Lastly, I was learning about the nature of Love. It wasn't about what I could get from a situation, it was about what I could bring. When I had expectations or demands I was usually let down. However, when I would strive to be of service, I was usually rewarded beyond my wildest dreams. I was starting to understand that the gift is in the giving and the joy is in the journey.

Josephine had truly become my friend, my lover, my teacher, my student, and my star. We would challenge, thrill, teach, accept, encourage, and love each other.

As we would finish our run I swear I could hear Dylan singing, " *It's a restless hungry feeling, that don't mean that I'm no good. When everything that I'm a-sayin' you can say it just as good. You are right from your side, I am right from mine.*"

CHAPTER SIXTY
SWEETHEART LIKE YOU
"PLAYING"

Josephine's birthday is January 6th. On the tenth we caught a show at the Fox Theater in downtown Atlanta. The show was a musical called *Stomp*. We enjoyed it and it was fun getting dressed up and going on a real date. Afterwards Josephine would take me to Krispy Kreme Donuts. I didn't eat any, but enjoyed watching her savor every bite of the freshly baked goodies as she drove us home.

On January 19th we drove to Hilton Head Island, South Carolina, for our first beach weekend trip. We stayed at the Westin Resort right on the beach. I got a forty minute run in on both Saturday and Sunday. We played, walked the beach collecting shells, and went dancing on Saturday night. Josephine is a great dancer. I seem to drift into my own world. We did find our rhythm and danced the night away. Like me, Josephine loved the beaches of Hilton Head. It was our number one choice of this weekend. Of course we had only been to one other beach together. We liked that fact that the beaches were clean and you could run, but overall the island was developed commercially and somewhat segregated. We were looking for something with a little more of a community feel. Our search would continue.

Some days when she got home from work early we would catch a five o'clock matinee movie and then grab some dinner. We both loved sushi and could easily convince each other to splurge. I was spoiled from the all you can eat sushi buffets in

Florida which usually ran about $15.00. In Atlanta you wouldn't even think of ordering sushi unless you had an extra $40-$60. I still had a road budget mentality.

On Friday the 26th we went to the Trinity Gallery in Buckhead for an art show. Josephine's friend, Sal Roberts was showing three of his paintings. It was my first show and I enjoyed it immensely. Afterwards we took Sal out for sushi. We instantly connected as insecure budding artists. It was amazing to see his work. He was very talented, but at the same time very insecure. While everyone sent him praise, he constantly was full of self-doubt. I could identify. Josephine had shared with her housemate, Linda, the Christmas story that I had written. While Linda had nothing but praise, I was totally unsure of my writing. Sal and I would talk for hours about this. One thing we both agreed upon; whether our works were good or bad, we had no choice, we must create, it's part of who we are. I was reminded of Rilke's *Letters to a Young Poet*. On a side note I should tell you Sal sold two out of his three paintings that night. Of course he focused on the one he didn't sell.

On Saturday night we went to a restaurant called Dave and Buster's or Buster and Dave's, I can never remember. It is sort of a grown up Chucky Cheese Restaurant. It was Josephine's Company Christmas party. They usually did it a month or so after Christmas I was told. We had a great dinner and the Company gave each person a credit card with over 1,200 tokens on it. Josephine and I each won about 8,000 coupons redeemable for prizes. She used all hers for a CD player, while I got some great stuffed animals for Sara and a limited edition Superbowl football, with the history of all previous Superbowls, for Joey. It was so cool, I got myself one too.

Every Sunday we were attending the Manifesting Meditation at the Dinner Place, I mean Inner Space. Since we both agreed that someday we envisioned living in a beach community we began to envision creating prosperity. We would focus on the flow of abundance and not the fear of scarcity. I called it our "beach relocation plan" and we would release any fears, any doubts, and surrender it to the Universe. Naturally, my new journal dated 1/28/01 was entitled Creating Prosperity.

Superbowl Sunday was super. We made love morning, noon, and night. I believe Baltimore beat New York, but I was a little dazed.

On Friday, February 3rd we went to Tybee Island, Georgia. We had gone over Thanksgiving weekend and decided to go again. We had a rough week. Josephine had a rash on her face and the doctors at work were worried her throat might close up, so they gave her some medication, which contained some kind of steroid. Josephine wasn't happy. She had suffered terribly with steroid medication during a past illness which required her to take steroids. It made her sensitive, irritable, and worried about gaining weight. She tried to tell me that she might overreact to any little thing, but I forgot. We got into some fight and were pouting in our respective corners before I even remembered about the steroids. The ride to Tybee was very tense. At times I wanted to go back to Atlanta. Josephine insisted we continue. I'm glad she did. We salvaged the weekend and realized what was happening with the medication and just tried to love each other. We stayed at the Super Eight Motel one block from the beach. I was able to get in a fifty minute beach run and enjoyed the sun. We ate our meals at Fannies By The Beach and I enjoyed the Neptune Pizza with lobster & shrimp toppings. We both decided Tybee was not for us. While it was less than twenty miles from Savannah and did have a small beach community feel, it just didn't feel right for us. The search would continue.

For Valentine's Day we attended the Fox Theater for the musical *Fame*. Once again we got dressed up and had a real date. Josephine got me thirty-nine valentine cards. One for this year and one for each year she missed. She's great at things like that.

In mid-February we went to a Mediumship Workshop at the Inner Space. The medium was a man named Jim Bellingham. Originally from England he was now living in the Atlanta area. I was somewhat skeptical. There were about fifteen people in attendance. Mr. Bellingham proceeded to go around the room asking each person whom it was that they wished to contact.

When it was my turn I gave him the name of my mother's father and the year he had died. I only had two memories of this man and was attempting to test the medium and at the same time see if I could learn anything about my mother. At first he said he saw a photo. No. I have no photos of my granddad. Then he mentioned a suit. No. My granddad was blue collar man. Then he mentioned a cane. Then it struck me. It's not my mom's dad. It's my dad's dad. My Grampie. I had one picture of him. It was of him and me and he was wearing a suit. Then of course, the cane. For years after Grampie passed away, I played with his cane. It was given to me by my parents. Could it be Grampie? Then Mr. Bellingham said, "I have a message." The message was, "Don't change what you believe for anyone." Sort of a generic message, yet, at the same time it was something that I personally struggled with all the time. I had abandoned many beliefs of the tribe and met much resistance walking my own path, following what I believed to be my truth. Later, upon reflection, I remembered my mother telling me after Grampie died, (when I was 7 or 8), that I had questioned her about why Grampie died. She did her best to explain and said I responded to her explanation by saying, "But Mom, doesn't God know that Grampie was my best friend?" Since then I would often wonder, "Was Grampie watching me? Was he helping me walk my path?"

A week or so later we attended a Past Life Regression Workshop with Mr. Bellingham. There were seven couples in attendance. Josephine and I were the last to go. He proceeded to tell us of an impression of a life we shared in Rome about 300 A.D. We were both male and best of friends. Later we journeyed to Bath, England and helped build that community. We had a strong friendship and were like brothers. We loved to play jokes on one another. We certainly displayed this characteristic in this lifetime. Overall this made little impression on me. I always felt we were lovers in France. Then he proceeded to tell us of a lifetime we shared as man and wife in Paris around 1920. Bingo. He had my attention now. He said we were financially well off. We traveled the world and liked to drink a lot. In this lifetime both Josephine and I had quit drinking many years ago. Perhaps we worked out some karma. He told us that we were not as well off in this lifetime as in the lifetime of prosperity, but not to worry, money would still not be an issue, as we had the capacity together to create our own prosperity in this lifetime. He knew nothing of our Creating Prosperity Meditation. Needless to say that night we made love for hours.

Was it real? Did we really have past lives together? We believed so.

Our Jykell Island trip the first weekend of March was cancelled. Josephine discovered that I had been there before and that I really didn't want to live there. She said, "Why should we bother if you know already that you don't want to live there?" Good point, I thought. We decided to go to Charleston, South Carolina instead. But the weather that weekend was heavy rain. So we cancelled that too.

For the most part the weather in February and March was warm. Even in the high sixties at the end of March.

The weekend of March 16th and 17th found us at our first wedding together. Trae was getting married. He was Beth and David's youngest son. We went to the rehearsal dinner on Friday and the Wedding on Saturday. We danced, ate, and eventually talked of marriage.

Josephine knew that I still had a problem with the idea of marriage. I think what scared me most was recreating what I knew marriage to be. We had both been married before and talked about creating something different. Could you really do that? My mind was full of fear. Additionally, I still associated marriage with divorce. If you get married, you will someday end up in front of the judge. It was a limiting belief I would sort out over the next few months. Finally, Josephine just said, "Look I'm not trying to get married tomorrow. I would just like to know if it is in the realm of possibility. I would like to get married someday and I hope we are heading in that direction." It wasn't an ultimatum. We agreed if I made a decision that I didn't want to get married I would tell her immediately. I thought of Johanna and our discussions about children. I never said no and she always had hope. But this was different. Josephine didn't want children. She just wanted a life partner who was committed to the relationship. I couldn't say yes and I didn't say no. Time would reveal more. Looking back I realize that I hadn't closed the door on my life in The Dub and wasn't willing to open another door until I did.

The last two weeks in Atlanta with Josephine were a little tense. We did manage to get to an Atlanta Thrashers hockey game and an Atlanta Hawks basketball game, but reality was setting in. I was hitting the road on April first. I was missing the beach and missing The Dub. Back in January there was a longing to stay and my heart knew there still were lessons to be learned with Josephine. I knew on a soul level it was the right path. Now it was the road I was longing for. We enjoyed ourselves for twelve weeks. I had practiced living in the moment. I had practiced self-care. I had practiced nurturing love. We enjoyed twelve weeks of discovery and still liked what we were discovering about each other. But the road still called. I wasn't finished. I wasn't ready to move on. I wasn't ready to give it up.

I longed for my own space. I had been visiting Josephine and was living in her space. Is this what Johanna felt on the road with me? I was craving my home on wheels. Perhaps someday we would have a home we called our space.

Closure. I couldn't start a life with Josephine until I put closure on the road. If I stayed in Atlanta, I feel I would have betrayed myself, my dreams, and my heart. I had started in The Dub in May of 1998 and it was now almost April of 2001. I was now dreaming of living in a beach community, running, writing, working, living, and sharing it all with a companion. No. Not a companion, but Josephine. At the same time I knew I wasn't finished with the road. If I stayed in her arms, I would always have one eye on the road. I needed to go. I needed to finish what I had started. I would need to leave the road on my own terms. I needed to put closure on what I had started. I needed to spend time in solitude. I needed to be true to my vision. I needed my home and my space. I needed Soul School-Playground Earth.

The tugging on my soul was still there. I needed to honor it. Happiness came from following my heart, not ignoring it. I knew I loved Josephine and I knew our love would survive. Lastly, I knew deep within that I wasn't finished with the road and that this was the right path, not only for me, but for us.

Back in January when we flew to San Francisco I had read Sophie Burnham's book *The Ecstatic Journey,* in which she talks of a Second Journey involving a search for new meanings, fresh values. She states that the Second Journey is a distinct period in a person's life when you set out in a new direction. It's not a fear based midlife crisis, but rather a call to end one life and strike out on a new way. I believe my Second Journey involved my journey in The Dub—the inner journey within the external journey. Perhaps my life with Josephine would be a Third Journey, but for now it was time to travel the Second Journey and finish what I had started.

I do believe we co-create with God. The God within will direct us, inspire us, empower us, leading us to a higher spiritual plane. One of the last things Josephine told me was that she believed that we could not go to a higher plane spiritually as a couple until I completed my journey. I valued her support and deep, deep within, I knew I needed to finish what I had started before I could commit to a new season.

On my last night I dreamt of a butterfly. What was it to be, the limiting world of the caterpillar or the limitless world of the butterfly? The choice is always ours to make. We must make it or it will be made for us.

CHAPTER SIXTY-ONE
GOING, GOING, GONE
"SENIOR TERM—THE ROAD"

The week before I left Atlanta, Josephine and I watched the movie *The Dead Poets Society.* In the movie the main character, played by Robin Williams, spoke of Thoreau and of living deliberately and sucking the marrow out of life. It was time to live deliberately again. It was time for The Dub.

On Sunday night, April 1, 2001, around nine at night, I left Atlanta for the coast. Letting go was painful. Josephine had tears in her eyes. I too was in pain, but the pleasure of following my heart was greater than the pain and grief of temporarily letting go. As my decision to stay for twelve weeks in Atlanta felt right, my decision to return to The Dub felt the same. My journey would unfold a day at a time. Besides Josephine and I had plans to meet in Edisto Beach, South Carolina, the following weekend.

The last book I read while at Josephine's home was James Van Praagh's book, *Talking to Heaven.* Mr. Van Praagh is a medium with the gift of being able to communicate with the dead. The book is full of fascinating stories with messages from beyond indicating that our time on earth is but a small portion of our soul's journey. Nothing happens by chance. All of life is a learning from experience. One message even stated, "Earth is a schoolroom. We come here to learn various lessons, and these lessons vary for every person. Each of us incarnates at a different level of growth, and each needs to go through different experiences in order to gain wisdom and expand our awareness of the bigger picture of life." This sounded a little familiar: schoolroom, lessons, growth, experiences, awareness, and big picture. Perhaps I was indeed heading in the right direction, walking the right path.

Dylan and I drove a couple of hundred miles until two in the morning and slept at a rest area on Route 78 in Branchtown, South Carolina, about ten miles west of Route 95. The next morning we drove to Edisto Beach and would spend four days alone parked in front of the house my friend, Jackie Davis, had rented for the weekend. She was hosting a small get together at the beach. She was from Carolina Beach, North Carolina, but each year rented a house on Edisto Island.

Immediately, we went for a 60 minute run on the beach. Dolphins were about ten yards off shore and Dylan chased the dolphins and birds. We easily slipped into a road routine of waking up early around seven or eight. I would feed Dylan and put on the coffee. The temperatures were in the high seventies and sometimes the low eighties. After coffee, we would take a walk on the beach, followed by some journal time and writing time. Around midday we ran. Afternoons were for reading and playing fetch on the beach. Dylan was becoming skillful at the game. Evenings we had dinner, did some reading, and were in bed by nine. The cottage had an outdoor hot water shower in the rear. What a bonus. We had four days before anyone would be arriving.

One of the first books I read while back on the road was by Charles Sides called *Motorcycle Enlightenment*. In the book the main character gets divorced, sells everything and buys a motorcycle, determined to travel from Pennsylvania to California seeking enlightenment. However, before leaving Pennsylvania he decides to go to the New Jersey shore and never hits the road. The irony is that all of his lessons still reveal themselves. My mind begins to tell me, "You never should have never left Atlanta." Then it catches itself, "No wait. That was his journey. I will walk mine."

Next, I read Rosemary Altea's, *The Eagle and The Rose*. Ms. Altea is a medium and spiritual healer. In the book she chronicles her journey and her process of discovery and development of her psychic abilities. She speaks of her guide, Grey Eagle, who leads her down the road of learning. He shares that the search for truth must begin within. We must listen to our inner selves. Now I'm feeling more comfortable about my time on the road. Yes, Napoleon. Listen to your heart. Many of the spirits who speak through Ms. Altea say, "We don't die. The spirit lives on and we continue on our journey and we continue to learn. Life is about learning." The soul never dies. The learning never ends. The journey is really just one series of journeys within journeys. Lessons upon lessons. She talks of gaining an understanding that life is an adventure, a learning experience that, if embraced, will help us grow. In that growing we can discover the spiritual self and truly know who we are. Problems are problems. The lesson is in how we deal with these problems. There are no chance meetings. All souls we encounter are for a reason. I thought of Lily, Corrina, Jane, Johanna, Angelina and Josephine.

I'm comfortable with the solitude of the road. I trust my time apart from Josephine is for a reason. There is no ache of loneliness like when I was in Key West back in December missing her desperately. I feel I'm in the right place at the right time. I'm on the path called my life.

It was Thursday and everyone was arriving the following day for the weekend. Dylan and I would go for our run on the beach and I'm sure I heard him singing, *"Then onward in my journey, I come to understand that every hair is numbered, like every grain of sand."*

CHAPTER SIXTY-TWO
DOWN ALONG THE COVE
"A SHARED WEEKEND ON THE ROAD"

The house Jackie rented contained seven bedrooms, was located on the beach, and was called Dolphin Watch. Josephine and Linda arrived around two a.m. early Friday morning. Dianna and Sean arrived around eight o'clock Thursday night, around the time Jackie and her boyfriend, Frank, arrived. Bobby from Chicago was in town with his girlfriend, Tori, from Boston.

Dylan and I had spent four days on the road and it was wonderful to be back home in The Dub. On Tuesday night it had rained. Usually when it rains I call it Dub Music. There is a steady beat of rain drops pounding on the roof varying in intensity. The beat is hypnotic and puts one to sleep quickly.

As we arrived in Edisto Island I was aware of again of the "New Town Discovery Process". Arriving in a new place there is a sense of apprehension. There is an undercurrent of fear. Everyone knows each other. You are the stranger. The roadways are a maze. Where will you sleep tonight? Is the town RV friendly? Is the town dog friendly? Then, you stay a few days, discover how to navigate the town, meet a few natives, get a feel for the energy, and finally it's time to move on. Pulling out, there is an air of sadness. You will miss the village. Then the process starts again as you pull into a new town. You are a stranger once again and the new town discovery process begins all over.

Friday, Saturday and Sunday were beach days. We all hung out and worked on our tans. Dinnertime was a group effort.

Josephine and I enjoyed the company of our friends, but more importantly we had survived our first week apart. We both agreed it wasn't that difficult. All week we had the weekend to look forward to.

At night we held each other and made love. It was only five nights apart, but I really did miss holding her at night. We are one of those couples who become entwined as we sleep. I did enjoy my bed in The Dub, but her bed was warm and full of love. I loved reaching out for her in the night. Some nights in The Dub I would hold a pillow and pretend it was her. In the morning we awoke with an ocean view and she brought me coffee in bed. She knows this is one of my favorite times of the day. Perhaps it's a rehearsal for our beach relocation plan.

On Saturday Josephine and I, along with Dianna (soul sister Dianna), Linda and Karen were hanging out on the back deck enjoying the sun. Dianna recently started a job at a bookstore. She goes in early and works seven to ten in the morning. She loves it because the store opens at eleven and she doesn't really have to deal with the customers. She jokes that each week she spends her paycheck on books. She says she has explored every section but the poetry section.

"That interesting," I say.

"Why?" Dianna asks.

Dianna had a difficult childhood. She has done a lot of healing work, but admits she still has a long way to go. After four years of therapy, she still awakes each morning with nightmares.

"Your creative child voice has been silenced," I tell her.

"No. I'm in touch with my inner child and she is really pissed."

"That's the girl who survived. What about the innocent one? The innocent voice buried beneath the survivor?"

"You're nuts and I hate poetry."

We're acting like brother and sister, roles we know well.

"Come on. Let's write a poem. We will play a game. We will write a five line poem. We will each make up a line, and Dianna you can finish it." I suggested.

I go first and say, "Sitting by the ocean with the sky so blue."

Josephine jumps in, "I looked into your eyes and knew it was you."

"Good. Now Linda its your turn," I prod.

"Miles apart and worlds away." She responds without missing a beat.

"Karen, anything?"

"As our hearts and spirits sway." She adds.

"Okay, Dianna you finish."

"Oh, how I hope to see you someday." She says triumphantly.

"Read it, Napoleon." Someone yells as I had been writing each line in my journal.

Sitting by the ocean with the sky so blue.
I looked into your eyes and knew it was you.
Miles apart and worlds away,
as our hearts and spirits sway,
Oh, how I hope to see you someday.

Dianna simply states, "Hey this poetry stuff is great. Let's do another one."

The second poem went:
Let's talk about the innocent one.
The one that went away.
Years have passed and days have gone.
What would I do? What would I say?
Perhaps this time I'll let her stay.

Later, while alone, Josephine and I decided Edisto Beach was not where we would like to begin a life together. It was very expensive and very remote. The nearest City was Charleston, about an hour away. The search would continue.

Josephine and Linda left Sunday at around two o'clock. Josephine had tears in her eyes when they pulled out of the driveway. Dylan just stared, as if to sing, *"If you're travelin' in the north country fair, when the winds hit heavy on the borderline. Remember me to one who lives there, she once was a true love of mine."*

CHAPTER SIXTY-THREE
BORN IN TIME
"THE JOURNEY UNFOLDS"

As we travel, I now burn candles and incense. Gifts from Josephine. Just lighting them reminds me of her and in a strange way, I feel her presence. I think of her and how she never tried to steal my dream. She loves deep enough to release me to the Universe. It pains her for me to be away, but she knows, this is the doorway of our being together. I think back to when I left Atlanta, and how the day before, she helped me clean The Dub. She even insisted upon washing the sheets and pillow cases. My comforter had grown old. She put it inside what I call a big pillow case, and it looked brand new. We even had lunch in The Dub that day.

Three years in The Big W and I'm still learning some tricks on the road. I made some morning coffee. I boil the water and then pour it in the French Press. This morning I boiled too much water. What to do with the excess? I hate to waste it. Then the idea. The new trick. Use the hot water to shave with. Three years and I have been shaving with cold water. A hot shave does wonders.

Clean clothes. Now there's another trick. Usually on the road I go a week to ten days without a hot shower. Swims in the ocean and cold showers at the beach give the illusion of being clean. But nothing beats clean clothes in the morning. Perhaps it's another illusion, but it feels good nonetheless.

Sunday night we drive north along Route 17 to Folly Beach, South Carolina. We find a Wal-Mart and pull in for the night. In the morning I journal:

I walk my path.
Others walk their paths.
I grow, I learn, I evolve.
Some come with me.
Some stay behind.
Walk on, Napoleon.

Who was I in past lives?
How many lives have I lived?
How many more will I live?
Can I remember?
Walk on, Napoleon.

Where am I on the journey of my spirit?
There is a universal plan.
It seems my soul group is very large.
What's real? What's an illusion?
Walk on, Napoleon.

Who are the characters I attract?
We all teach, we all learn.
Be still. Be aware.
Listen to your heart.
Silence the mind.
Walk on, Napoleon.

Walk, live, learn, play, dream, love.
Life is good, enjoy the ride.
The ride never ends.
No limits.
Walk on, Napoleon.

Onward. Upward.
Be still, listen, more will be revealed.
Trust. Don't let others dictate your thoughts.
Believe, Believe, Believe.
Action, Action, Action.
Walk on, Napoleon.

Challenges await, rewards are great.
Time to learn, time to grow, time to play.
Be still, listen and learn.
Experience is true wisdom
Trust your experience.
Trust your past, walk into your future.
Walk on, Napoleon.

The journey never ends.
God is within.
Has been and will always be.
Silence the doubts and all the doubters.
Walk on, Napoleon.

The journey is real.
The lessons are real.
Love is real.
Fear is an illusion.
Walk on, Napoleon.

Be still and listen.
Walk on.

Random thoughts on a not so random journey. In the morning I love to journal over coffee. Some days I report, some days I have insights, and some days I create.

We spent three days in Folly Beach. The beach is flat and hard packed near the ocean, which is ideal for running. Dylan chased the birds, as there were no dolphin sightings. We hung out at a place called "The Washout". It is where the locals do most of their surfing. The weather was great. Around 85 degrees and the days flew by. The beaches were dog friendly at the north end of the island. Late in the afternoon we would either drive The Dub or walk through the neighborhoods exploring. Folly Beach was now on my A-List. It was a small beach community and had a small-town feel to it. There was a local fishing pier and just a little commercial development. You could probably still get a pizza at ten at night. I scanned the real estate listings and the prices seemed somewhat reasonable. I was thinking perhaps we could buy a place, live in it nine months a year, and rent it out during June, July, and August, to pay for the debt service. Over the summer perhaps we could travel in a Jumbo Dub. The bonus was that Folly Beach was only fifteen minutes from downtown Charleston. Josephine would definitely have to visit. Folly Beach was my number one choice. The only negative was that there was no ocean sunset on the Atlantic Ocean side of the island. I still was very fond of the sunsets on the Gulf of Mexico on the west coast of Florida. More would be revealed.

Our days in Folly Beach were marked by waterfront property by day, Wal-Mart parking lots by night. Since we spent most nights at Wal-Mart we tried to buy all of our provisions there. Karma, I guess. We bought bottles of water for me, and gallons for Dylan. When we left, the temperature was 89 degrees. Between our runs and games of fetch, Dylan drank nonstop.

We pulled out of Folly Beach and drove north on Route 17 through Charleston during rush hour. The traffic was light and I could envision building a home with Josephine here.

We ended up driving 100 miles north to Myrtle Beach, South Carolina. The first 50 miles were pretty boring with nothing of interest until Georgetown. South of Myrtle Beach was Pawley's Island, Litchfield Beach, Garden City and Surfside Beach. We couldn't find anywhere to spend the night, so we drove to the Wal-Mart in Myrtle Beach. It was the first time I ever saw a sign saying NO RV OVERNIGHT PARKING. We parked anyway. I concluded it must be because there are RV campgrounds all over the Myrtle Beach area and the town officials made Wal-Mart post the signs so as not to compete with the campgrounds. No one ever bothered us and later I was able to confirm my campground theory accuracy with a manager.

We spent a couple days in Myrtle Beach. While we did get to run, the area was a tourist trap. Route 17 was all restaurants, mini-golf sites, and beach super stores. I made a mental note that the kids might like it someday to visit, but it was no place I wanted to live. Folly Beach was still number one.

At night I was re-reading the novel 2050 *A.D.*, by Thea Alexander. My friend Tom Bright from Naples, Florida, had given it to me. In the book, Ms. Alexander talks about how each love we share prepares us to more fully experience the better one which lies ahead if we just evolve enough to be willing to take the risk of loving again and again as long as we live. I was thinking of Josephine. Had all my past relationships led me to her? I believed so. All the lessons of my life were being applied with Josephine and new ones were emerging. Ms. Alexander talked of the micro man and the macro man and the journey from a limited thinking man to an unlimited thinking man. The macro view of awareness – all is one. She talked of past lives, and that all learning was really a remembering. What I found most fascinating was the concept that our other lifetimes were all occurring at the same time. She stated all time is happening simultaneously. Linear time was how the limited man, the micro man viewed life. My mind was spinning. Time is an illusion. Earlier I had read how Richard Bach described alternate realities based upon alternative choices made. Did each decision create an alternative life with alternative lessons? The possibilities were endless. Was there a Napoleon who stayed in Atlanta? Was there a Napoleon with Lily? Corrina? Jane? Johanna? Angelina? Was there a Napoleon still married and living with Joey and Sara?

Still heading north after spending two nights in Myrtle Beach, we awoke and drove to Sunset Beach, North Carolina. We had a great 64 minute run in the morning and had planned to spend the whole day there, but the clouds came in for the afternoon and spoiled our plans. We proceeded north along Route 17 then west on Route 211 to Southport. We found a Wal-Mart and were going to spend the night, but the clouds were still looming. We decided to take the ferry across from Southport to Carolina Beach across the Cape Fear River. Despite rumors that actor John Travolta was in town filming a movie, we still continued north. If Mr. Travolta had spotted The Dub, I was prepared to serve dinner.

It was the second ferry ride for The Dub. Dylan nearly jumped off as the seagulls were flying nearby. We arrived in Kure Beach and within ten minutes had reached Carolina Beach, North Carolina.

We parked in front of Jackie's condo for the night in a guest parking spot. At least three of the neighbors stopped by to see who we were. She was staying at her boyfriend, Frank's home for the evening. However, she did come by and give me a key to her apartment. That evening and in the morning I took a bath. Lots of bubbles and of course, hot water. It reminds me of Josephine and the many baths we had shared together. Josephine had baths salts, bubbles, little ducks, and these great sponges. All Jackie had was shampoo. Still I was grateful and clean.

Carolina Beach was a small community about 20 miles south of Wilmington. It would be a nice place to live, except the beaches are terrible for running. They have lots of loose sand and slope abruptly towards the ocean. However, Dylan had fond memories, as he had is first ice cream cone in Carolina Beach. Actually it was in a cup. I wanted to get him Turtle Tracks, but the vendor suggested straight vanilla. Being his first time, I went with the vanilla. He attacked it and ate the cup right along with the ice cream. We'll have to work on that.

The next three days we spent at Wrightsville Beach just outside of Wilmington and parked at the Wal-Mart in Wilmington at night. Wrightsville Beach was a little better for running, especially at the south end. However, overall I knew it wouldn't cut it. The biggest strike against it was the numerous "No Dogs Allowed" signs.

Sunday morning the fifteenth we left the Wilmington area and continued north along Route 17. We eventually headed east on Route 210 and stopped on Topsail Island. We drove to the south end of the island and found public parking for Topsail Beach. It wasn't really a beach day, but it wasn't raining. We managed a 60 minute run and a quick swim. Looking for a place to park overnight and finding none, we drove to Surf City. Still nothing.

Heading north in Holly Ridge, North Carolina, I

instinctively knew that the car up ahead pulling onto Route 17 was going to cut me off. No respect. The Dub gets no respect. Everyone is always pulling out in front of me. I can see the person in the car up head inching out and looking away from me. I see her easing off the gas and slowing down. She is pulling out and turns to see me. Oh, shit. She hits the brakes. Nobody hits the brakes. They just cut me off and zoom away. She froze when she saw me. I hit the brakes too. Fortunately I was only going about 25 mph when I originally saw her and by the time I slid into her I was barely moving.

The police were there in minutes. Photos were taken and markings were made on the street. A fire truck and ambulance arrived. It reminded me of the song by Arlo Guthrie *Alice's Restaurant.* Nobody was hurt. The seventeen year old, rookie driver, was given a ticket for pulling out in front of me. The Dub's bumper, hood, and front quarter panel were dented and rippled. She was still drivable though. My first accident in The Dub. The police took all of our auto information and filled out the accident report. An hour later I was underway.

Shock. I was in shock. I wandered north and decided to drive inland to Jacksonville. I knew there was a Wal-Mart there. I started to think about the accident. I wasn't attached to too many things in my life. But for some reason I was upset after the accident. Later, I realized The Dub is my home. It is not just an automobile for transportation. It is my sacred space. It's where I feel at peace. It's where I feel safe. It is my home. In one quick instant it was almost taken away. Why had this happened? Was it a chance encounter with the young driver named Steffanie? Was she to learn a lesson? Was I to learn a lesson? Or was it all just a coincidence? I guess it's all in what one believes.

What would I have done if The Dub could no longer be driven? Would my external journey have ended? Would my inner journey have ended?

No.

Each journey would have continued.

Perhaps The Dub is an illusion. The external journey in this lifetime will continue with or without The Dub and the inner spirit journey never ends.

We are all on the same journey. We have different landscapes, but the same lessons. I was convinced that somehow my inner journey was connected to my external journey and travels in The Dub. If I gave up the Dub, I would give up the inner journey.

Not true.

Now, I was grasping deep within, that the journey would never end.

Perhaps in the beginning I needed The Dub. I needed the space. I needed the time to get away from the noise. But now, deep within, I knew the journey never ends.

My spirit had awakened, my sleep had ended, and I knew the journey never ends.

People would always try to distract me, to lure me away from my path, to join the sleeping masses, but I knew, the journey never ends.

There would always be challenges, there would always be hurdles, there would always be decisions to make, but I knew, the journey never ends.

One lifetime, two lifetimes, or many lifetimes, the fact was that I was living this lifetime, and I knew the journey never ends.

One soul mate, two soul mates, or a soul group, we were all students, we were all teachers, and I knew the journey never ends.

Each day, each encounter, each moment, offered the chance to create, to walk a path, to love. And I knew "THE **JOURNEY NEVER ENDS**".

CHAPTER SIXTY-FOUR
NEVER GOING TO BE THE SAME
AGAIN
"THE UNIVERSAL PLAN"

Was the external journey an illusion? Was the inner journey the only real journey? To live in The Dub or a beach community with Josephine; it didn't matter, the journey never ends.

My fears were falling from me. Live in the truth, live in the journey, follow your heart, evolve, become aware, grow, and love. Was I putting closure on this part of the journey? Was I preparing for the next season? I think so. I traveled in The Dub and I knew there would be life after The Dub.

While in Wilmington, someone asked me if I was freaking out because I would be turning forty this summer. "No," was the answer. I wasn't "Freaking Out". What was I? I was actually very excited.

That night in Jacksonville I would reflect on the decades gone before.

I concluded that my first decade of life from one to ten years of age was when most of the programming was done to my mind without my consent. The innocent child, the newly arrived spirit in human form, was quickly initiated into the tribe. I was numbed and disconnected from my heart and following the pack with a polluted mind.

My adolescence and the majority of my second decade, were about rebellion. It was a teenage revolution against authority and the programmers of my youth. The problem was that it was mostly alcohol and drug inspired. There was relief, but no growth. I was still numb and disconnected from heart. Looking back I realize that this form of rebellion could be fatal.

My twenties and third decade were about living the script. No longer turning to drinking and drugs, I was conforming. The job, the wife, the kids, the home, I had arrived, but was still disconnected. I was living an external journey with no real inner spiritual joy. I had lived another's dream, another's script, and another's definition of success. From the exterior you would judge me as a success. Spiritually, I was lost.

My thirties were about chaos and clarity. The marriage ended and the script dissolved. The external trappings of success came tumbling down. Of course they would, there was no inner foundation. Then, The Dub, the tugging on my soul, the awakened heart, the journey of the road, and the journey to my essential self.

Now. Anticipating my forties, I was excited for my fifth decade. The inner and external journey would continue, but with a sense of purpose. I was aware. I was awake. I would walk my path. I would live my dreams. I would co-create with the universe, with the divine spark within. The big sleep had ended. I loved Joey and Sara. I loved Josephine. I loved the beach. Somehow, the Universe would bring it all together. The journey would never end.

Lastly, as I reflected over my life and over my journey in The Dub I had the sneaking suspicion that my time in The Dub was really preparing me for my fifties and sixties. More would be revealed.

For now, we headed north, me in the driver's seat and Dylan with his head out the window singing, *"For the loser now will be later to win, for the times they are a-changin'."*

CHAPTER SIXTY-FIVE
WHEN THE SHIP COMES IN
"EVERY NEGATIVE HAS A POSITIVE"

Monday morning we left Jacksonville and headed for the North Carolina coast. Travelling east along Route 24 and then turning to the beach on Route 58 to Emerald Isle, we found a public parking lot and we went for our beach run. Afterwards, a cold shower at an outdoor rinse off station. In the afternoon we headed along the coast to Atlantic Beach just outside of Morehead City. Alternating between reading on the beach and playing fetch with Dylan, we spent the afternoon in the sun. That night we found a Wal-Mart in Morehead City.

Tuesday, April 17th was Dylan's birthday. He was one, but still all puppy. Gathering provisions in Wal-Mart, I found him a birthday treat; a gigantic bone with a knuckle on each end. The weather was windy and cloudy, not much of a beach day, so we went to an autoparts store and replaced the left headlight and blinker. Fifteen minutes and $12 was all it took. I was beaming. No pun intended. My whole childhood I was told I wasn't mechanically inclined. So much for that tape.

Wednesday was again cold. We found the Morehead City Webb Library. I was hoping to plug in my laptop and recharge the battery while getting in a little writing. Not only did they let me plug in and have a room to myself, they also had a computer set up where you could go online for free and check your e-mail. Thirty-three e-mails. Mostly junk. However, there was one from my dad stating that Farm Bureau Insurance was trying to get ahold of me and to please call and speak with Amy.

Farm Bureau was the insurance company of the young girl from the accident. I called Amy. She informed that on Tuesday there were several tornados, which had touched down in Morehead City, and that the regional adjuster was in that area and carried a checkbook. She wanted to know if I wanted to meet with him and have him look at my vehicle. I knew it was windy, but I never saw any of the tornados. Did she say checkbook? I made arrangements to see the adjuster Thursday morning. That night I found their office in Morehead City and parked in their lot overnight.

After the accident in The Dub I was just grateful I was able to keep driving. The damage, while it didn't look pretty, had no effect mechanically on The Dub. Also, I was grateful for the lessons, for the thoughts I had about The Dub and my journey. I had no intention of ever making any repairs beyond the left headlight and blinker. The Dub's dents would be battle wounds. Besides it gave her a little more character.

Thursday morning I met the adjuster at eight-thirty. He took photos and inspected the damage. His estimate would be based upon used parts and local labor rates, he informed me. By nine o'clock he handed me his estimate for damage and a check for $1,278.67. The ink wasn't dry before I was at the bank and cashing the check. I had signed off for vehicle damage only. My right ankle was sore. I wasn't sure if it was from driving, running, or the accident. Later I took the estimate to two repair facilities and confirmed they could indeed do the work for $1,278.67. I felt reassured that I didn't leave any money on the table.

The money came in handy. Money was running a little low. I knew I had funds to last through June, but now July was looking pretty good. Plus, we intended to go to the outer banks and suspected we would have to rent a few campsites. The accident in The Dub was negative at first, but the positives were now surfacing.

We stayed in Morehead City until Sunday. The weather wasn't that great and I didn't want to get too far north in the cold. We spent our days in The Dub, the library, and exploring nearby Beaufort. With my new found riches, we splurged and got some cigars. Later we went to Radio Shack and purchased a portable charger for my laptop. We were living large. As I sparked up a cigar, Dylan just sang, *"Money comes and goes, money comes and goes, my money comes and goes, and rolls and flows and rolls and flows, through the holes in the pockets in my clothes."*

CHAPTER SIXTY-SIX
THE WATER IS WIDE
"THE OUTER BANKS"

Sunday was a beach day. We drove over the Bogue Sound back to Atlantic Beach from Morehead City and spent the day in the sun. At around three in the afternoon we headed north along Route 70 and Route 12 to Cedar Island. We arrived around five o'clock and got in line for the ferry from Cedar Island to Ocracoke, North Carolina. They measured The Dub. It was under 20 feet, so we paid $10 instead of $20. A half a tank of gas savings.

They called it the sunset ride. We were finally on our way to the outer banks. The ride lived up to its name. The sunset was awesome. Arriving in Ocracoke, Pirate Blackbeard's stomping ground, we were pleasantly surprised to find a 72 hour public overnight parking lot.

Ocracoke is a small beach community with a winter population of less than 1,000. Over a million tourists pass through in the summer season. We spent Sunday and Monday nights in the 72 hour lot. During the day we found the beach. Absolutely beautiful. The waves were incredible. Resting my leg, we chose to go boogie boarding instead of running. Dylan would chase me out in the water and watch in amazement as I rode the waves. He was becoming a talented body surfer in his own right.

On Tuesday we ventured north. After sixteen miles we had to take another ferry to Hatteras, North Carolina. We were slowly going to work our way up the outer banks.

Hatteras didn't feel right. We continued on and found our first campsite. For $36 we had a waterfront site at the Frisco Woods Campgrounds in Frisco. After a quick twenty minute run and a swim for Dylan, I went to the pool. Yes, a pool. Hot showers, too. I was getting my money's worth. It was blue sky and 80 degrees all day.

Wednesday was rain, rain, and more rain. To make matters worse it was cold and windy. We drove north to Avon and found the Sands in Time Campground. For $18 we had a place to park and could plug into the electric service.

I was happy we had the accident money, as I didn't expect to find any Wal-Mart's on the outer banks. For now I was just glad they were RV and dog friendly in the outer banks.

CHAPTER SIXTY-SEVEN
DON'T FALL APART ON ME TONIGHT
"JOSEPHINE IS PISSED OFF"

Sunday night and Wednesday nights were date nights. No matter where I was, I would give Josephine a call and we would have a phone date. It was Wednesday, April 25, 2001, I was in Avon, it was cold and wet, and instead of waiting until nine I called at a little after six.

Usually the first few minutes of the conversation were spent updating Josephine as to my travels and where Dylan and I were at the moment. Tonight's call was typical. Then I asked how Josephine was doing.

"Not good," she responded.

I knew immediately she was upset.

"What's the matter?" I asked.

"I'm full of resentment. There is no reason for us to be apart."

Silence.

"This is not what I thought it would be."

Silence.

"Sure, intellectually I told myself this was something you needed to do. I thought I knew what it was going to be like. It's not what I thought. I'm pissed. I'm lonely. I miss you."

Silence.

"There I said it. I knew you wouldn't want me to hold it in. We told each other we would always be honest, even if it was something we thought the other person didn't want to hear."

Silence.

"Okay, I feel better. I was afraid to tell you how I really felt. I was afraid you would think I was trying to tell you to come back. I'm not saying that. I'm just saying that I'm hurting, I miss you and I need reassurance you are coming back."

"I love you, Josephine."

"I know. I love you, too. I just need to know you still want to build a life with me."

"I do want to build a life with you, but not in Atlanta. I love you."

We talked like this for about an hour. She needed to get it out. It's funny, I never felt like she was trying to get me to come back. I just knew she missed me. She was struggling with our separation. It had nothing to do with bringing me home early. She was just in pain. Also, I never even thought about returning. I never thought, "Drive to Atlanta, fix her pain, make her happy." My mind never even spoke. Only my heart. Compassion for her pain. It wasn't my job to fix it. I was at peace. I knew I was exactly where I was supposed to be. Her resentments and ranting had nothing to do with me. I simply reassured her that I loved her, that I missed her, and still wanted to build a life with her. I didn't need to go into a lengthy explanation of the big picture, of putting closure on the road, of finishing my time in The Dub on my own terms. No, I simply let her know that I loved her.

She knew, too. She was, as she said, "Stuck in the little picture and hated being so needy." She thought neediness was so unattractive. I told her that I loved her most when she was vulnerable and not a know it all. She didn't have to be so strong. She stated her true feelings and was still teaching me to do the same. I respected her for that.

The last thing she said to me was, "Well at least you'll have some new stuff for your book."

Soon my love, soon.

CHAPTER SIXTY-EIGHT
DIGNITY
"CROUCHING TIGER, HIDDEN DRAGON"

After the phone date with Josephine I decided to go to the movies.
I had passed the theater in Avon earlier in the day. I was actually
shocked to see a movie theater on the outer banks. I hadn't seen
Crouching Tiger, Hidden Tiger and decided to go.

The next morning we awoke and the rain had stopped.
The sun was shining, but it was still very windy. We decided to
continue north. The speed limit was 55 mph, but we couldn't get
The Dub past 46. There was a strong headwind and it reminded
me of New Mexico with Jimmy. Life in the slow lane.

About 20 vehicles passed me like I was standing still. All
rushing by to some important appointment, I'm sure. Only one
gave us the finger, but they all gave us strange looks.

We pulled into Waves, North Carolina, and found a
campsite for $22. We plugged into the electric service and
walked the 50 yards to the beach. The surf was pounding and
the sand was blowing, but at least the sun was shining. I sat
in the dunes, while Dylan ran and inspected the entire beach
within 300 yards in all directions.

As I sat, I thought about Josephine and our talk. I was sad
that she was sad. But I was also very much aware of how happy I
was at the same time. In the movie there was a line spoken near
the ending of which I couldn't get out of my head.

The line went something like this, "PROMISE ME,
WHATEVER PATH YOU CHOOSE IN LIFE, YOU WILL
BE TRUE TO YOURSELF."

True to yourself. That's how I felt. Yes, Josephine was sad. She was lonely. She was angry. At times she was confused. I could do nothing about that. She would have to walk her path. But for now, I knew which path I had chosen and I was being TRUE TO MYSELF.

I could hold my head high and my heart was at peace.

I stared at the ocean. I was safe. I was true. I was peace. I was content. I was happy. I was alive. I was love.

There is nothing to fear, we are all love, and love is all there is.

CHAPTER SIXTY-NINE
BROKE DOWN ENGINE
"THE DUBS MEDICAL WOES"

Returning from the beach I couldn't help noticing all the fancy RVs at the campsite. I called them luxury rides. Some are as nice as hotel suites, but on wheels. The Dub has character. Almost always, heads turn when we pull in. And sooner or later the bumper stickers, historically documenting the journey, draw a crowd. To be fair, I also have to mention those who travel and camp in tents. They dream of luxury RVs, but their pocketbooks are empty. I share with them the price tag of The Dub and their eyes light up. Do they ever take action? I'll never know. But I hope they do.

Looking at The Dub's latest battle wounds from the Holly Ridge accident, I begin reflecting on all her medical treatments over the years. She was born in 1981, but I didn't start attending to her until 1998. First off, we immediately had a tune up, an oil change and a new exhaust system. Her first major problem was in December, 1998 when the clutch stopped working as I was paying a toll on the Florida Turnpike. She looked so sad being towed. We had no real problems until July of 1999 when the alternator went in Chicago. Over the summer we had another tune up and tried to have her oil leak fixed to no avail. In October 1999 on Route 95 heading north in North Carolina I ran over a piece of a truck tire sitting in the road and her waste tank plumbing was ripped off. I didn't discover it until the next morning as I was coming out of a Wal-Mart. From a distance I saw a puddle under her. Bending down and examining her more closely, I realized that my morning pee went in the toilet and straight to the parking lot. Four new tires were acquired in Kansas in November and a new coach battery was installed in December in California. Summer session II in 2000 we tried again to fix the oil leak. No luck. Another tune up and we also had a leak in the gas tank repaired. In September 2000 in Sedona we lost the rear bumper and in Las Vegas we had her shocks examined, but were told there was nothing we could do as the previous owner had done a little of his own maintenance and had welded some high tech attachments to The Dub. We would need a specialty shop to take a look at her. As a result of never having the shocks fixed the interior suffered some damage we never fixed. Both the shower rod in the back and a bookcase over the bed fell down and broke beyond repair. In December, 2000 in Atlanta we had the brakes fixed and her fourth tune up. Now with the accident in April 2001, she was looking pretty beat up.

I had paid $4,500 for her and estimate I put another $4,500 into her over three years. Subtract the $1,278.67 we received from the accident and I was into her for less than $8,000. But I had no rent, no phone, no cable, and no electric bill. She owed me nothing. When the journey ended would I ever sell her? I guess a better question is, "Would anyone ever buy her?" For now I just dreamed of giving her to Joey and Sara and letting them use her as a clubhouse parked in the backyard.

She had character and to me she was still sacred, still my sanctuary, still my home.

CHAPTER SEVENTY
TOMORROW IS A LONG TIME
"ASTRAL TRAVEL"

It seemed like the Universe Librarian was busy at work. Over the past several years I had the opportunity to read many books. Each day I was reading exactly what I needed to read. My life had changed so much since my purchase of The Dub back in 1998.

Thursday night at the campsite I finished Jess Stern's *The Search For a Soul, Taylor Caldwell's Psychic Lives.* I had previously read his book *The Search For The Girl With Blue Eyes.* Like my own experiences with past life regressions I was fascinated with reading about other's experiences. I particularly liked reading the many writings of Edgar Cayce. I had read several of Ms. Caldwell's novels as a teenager and when I saw the book at a used bookstore, I immediately purchased it. Many of Ms. Caldwell's descriptions in her books of places, people and medical procedures were so accurate and so real people would often wonder where she received her information. She admits she doesn't know. Many nights she would just sit at her typewriter and the words would magically flow. I think they call it automatic writing. Mr. Stern's book essentially details the hypnosis sessions of Ms. Caldwell and many of the past lives she lived. While Ms. Caldwell still remained skeptical, I was not. For me the most intriguing parts were when she would recognize her deceased husband, Marcus, while reliving other lifetimes under hypnosis.

I would think of Josephine. How many lives had we shared?

Was our separation as I traveled the road related to a past life? I remember when she walked into the restaurant last May. Our eyes met and there was a deep recognition at a soul level. You couldn't explain it, you just knew.

I had also recently finished Chris Griscom's *Time is an Illusion*. Shirley MacLaine had spoken highly of Ms. Griscom in some of her books. She was a spiritual healer and teacher and in her book she talks of the "experiment of life". She states that death is a passage and we experience cycles of life and death. Like, Dr. Weiss, Mr. Stern, Edgar Cayce, Mr. Praagh, and Ms. Altea, and so many others, she indicated we could learn lessons and experience healing by reliving and understanding our past lives, whether through hypnosis or mediumship. The journey of the soul and never ending evolvement continued through many lifetimes, many cycles of life and death. Dr. Weiss had previously stressed that he believed whether or not these past life memories were real or imagined, the healing would still be real. Ms. Griscom stressed that if we followed are own knowingness, our hearts, our inner voices will guide us along our paths. This I knew to be true. She emphasized sticking to our choices, not believing the masses and trusting our heart voice. We could participate in the divine plan and co-create if we developed the courage to stand alone. This too I knew to be true.

I was fascinated with her notions of linear time being different from the time of the "spirit world" and her experiences with astral out-of-body travel. The ideas weren't new to me. But for some reason the idea of astral travel was stuck in my head. Mr. Bach, Ms. Altea, Ms. MacLaine, Ms. Alexander and so many others had discussed the idea. Even Michael Crichton in his book *Travels* had discussed astral travel. Ms. Griscom said anyone could do it.

I remember when I first began meditating and thinking I would never be able to reach an altered state. But with practice and repeated effort, by the end of my stay in Atlanta I was regularly meditating for 45 minutes and feeling like only 10 or so minutes had gone by.

Also, when Dylan and I were in Morehead City we were walking the beach and saw 25 to 30 seagulls hovering above a fallen gull at the edge of the ocean. The bird could not seem to get on it's feet and was being tossed about in the waves. We were about 50 yards away and I told Dylan we should send healing energy in the bird's direction. Miraculously or coincidently, by the time we reached the gull it was standing on one foot. As we got closer and telling Dylan to send the fellow animal love and energy, I closed my eyes, turned to the sun with arms outstretched and imagined flying as the wind was gently caressing my face. Seconds passed and I opened my eyes just as the seagull flew and joined the awaiting flock. Did we heal the bird? Was it just perfect timing and a coincidence? I have no idea, but it certainly made our day.

So why not try astral travel? I had told Josephine that if I managed to do it I would come visit her at night. I indicated that as a sign of my being there I would move certain things in her room.

Anyway, as of this date we had no luck yet.

Soul School – Playground Earth would continue again tomorrow.

CHAPTER SEVENTY-ONE
A SATISFIED MIND
"IS THE BATTLE OVER"

Friday morning as we awoke in Waves we discovered the wind had gone and the sun was shining bright. It was a beach day. I made the coffee and fed Dylan. By eight o'clock we were walking the beach. The waves were enormous with white caps stretching out for eight or nine waves deep. I am amazed at how many people have dogs in this campsite. Dylan can't control himself. Dogs are everywhere and he wants to play with them all. I let him run free. It's a beautiful day in the outer banks.

Travelling north in the outer banks reminds me of both Cape Cod in Massachusetts, where I spent a lot of my time as a youth, and also the Florida Keys. The sand, grass and even many of the homes have that Cape Cod feel. But travelling north along Route 12 in the outer banks, with the Atlantic Ocean on the east and the Pamlico Sound on the west, most definitely, reminds me of The Keys with the Atlantic on one side and the Gulf of Mexico on the other. In my anticipation of the outer banks and while at the Maritime Museum in Beaufort, I had purchased Terrance Zepke's book *Pirates of the Carolina's* hoping to discover a little history and folklore of the days gone before. Now as I traveled I tried to envision the great pirate ships just off the coast and the tales they could tell of great journeys upon the sea.

I had hoped to visit Josephine last night, but my attempts at astral travel failed again. Anyway, I hope she is well. I reviewed some of my journals and was reading about my times in Sedona. I discovered some writings, in which I indicated that perhaps all roads led to Josephine. I had called her one night while in Arizona and shared these thoughts with her. Ironically, she had just written in her journal the following:

Where are you?
I am here with the memories of you.
You're on the road again. Off to find the wizard.
When will you realize there is no place like home?
Click your boots together; speak the truth.
I am here waiting for you.

Now months later I knew she was still patiently waiting as I was off again. Sure she had a rough night a few days back, but that's not really who she is. I'm learning love isn't about caging someone. It's about releasing them. Allowing them to grow, dream, be alive, and walk their path. Josephine has shown me true love.

By ten a.m. we have walked the beach and I enjoyed the luxury of a hot shower. We hit the road and headed north on Route 12 in the Outer Banks. Nothing of interest in Nags Head, so we drove straight to the Kitty Hawk fishing pier.

I paid the six dollar fishing fee and bought some squid bait for one dollar. Heading out to the end of the pier, I'm a little nervous. Does everyone else seem to know what they're doing or is it my mind just questioning my fishing ability? I find an open spot and bait my hook with the frozen squid.

Nobody talks. Then suddenly someone reels in a three foot sand shark. It's like everyone has known each other for years. Then a few minutes later, silence. Everyone has withdrawn into their own private worlds. Finally, after an hour I catch a "skate". It's a garbage fish, a throw away. One guy called it a Carolina flounder. But, for now I'm in "The Club". Nobody says it out loud, but everybody keeps track and you're not in "The Club" until you catch something, anything, even a Carolina flounder.

As I sit and fish, I watch the waves. I've seen four dolphins. But it's the low flying pelicans that hold my attention. They cruise in low and just ride the waves.

I'm in Kitty Hawk and of course I'm thinking of the Wright Brothers. No one believed they could fly, but they believed. While the masses were full of doubt, they persisted, and now worldwide airplane travel is commonplace. I wonder if astral travel will someday be the same.

Paul from Virginia has broken all the rules. He hasn't caught anything yet and he's officially not in "The Club", but he starts talking to me anyway. Seems last week he caught a few fish at the Nags Head fishing pier. Somehow he confuses his membership in that club with this club. Anyway he asks where I'm from. When I first started travelling I would sometimes respond, "I'm on a spiritual walk about." Most people just kind of shook their heads and walked away. Then I started saying, "Oh, I'm retired." This seemed to bother people even more as they suggested that I wasn't old enough. Later, I would respond, "On vacation." But this didn't ring true for me. Now I simply say, "I'm living on the road." Then as the puzzled look appeared on the stranger's face I would add, "and writing a book." Relief. That's what was now written on their faces. It seems it's okay to travel and live on the road as long as you have a legitimate purpose. But to just travel and live, that's unthinkable.

Later as Dylan is having his dinner, dog food not fresh fish, I study the maps. I love to read and re-read the maps. Where shall we go? Where have we been? What roads should we travel? While at Josephine's I used to love to watch the weather channel. Great maps showing the weather of the entire country. I would scan the map, the colors, the temperatures, and dream of friends scattered throughout the country.

We decide to head north to Virginia. I heard there was a Wal-Mart in Chesapeake. We head north along Route 158 to Route 168 and cross into Virginia. All day I have been having the urge to call Josephine. I pull over and make the call. She says, "I've been calling you all day. I'm glad you finally heard it. I'm so happy you called. I need you."

Turns out her friend Beth's mother, Meg, passed away earlier in the day and Josephine found her. She had been sick for about a month with cancer and had moved in with Beth.

Her condition declined rapidly and Josephine was helping out quite a bit. Now, she was crying and having an extremely rough day. Meg was in her eighties and had a great life. Josephine and I both believed in the never-ending journey of the soul, but she was emotionally drained from the experience of attending to the ill woman. She had spent a great deal of energy caring for Meg and being there for Beth. I told her I loved her and about the urge to call all day. There wasn't much I could do, but let her know that I loved her.

Before I hung up she told me she was doing better with our separation. While she wished I were there, she knew my time on the road was necessary for our long-term happiness. She just needed to acknowledge her feelings earlier in the week and share them with me. She was at peace again with our separation.

As we pulled into the Wal-Mart in Chesapeake, I considered driving through the night to Atlanta. Should I be there for Josephine? Joey's Birthday was May third, next Thursday, and I was heading north to celebrate with the kids. I decided to stay my course, but would call each day for a few days. There was no real battle between my mind and my heart in making the decision. I loved Josephine and was sad for her, but I loved Joey too, and knew I needed to continue my journey north.

I was content. I was satisfied. I was true.

CHAPTER SEVENTY-TWO
GOTTA TRAVEL ON
"STILL HEADING NORTH"

Saturday morning we drove into Virginia Beach. The sun was out and while my ankle was still sore we skipped our run and played fetch on the beach around 30th street. Afterward I went to a local breakfast joint and had some French toast and eggs. We spent several hours on a bench on the boardwalk and did some people watching.

Couples everywhere. Naturally my thoughts were of Josephine. Near the water was a man taking photos of a black male in extremely good shape wearing a skimpy, tight bathing suit. Eventually Dylan had to go check it out. Surprisingly, they invited Dylan into the shoot. Turns out it was for the magazine *American Health and Fitness.* I'll have to pick up an issue and see if Dylan makes his debut.

Later in the day we head over to the A.R.E. founded by Edgar Cayce on 67th Street. I had had a massage there last August and was hoping to drop in and get one. No luck. No openings. With Dylan in The Dub, I went in and watched a movie on Mr. Cayce. After the movie, a trip to the bookstore.

On the road I spare no expense when it comes to books. I bought seven. I enjoyed Kevin Todeschi's book on soul mates and purchased his book entitled *Edgar Cayce on the Akashic Records.* The other books were called *Edgar Cayce on Dreams, Edgar Cayce on Atlantis, Edgar Cayce on Channeling Your Higher Self, The Edgar Cayce Encyclopedia of Healing, Edgar Cayce on The Power of Color, Stones and Crystals,* and finally *Edgar Cayce, You Can Remember Past Lives.*

As I was paying the girl at the register said, "Wow. You got some really good stuff."

I responded, "Yes, and I deserve it."

"Boy I wish I felt that way about myself," she said.

Later I would think about this. I knew deep within I did deserve it. But sometimes it was difficult truly believing and acting as if I did. I learned that there were times where I would have to fake it, until I could make it. Saying it out loud to others made it real. I did deserve it. I'm worth it and so is the girl at the register.

I immediately read the book on the Akashic Records as many of the other authors I had read had briefly mentioned these records. Cayce stated that when he gave a reading, it was the Akashic Records which he accessed for knowledge. According to Mr. Todeschi, Cayce believed that the Akashic Records contain the history of every soul since the dawn of creation. Not just deeds done, but thoughts, emotions and intentions. Cayce's readings stated that each of us writes the story of our lives through our thoughts, our deeds, and our interactions with the rest of creation. The data contains a record of lessons learned, opportunities lost, faults acquired and experiences gained. Mr. Todeschi spoke of how Cayce believed all of life was the gathering of experiences whereby an individual is challenged to become a better person. He stressed that we had a personal responsibility for our lives, as we are the co-creators of the unfoldment of our life's journey. Cayce believed it was not important as to who we were in the past, but who we were becoming in the present. I was reminded of Mr. Praagh's message of life being an experience, whereby we learn and grow. Additionally, I was reminded of Ms. Altea's message that it was not the situations in our lives that were important, but rather how we responded. Mr. Todeschi further pointed out that the Cayce readings stated that patterns throughout lifetimes would repeat giving us the option of making new and different choices leading to higher levels of evolvement.

After an evening of reading, we hit the road around ten o'clock on Saturday night. We paid $14 and rode the twenty mile long Chesapeake Bay Bridge & Tunnel to the eastern shore of Virginia along Route 13. At midnight we had reached Maryland and stopped to sleep in the visitor information rest area. In the morning we found Route 113 to Route 50 and drove through Ocean City, Maryland. Having been there, done that, we continued north along Route 1 into Delaware.

By noon we found the Delaware Seashore State Park at Indian River and decided to try our luck at fishing again. It was a "noon until five p.m. free buffet" for the fish. I really expected to catch something and was disappointed. I thought of what Jimmy Day used to say, "Keep your expectations tiny, and you won't be so whiny." Tired, we drove to Lewes, Delaware, with plans of taking the morning Ferry to Cape May, New Jersey.

Monday morning at seven o'clock sharp Dylan was ready to eat. Plenty of time to catch the 8:40 ferry. The seventeen mile crossing took a little over an hour. For $18 we got to cross the Delaware Bay and watch ESPN Sportscenter. I was amazed. I didn't realize the NBA and NHL playoffs were going on. Sometimes on the road I go months without TV or a newspaper. The world still seems to manage to go on without me.

Being from the northeast part of the country, the most I had ever really seen in New Jersey was the Garden State Parkway and Route 95 while rushing south. Cape May really surprised me. I had heard about the Jersey Shore, but had never envisioned how beautiful it was. We walked the beach, had some coffee and explored Cape May.

By noon we decided to head north along Ocean Boulevard and see the coast. Within fifteen minutes the roads were unbearable. At Atlantic City we headed west to The Jersey Turnpike. This was no better. My mood was foul. It seemed every time I turned a corner I was paying a toll and could find no evidence of this money being spent on the roadways. By one o'clock I just wanted out of the state. We found the Garden State Parkway and continued north. We drove through Patterson, New Jersey.

I had seen the movie and read the book *Hurricane, The Miraculous Journey of Rubin Carter,* by James Hirsch. In 1967 in

Patterson, New Jersey, Rubin Carter was convicted of a triple murder by an all white jury for an act he never committed. Eventually, many years later he would be freed. I always remembered it was the falling apart of his external world that led him on his inner journey of self-awareness. In the book Mr. Hirsch shares a letter that Mr. Carter had written which states:

"So you see why it takes a very courageous heart to look at oneself without being afraid... The beautiful thing is that we can be different; we can change. We can be more powerful, and more intelligent, and more trustworthy, and more respectful than anything we have ever known before or could have imagined."

With the courage to listen, the inner heart voice leads us to our higher selves. But for now I left Patterson just wondering if any of the toll money I was spending was somehow ending up in the corrupt pockets of those in Patterson who had convicted Mr. Carter.

By four o'clock we were at the last New Jersey service rest area on the Garden State Parkway and getting ready for the New York Expressway traffic over the Tappan Zee Bridge crossing the Hudson River. I decided to give my friend, Paul Almay, a call. He lives in Palisades, just this side of the bridge. I got him on his cell phone and got directions to his house. Dylan and I met him at his home a half hour later.

It was great to see him. I quickly fed Dylan and went in to shower at Paul's insistence. I think it was the "road odor". Anyway, we had a great, relaxing night after the roads of Jersey. Following a sushi dinner as Paul's treat, we sat and smoked a cigar while talking of love and relationships.

He is friends with Josephine and had spoken with her the day before. He joked with me and asked me when I'm getting married. I explain about my "closure to the road" theory, but also tell him that I am very much excited about building a life with Josephine and share my excitement about Folly Beach and the Charleston area of South Carolina.

Before I left Atlanta my "closure to the road" theory was just a theory, but now a month later it is more than that. I can actually feel the closure. It's not just a theory, it's real. I am closing one door in preparation of opening another.

Paul joked and told me that he told Josephine that 80% of all marriages without children last. I don't know his sources, but it appears reasonable.

At nine o'clock we turn on the television and find the show *Ally McBeal.* It's Josephine's favorite show and we used to watch it together when I was in Atlanta. I give her a call on the phone and let her know that tonight I will be watching with her. Eventually, I would call four times during the show. We would laugh and enjoyed a night of TV together, even with the miles between us. Paul just shook his head and laughed.

On Tuesday morning, May 1, 2001, after coffee and a cigar with Paul, we crossed the Hudson River with no traffic on the Tappen Zee. We planned to travel Route 287, to Route 684 to Connecticut, and finally Route 84 to the Massachusetts Turnpike and Worcester. It was three years ago today that I purchased The Big W and the journey began.

Somewhere en route I begin thinking of Mr. Todeschi's book *Edgar Cayce on Soul mates.* Mr. Todeschi stated that sometimes people requested a reading by Mr. Cayce seeking advice on marriage. Some would even say, "Should I marry this one or that one." Cayce responded, "You could be successful with your pick of several to marry." The readings stated, "Sometimes marriage provides the structure to best work things out between soul mates. However, there will be no harmony without a "oneness of purpose". "The working through of challenges and problems, which all relationships certainly have, is done when home is first and most important. The purpose of soul mates, marriage, or any lifelong commitment to another person is primarily to enable each individual to grow, to evolve, and to assist one another in spiritual development." Would I get married again? As I felt the closure of the road I pondered this "oneness of purpose", this "structure" to best work things out between soul mates. What would be best for my growth? What would be best for Josephine's growth? What would be best for our growth? I knew I still clung to many limiting beliefs about marriage, but I did believe in this "oneness of purpose", in a unified "vision" of a life together. My heart would lead me, as my fears would fall.

We arrived in Worcester around three o'clock. A quick trip to my insurance agent, a call to my dad setting up breakfast in the morning, and we were now ready to see the kids the next day. We were back in the northeast and as we drove to find a place to spend the night, I could hear Dylan singing, *"Why wait any longer for the one you love, when she's standing in front of you."*

CHAPTER SEVENTY-THREE
JOEY
"BIRTHDAY NUMBER ELEVEN"

We slept in front of my friend Gill's old apartment in Worcester. He had since moved, but I knew no one on the street would complain. At eight a.m. we met my dad for breakfast. He had brought some mail for me and we spent an hour eating and talking. As usual, he was interested in when I would be settling down. I told him all about Josephine and all about Folly Beach, South Carolina. I still had some travelling to do, but I was getting close. He looked relieved. Then of course there was the job question. What would I do for a living? My dad was happy that I was happy, but my road lifestyle still had him a little confused. By now I was telling people I was writing my first book. I used to say, "I'm writing a book," but everyone would respond, "What if that doesn't work?" I stopped entertaining that notion and simply assumed this would be my first book as I had a head full of ideas just begging to be put on paper. My dad wished me luck.

It was great to see him. After breakfast Dylan and I headed out to Barre to wait for the kids to get out of school. On the way we found a lake and stopped for a few hours. My running was practically nonexistent for the past two weeks. We tested the ankle with a 32 minute trail run. It was hot, 83 to be exact. After a successful run we went swimming and hung out at the lake for a couple of hours.

By three o'clock we were waiting in front of the kids' house. Right on schedule at 3:15 Joey hopped off the bus. Sara was at Girl Scouts until five. We hugged and played catch of the day. It was awesome to see him. Tomorrow he would turn eleven. At five we picked up Sara and went to Joey's Little League game. The level of play was higher than last year's team. Joey played second base and made some good plays in the field. In the last inning he hit a grounder and ran it out and was safe at first. After the game they went home with their mom and step-dad, while Dylan and I drove to the local Wal-Mart. It was hard to believe it was two years ago that I cried in Jimmy's arms as I gave him a baseball on Joey's birthday.

We had plans for each day, but everything could change in a moments notice as their mom was pregnant and due on Sunday. She looked ready to pop and couldn't wait.

Thursday at 3:15 Joey hopped off the bus. Sara was at karate. "Happy Birthday," I shouted as I threw him his glove. We worked on a few grounders and after a few games of chess Sara was home at 4:15. She had a new dolphin book and we sat in The Dub while she read it to us. At 5:30 we went for dinner in a local pizza shop and then had cupcakes and ice cream in The Dub to the singing of Happy Birthday. Joey especially liked giving Dylan a plate of ice cream. Miraculously, Dylan didn't eat the plate. At 7:00 it was time for Sara's art show at her school. We toured the halls and saw many of her drawings and creations. I took lots of photos and always had doubles printed.

While at the show, Joey suggested that he and Sara get out of school and that I pick them up on an early dismissal on Friday. Jokingly I said, "You should just skip school." I told him whatever was okay with his mom was okay with me. Later, his mom told me that Joey told her that I wanted them to skip school and spend the day with me. In the end it was agreed, I would pick them up at their house at nine a.m. and there would be no school on Friday.

Later that night I checked into the ColdBrook Campground once again. Three nights for $69. It was three miles from their house, had electric plug-ins, and hot showers.

At night I reviewed my journals. On the ferry ride across the Delaware Bay I had written:

Embrace the journey of the road. Sometimes I have loneliness, fear, and questions, but for the most part I have a sense of closure. It's not just a theory. It's real. I am finishing what I started three years ago. I am finishing the journey of the road on my own terms. I haven't abandoned the road for the comforts of a relationship. Josephine and I have endured this period of separation. One door must be closed before another can be opened. One path must be traveled completely, before another can be traveled. I have honored my heart, I have honored my soul, I have honored my dream, I have honored the God within, I have honored my path, I have honored myself, I have honored Josephine. I am free. I am free to choose a new path. I am free to live. I am free to dream. I am free to love. I am free.

It was a great birthday and I was glad I was in the northeast.

Friday the kids played hooky. We spent ten hours together. In the morning we just hung out in The Dub and played games. Later, we went back to what I called "The Barre Townline" fishing hole. We played catch with the poles baited and lines in the water. Joey caught a 15 inch Carp. At least that's what his step-dad called it. At four o'clock Joey had baseball practice for two hours, while Sara and I hung out in The Dub and read together. After practice we had ice cream for dinner.

On Saturday I again picked them up at nine a.m.. This was to be our sleepover night. In the morning we went birthday shopping at Wal-Mart (more karma). Joey purchased a CD, a game for his gameboy, and a Red Sox baseball jersey. In the afternoon we went to the movies. I remember seeing a listing of all the movies showing and seeing the third Crocodile Dundee movie called *Crocodile Dundee in Los Angeles.* I remember thinking, "Who the hell would go see that movie?" Wouldn't you know that's what the kids chose to see and there I was seeing the movie I envisioned no one ever seeing. Never say never. In the movie, Mick Dundee and his girlfriend have a child about eight years old. The boy, who is named Micky, eventually asks Mick why he hasn't gotten married. Mick responds saying that the boy's mom and he are sort of married; they just haven't done the legal thing. Ironically, that's my biggest limiting tape; the legal thing, the judge thing. At the end of the movie with his girlfriend's life in danger, Mick proposes marriage after truly realizing what she means to him. The Universal Movie Guide at work.

All day we had been checking in with the kid's mom every two hours for the baby alert. After the movie we called and found out that Liza was indeed heading to the hospital. The kids were excited and we drove to the campground, checked out, and parked in front of their house awaiting further instructions.

False alarm. By eight o'clock Liza had returned home. We decided to have a camp out in The Dub in front of the kid's house. We played games, made popcorn and by ten o'clock it was lights out.

As we lay in the dark Joey and Sara started asking questions about the many pictures on The Dub walls and the places I've been.

"What's your favorite place you've been to Dad?"

This was tough to answer. I had loved my routine in Key West. Camping and fishing in Breckinridge was awesome. Running with Dylan in Sedona was exciting. The California coast was fun. But my all time favorite was bringing The Dub onto the beach in St. Augustine, Florida, at Anastasia State Park.

"What was the favorite place you ever ate?"

No question. The Fish Market in Islamorada, Florida, at mile marker 80 in the Keys. It is an outdoor restaurant on a boat dock. At sunset the dishwashers come out and feed the fish and at least eight to twelve sharks about five feet long come out of nowhere to eat.

"Where was your favorite sunset?"

Another tough one. I love the sunsets over the Gulf of Mexico. But once travelling through Nevada I saw one over the mountains that ranks as number one. With the clouds and the mountains I saw blues, oranges, pinks, purples and a variety of other colors.

"What was your favorite beach?"

Tough. Hawaii was nice, both the north shore and Waikiki. The Carolina's have so many good ones; Hilton Head Island, Folly Beach, and the outer banks. In Florida I liked Destin, St. Augustine and Naples. Virginia Beach north of the tourist area is nice. Laguna Beach in California was scenic, but you can't really run. My favorite would either be Folly Beach or St. Augustine. Both ideal for running, body boarding, and of course Dub access at St. Augustine.

"What was your biggest surprise on the road?"

A no brainer. The Gulf Shores of Alabama Didn't even know there was a coast there. Also, finding Cape May in New Jersey was a big surprise.

"What was the coolest thing you did?"

I had done many tourist things. I had toured the White House, walked Bourbon Street in New Orleans, run across the Golden Gate Bridge, camped in the Grand Canyon, saw musicals in Las Vegas and New York City, saw Niagara Falls, slept on a boat in Catalina, stood under the Arch in Missouri, attended numerous baseball parks, drove The Dub into Mexico and Canada, toured the Mormon Tabernacle in Salt Lake City, saw Dylan at the Hollywood Bowl, hiked in Arizona, snorkeled in Hawaii, and played on the beaches throughout the country. But the coolest thing was to stand at the point where the four states of Arizona, New Mexico, Colorado and Utah merge, and put my hands and feet in different states. Naturally, I did a quick loop and had a four state jog.

"What was your favorite road?"

Nothing beats the ride from Flagstaff to Sedona, Arizona.

"What is the one place you wanted to go and didn't?"

Montana. I wanted to go last September when I was in Colorado, but it got too cold. Someday I'll get there. Hopefully in the month of July.

This could have gone on all night. But it was time to sleep. As I drifted to sleep in the upper bunk with the kids on the lower bunk and Dylan on the floor, I reminisced about the road.

The question they didn't ask that I thought of was: "What was your favorite billboard?"

"The Pig Out Palace" in the Midwest, "Happy Harry's Discount Drugs" in Maryland, and "Dirty Dick's Crab Shack" in North Carolina.

CHAPTER SEVENTY-FOUR
DRIFTING TOO FAR FROM SHORE
"BEACH BOUND"

On Sunday I left the kids at noon. We had breakfast in The Dub, played some games, and said our goodbyes. It was Liza's actual due date and everyone was just hanging out waiting.

I had told the kids that I was getting close to being done with living on the road. They liked the idea of me setting up a home in the Charleston, South Carolina area, or any area for that matter. We talked of monthly visits with both me flying north and them coming south. They saw the many pictures of Josephine on the walls of The Dub and were looking forward to meeting her. Perhaps Christmas, I suggested. As for what to do with The Dub after I completed my road time, they were all for keeping her at their house. We'll see what Mom says. It was another magical visit. Coincidently, Liza had a baby boy named Zak at around three in the morning.

Dylan and I headed north out of Massachusetts and drove 200 miles to Burlington, Vermont. Once again I headed north to go south. It was strange and reminded me of my initial beginning on the road. The whole trip north this journey had a sense of saying goodbye. The reason for the trip to Vermont was that I told Dylan we would go to see his mom. Zoey was home and mother and son were reunited. After a quick hello, Dylan seemed more interested in his Uncle Jake. They played as Zoey stood and watched. Eventually, Dylan tried to mount Uncle Jake. So much for the $100 I had spent on getting him neutered. Afterwards we looked up Jimmy Day and Don Kaplin. Neither we're at home. We hung our for a few hours, but I was getting itchy for the road. I left a note at Jimmy Day's and told him I would call him during the week.

It was good to be in Burlington. It reminded me of the acceptance energy of Key West, San Fran and New Orleans. As we had driven up Route 91 and 89 I thought of my early days in The Dub and some of my early adventures. After the purchase in May of 1998 and before hitting the road in November fulltime, I had taken many small exploratory trips in The Dub to Vermont. We had stayed in both Brattleboro and Burlington, Vermont. There was a camp out at Swanzey Lake in New Hampshire, an overnight trip to L.L. Bean in Freeport, Maine, and numerous outings to Cape Cod. I remembered how I drove into my first campground and didn't know you needed to bring your own extension cord, sewer hose and water hose. It seemed like a lifetime away.

At seven o'clock we headed south on Route 7 along Lake Champlain with the mountains in the background. Driving by the Vermont Teddy Bear Factory I thought of Johanna. Once again I felt like I was retrieving pieces of my soul. By eight we were on a bridge crossing the lake into New York State with the sun setting on our left and a full moon rising on our right. Sunsets still remind me of Corrina and the full moon and stars remind me of Josephine. Two of the most powerful soul connections I have ever felt. The lake was beautiful. Jimmy Day would always say, "It's not a Great Lake, but it's a Good Lake."

As we drove, I was very aware of the strong sense of closure in the air. There was a sense of sadness. It wasn't like a death or a loss, but rather a completion. Sort of like graduating from High School, or was it Soul School? My time on the road was ending. It was time to move on. The natural progression of the lessons of life were unfolding and leading me into new territory. The road wasn't being taken from me and I wasn't giving it up; rather, I was nearing a completion. It was time for a new season, a new dream, a new vision. The tugging, the road, and this season had taught me all that it could. It was time to move on. Closure, was all I could say. But deep within I knew Soul School – Playground Earth would always continue.

We eventually spent the night at a rest area somewhere on the New York Expressway Route 87. In the morning we drove out of New York, through New Jersey, over the Delaware Memorial Bridge and turned south on Route 13 in Delaware. We had spent a week away from the beach and I was aching to get back. With only two runs in while in New England we longed to run on the beach again. We stopped at the Indian River in Delaware and this time landed two fish. There was no free buffet today. We threw back a twelve inch and a thirteen inch Rock Bass. Both just short of the fifteen inch minimum. While many anglers promote a "catch and release" philosophy, I'm all for "catching and eating". Dylan, of course, just wanted to play with the fish.

We drove on and eventually slept at the rest area on the Maryland-Virginia border on Route 13. In the morning we continued south to Virginia Beach and stopped at the A.R.E. founded by Edgar Cayce. I spent several hours in the library typing and later played fetch on the beach with Dylan before departing. Naturally, I couldn't stay out of the bookstore. I had purchased a book by Rachel Runnels based on the Edgar Cayce readings and entitled, *Marriage and The Home.* The thing that struck me the most was where Ms. Runnel states that the "Home" is a most radical opportunity for the playing out and the working out of creative force; it is a place where lives intertwine and unfold together. She states that the Cayce readings suggest that man's highest achievement in the earth is the creation of the home. She talked of the home being a sacred haven and I realized I had achieved this in The Dub on my own, now perhaps the challenge was to create this with another.

At nightfall, more driving. We headed west along Route 58 out of Virginia Beach and connected with Route 95 South. At exit 97 we stopped at JR's Outlet Shopping in North Carolina for a box of cigars for the upcoming bash Mark and Glenn were hosting in Cocoa Beach, Florida beginning on the 17th of May. For dinner we dined at the Waffle House. To a boy from up north the Waffle House is a real treat, grits and all. While eating, the jukebox played a song by Sade called, *By Your Side.* I thought of Josephine and the sense of closure grew stronger.

The next hundred miles south to exit 181 in South Carolina were anxious. The red light signaling that the alternator had gone was flashing. As I pulled off the exit ramp, The Dub stalled and died. The battery was dead. Out of nowhere a man named Tom Hyde pulled up with a battery for sale at the price of $60.00. It was midnight and he even offered to install it. A sweet deal anyway you look at it. A half hour later I was parked at the Flying J Truck Stop. We would deal with the alternator later. For now The Dub was drivable only during the day, as the headlights would drain my new battery. I thought perhaps Tom Hyde was an angel, but then thought, "Would an angel have charged me?"

Another question for the kids, "What's your favorite rest area?" The Flying J of course. Free overnight parking, cheap gas and a free cup of coffee with a fill up, and $5.00 showers in the morning.

After my morning shower we drove 150 miles along Route 95 South and Route 26 East in South Carolina, and by noon arrived at Folly Beach. It was Wednesday and we planned to spend three days at the beach before Josephine would meet us on Friday night. It was hard to believe it was May 9th already and it was one month to the day that we had been at Folly Beach the first time.

I had shared my enthusiasm with Josephine about Folly Beach and the greater Charleston area on our phone date nights. We had plans to see each other the following week in Cocoa Beach, Florida, but were equally missing each other and when I suggested she make the trip from Atlanta to Folly Beach after work on the 11th she didn't hesitate. The plan was for Dylan and I to hang at the beach and run during the days and sleep at Wal-Mart at night. Sometime around eleven at night on Friday Josephine would meet us at Wal-Mart. She would spend a night in The Dub on the Road and on Saturday we would treat ourselves to a hotel room and a reunion fitting of lovers who had been apart for a month.

The weather was stunning and Dylan and I were able to run each day. Surprisingly the beach was packed. Last month we seemed to have the place to ourselves. It appears the local colleges had completed their terms and the summer season was well underway at Folly Beach.

On Wednesday night I called Jimmy Day. His wife, Kate, had left him after almost two years of marriage. It happened about three weeks ago. Jimmy was willing to work on the marriage, but she was resigned to the fact that it was over. All in all he was doing okay. Apparently, neither was truly happy for sometime. I told Jimmy I would start calling him weekly. I considered him my best friend, even though we hadn't talked that much in the past year. It was one of those relationships where time didn't matter. Regardless of the time, we always just picked up where we had left off.

It's funny, as I am considering a new life with Josephine, my friend Jimmy's marriage is ending and just three weeks ago I received an email from Amy in Denver stating that she had moved out of her home with Jimmy Walker and they had broken up. Normally, this kind of news would send me into a panic. My mind would start blabbering, "See relationships don't last", "Why commit to Josephine, they never work", "Get out now before it's too late", "Remember once how you envisioned a series of sexual relationships around the country with no strings attached. Go for that. No commitment. Nothing to lose". But that didn't happen. I was at peace. Perhaps, the mind is really starting to be reprogrammed. My heart just whispered, "You are love and have no need to fear love."

I still felt strongly that my time in The Dub was nearing its end and I would be enrolling in a new adventure, an adventure of love with Josephine. My time in The Dub and my time with Lily, Corrina, Jane, Johanna, and Angelina, were all part of my path. I was discovering my true inner essence, my power to co-create with the Universe, my heart voice, and my soul mate, Josephine. The distractions of the world were abundant, but with effort, with stillness, with faith and perseverance, the journey would unfold. I had nothing to fear.

I am love and love is all there is.

I was waking up. Life was good and I was enjoying the ride.

My thoughts would create my reality and my thoughts were now free of fear. My time on the road, gave me time to examine and discard many limiting beliefs held for so long within my mind. I listened to my heart, I trusted my heart, I expressed my heart, and I lived by my heart. There would be no limits. There would be no programmed voices from the past. I would trust the Universe to orchestrate my highest good.

Yes, my time in The Dub was nearing its end; but the real journey, the inner journey, never ends. In Josephine I had found a lover, a friend, a teacher, a student, a companion, and a partner. She had found the same. It was time to take it to a new level. She challenged me to grow, to be present, to love and be loved. I also challenged her. Soul School–Playground Earth would always be, and I had found my soul playmate.

My heart just whispered, "The journey never ends. Learn your lessons, live your dreams, and enjoy the ride. You need not fear love, you are love."

CHAPTER SEVENTY-FIVE
SOMETHING THERE IS ABOUT YOU
"AWATING JOSEPHINE'S ARRIVAL"

Dylan and I had three glorious beach days while awaiting Josephine's arrival. We awoke on Thursday and Friday mornings by 6:30 and were parked at the beach by 7:00. Between seven and nine Dylan would eat and chase the birds while I had coffee and journal time. Our runs for the week were 35 minutes, 40 minutes and 45 minutes. Slowly crawling back to form. At night we parked at Wal-Mart and spent our time reading and writing.

Friday night we awaited Josephine's arrival. I reviewed my journals. Yesterday morning in the early sunshine at the beach I had entered:

> My thoughts create
> My desires surface
> Time unfolds
> Seeds are sown
> The harvest is reaped
> The journey continues
> Lessons are mastered
> Embrace my humanness
> My soul has chosen this experience
> Wisdom is gained
> Lifetime upon lifetime
> Dreams disguised as desires
> Companions are teachers

The light shines bright
Awareness dawns
Scenery changes
Co-create, build, nurture love
We are powerful beings with no limits
Distractions and noise cloud the path
But the voice will not be silenced
Be still
Listen, trust, express
Dream on and create

I was excited to see Josephine. She had only stayed in The Dub one night prior to this and that was the weekend she flew to Virginia Beach. The Dub was my home. I had visited her home, now she would visit mine on the road once again. But soon, we would create our home.

As I read my journals the sense of closure was great. I felt like I was transitioning from one world to another. What would we create with the Universe? Would we end up in Folly Beach or another beach? The opportunities felt limitless.

I found a notation I had written after reading Richard Bach's book *Running From Safety*. His wife Leslie was talking about love and marriage. She said, "When you look at us, when you look at anybody long term, we really love only once or twice in our lives. Treasure that love. That's my secret to marriage."

I thought of Josephine and felt I had found a "treasure" to be loved and "love" to be treasured.

After reviewing my journals I picked up the latest book I was reading, Marianne Williamson's *A Return to Love*. Nothing is by coincidence, and again the Universe Librarian was busy at work. In her book, Ms. Williamson shares her thoughts on Love based upon her experiences with the teachings of a *Course in Miracles*. She talks of how Love is what we were born with and Fear is what we have learned. The spiritual journey is the unlearning of fear and the acceptance of love back into our hearts.

Yes, that was my experience, my journey. The Dub gave me

time, and a place to begin to unlearn the fears of my mind and let the love within, the divine within, grow and blossom in my heart.

Later she discusses how so many of us, myself included, think there are different categories of life; such as finances, health, relationships, spiritual, etc. Boy did that look familiar. Her answer was to invite Love into all these areas. Love is real and all else is an illusion. She states that there really is only one drama going on in life; our walk away from God, and our walk back. I realized my limited programmed, fear-based mind led me away and my inner, limitless heart voice led me back. Now my job was to try to live each day in that awareness.

The last thing she discussed that really made an impression upon me was when she stated that the *Course in Miracles* says that there are three levels of teaching in a relationship. They are; the casual encounter, the more sustained relationship, and the "lasts all our lives relationships". Sounded like a reason, a season, or a lifetime.

I thought of all the books I had read which stated that there are no chance meetings and that everyone offers us a chance to learn something. Each moment is valuable. I thought of the strangers on the road who taught me little lessons about myself. Was my soul contact with these strangers kindness or anger? Was I helpful or was I in a hurry? Was our meeting pleasant or distasteful? These casual encounters gave me the opportunity to practice what I preach. I thought of Lily, Corrina, Jane, Johanna, and Angelina and how I had shared with each a season and how each taught me lessons before our time of separation. Each came into my life for a reason and a season. Each allowed me to grow more in my awareness of love. Each led me deeper into the journey to myself. Lastly, I thought of Josephine.

Ms. Williamson stated that someone whom we have a lifetime's worth of lessons to learn is someone whose presence in our lives forces us to grow. That's exactly how I felt about Josephine. She challenged me to grow. I never felt like we completed each other, but rather we complemented each other. We were not two halves looking to make each other whole, but rather to individuals coming together assisting each other on the journey of wholeness. My journey in The Dub and my journey in Life had led me to her. Now we had the opportunity to help and support each other to higher and higher levels of self. We could share a life, build a home, live our dreams, and grow more aware, not only of the journey we share together in this lifetime, but of our individual inner journeys and return to love.

I pulled out my journal and wrote the following:

As I traveled deeper and deeper into the journey, the fear based voices of the mind were slowly being reprogrammed as my heart spoke louder and stronger each day and I now realize that in every moment I have the choice to focus on love or focus on fear. My experience has shown me that we are powerful beings, and what we focus on, what we allow our thoughts to be, we will create. To read about it is one thing, but to live it is another. Soul School – Playground Earth and my time in The Dub gave me the chance to read many books, but mostly it gave me the chance to learn from experience, and everyone knows experience is true wisdom. I have met many in my travels and each has taught me more about self. While the inevitable closure to life on the road and life in The Dub is looming, my heart knows my education in the journey of my life, the journey of my soul, is far from over. Perhaps, it's all just been a sort of a "kindergarten" and the real lessons are just beginning. Time will tell.

CHAPTER SEVENTY-SIX
ARE YOU READY?
"JOSEPHINE AND FOLLY BEACH"

I had called Josephine's cell phone at seven o'clock Friday night.
She was in Augusta, Georgia heading east along Route 20 and
planned to arrive at 9:30. I told myself I wouldn't start to worry
until ten. At 10:15 p.m. I called her cell phone once again.

"I'm fifteen miles outside of Charleston on Route 26 and
I've been sitting in "fucking" traffic for an hour," she vented.

She had worked all day and this was the last thing she
needed. My mind quickly conceded the weekend would be
ruined.

"No," responded the heart. "She'll make it and we will get
through this tiny setback."

Back in The Dub I expected to see her at midnight. At
eleven she pulled up next to The Dub in the James Island Wal-
Mart. It appears that right after she got off the phone with me
the traffic let up and she cruised the rest of the way.

It had been 32 days since our last embrace. It was good
to hold her again. She changed into some comfortable night
clothes and we climbed into the upper bunk, chatted for about
an hour, and fell asleep in each other's arms.

Dylan was up Saturday morning at seven and a half hour
later the three of us were at the beach sipping coffee and
playing fetch. The day before it rained in Atlanta and the storm
was heading east. I was grateful the sun was shining in South
Carolina. We stayed at the beach until two o'clock enjoying
over six hours of prime sun. Josephine became a golden brown.
She looked beautiful.

She loved Folly Beach. I was glad. As the day unfolded we were slowly becoming entwined once again. I shared my adventures on the road and she updated me on things in Atlanta.

At two o'clock we left the beach and went and found a hotel in Charleston on Route 17. We took her car and would go back for The Dub and Dylan after our late lunch. While eating our meal the storm from Atlanta arrived and there was a mass exodus from the beach along Route 171. By four we were back in The Dub and decided to take a nap, hoping to wait out the traffic. The plan worked and by six we were showering together in our hotel home for the evening. Afterwards we made love.

Exhausted and lying in Josephine's arms I thought of how in the past, when away from my lovers I would make love upon being reunited and then hope to make a reconnection. Things were different. Josephine and I spent almost an entire day together getting reconnected emotionally before having sex. Our lovemaking was an extension of our spiritual and emotional connection. This was new for me. But then again, so much with Josephine was new and different for me.

We spent an hour lying in each other's arms, kissing, laughing, and watching the weather channel, my favorite. We were going to go explore Charleston that night but by eight o'clock we decided to just stay put and have some Chinese food delivered. We made love again and awaited our meal.

At nine we decided to watch the movie *The Patriot* on HBO. Josephine fell asleep with her head on my chest while I enjoyed the movie about the South Carolina militia and the battle with the English for America's independence. Once again I was surprised by the Universe Movie Guide. The ending of the movie spoke to me. The Patriot, played by Mel Gibson, was a hero and a great leader. The battles were fought in and around the Charleston area. To me the English represented the outdated thinking of the old world, the polluted mind. The militia represented the voice of the heart, the dream of freedom, and a life lived on one's own terms. After defeating the English in the name of Freedom, The Patriot returned to his land with his family. To his surprise, the men he commanded in battle were on his land constructing a house. In the war, the Patriot had lost two sons. One was a soldier named Gabriel. As he questioned his former comrades as to what it was they were doing, a freed slave responded, "Gabriel said that if we won this war we could build a whole new world. We just thought we would get started with your home."

A new world. A new home. That's exactly what I was contemplating doing with Josephine. I was free from the tapes and beliefs of my past that were lodged for so long in my mind. The war was won. The heart was victorious. I could build a new world. I was free. There was nothing to fear. Love is good.

In the morning we awoke kissing. After coffee and a shower we were off to downtown Charleston for lunch at the East Bay Crab Shack. Josephine had a Ceasar Salad with shrimp and I tried the Shrimp and Grits. Yes, Shrimp and Grits. Afterwards we wandered the streets exploring and talking.

By two o'clock it was time for the road. We said our goodbyes and Josephine drove west to Atlanta and I drove south to Florida. We had plans for Cocoa Beach, Florida, the following weekend and my road closure was entering the final weeks.

CHAPTER SEVENTY-SEVEN
NOBODY 'CEPT YOU
"COCOA BEACH"

Dylan and I left Charleston heading west on Route 17 and turned south on Route 95. We were on the road again. We cruised out of South Carolina, across Georgia and into Florida. About thirty miles north of Daytona we stopped at a rest area for a Dylan break. Trying to head as far south before nightfall we climbed back into The Dub. Dead. The battery had died. Fortunately a state trooper was parked in the rest area and we asked for a jump. We made it to the next exit before dark and stalling rolled into a full service Mobil Gas Station. Closed for the evening, Dylan and I were resigned to spending the night and having The Dub fixed in the morning.

At eight o'clock on Monday morning the mechanic showed up and we explained our dilemma. Six hours later The Dub had a new alternator, regulator, and battery, at the cost of $600. Ouch. Little problems turn into big problems when you pretend they don't exist. A lesson of life and a lesson for relationships. So much for the quick accident money we received in North Carolina. By three o'clock we were heading south on Route 95 and drove straight to Cocoa Beach for dinner.

I called Jamie and Charlene Strauss from Plantation, Florida, and found out they would not be heading north for the weekend gathering. It was now six o'clock and Dylan and I told them we would be driving the 180 miles to their home and should arrive by ten.

It was great to see them again. It had been well over a year since my last visit. We stayed up until midnight with me filling them in on my travels and love life. While Jamie went to work on Tuesday, Charlene, Marena,, Kalysta, and I spent the day at their pool catching up. The kids were happy to see The Dub.

Once again the sense of retrieving pieces of my soul was strong. I had been at their home with both Corrina and Johanna, and also used it as a haven when I left Jane in Naples. Now I had returned solo. Additionally, it seemed only fitting to end my term on the road with a visit with Jamie and Charlene.

Dylan and I ran both Tuesday and Wednesday. Only four miles on each run, but we were running again. At night Jamie and I took the kids for ice cream.

On Wednesday afternoon we headed north again and drove to the Cocoa Beach Hilton. Glen and Mark had planned a beach weekend and invited friends from around the country to attend. Josephine would be flying in on Thursday night. Sean and Dianna arrived shortly after I did and decided to spend a night in The Dub. It was awesome having them in my home after visiting them so many times. Dianna loved it and was tempted to spend the weekend in the parking lot. She was also very much excited about the possibilities of my moving to Folly Beach. She planned to visit often.

Zeke and his wife, Karen, from Boston flew in on Thursday morning, Susie and Rick drove up from West Palm, Tim from Atlanta drove in, Jake came with a crew from North Carolina, and I met many others I hadn't known before.

Josephine's flight arrived at nine o'clock Thursday night and I picked her up in Tim's car. We embraced and returned to our hotel room at the Hilton. Our days were spent on the beach and at the pool. Friday, Saturday and Sunday were hot and sunny, the way I like it. Dylan and I managed to run, despite the numerous warnings and anti-dog beaches. It was great seeing everyone and Josephine and I shared with our friends our dreams of someday living at the beach.

The highlight of the weekend was on Saturday night. After dinner all of my friends, and even those I was just meeting, asked me to share about my travels. I spent an hour telling my tale and shared how I decided to journey in The Dub, how I traveled the country, and the lessons of love learned. I explained my dream of living on the road and the journey from my head to my heart. I spoke of my dream of writing and eventually of my sense of closure of a lifestyle on the road and my new dreams of creating a home with Josephine.

When I was finished relating my adventures of the last few years I had a deep sense of knowing. I knew I was done with the road. There was something about sharing my story with my friends. It was completed. My journey was real. The road was real. My heart voice was real. My "closure theory" was real. My "soul retrieval" theory was real. Soul School-Playground Earth was real. I found myself again at another sacred crossroad of my life. The last leg of my journey would be from Cocoa Beach to Atlanta.

CHAPTER SEVENTY-EIGHT
BRINGING IT ALL BACK HOME
"THE LAST LEG"

I awoke Sunday morning in our hotel room and invited Josephine to drive with me to Atlanta. She had a ticket to fly from Orlando to Atlanta, but joyfully agreed to ride in The Dub. She had spent two nights in The Dub, one in Virginia Beach and one in Folly Beach. Now she would travel 500 miles with an overnight in the middle.

At six o'clock Sunday evening after a visit to Ron Jon's Surf Shop (more soul retrieval) we headed west on Route 528 and then turned north on the Florida Turnpike. We drove 260 miles and eventually stopped at the visitor center on Route 75 at mile marker four in Georgia at midnight.

The ride was awesome. We drank coffee, laughed, and talked of the past and of the future. But mostly we just lived in the moment. She would share my last night on the road with me. That night we made love in The Dub for the first time while parked at the Georgia visitor's center.

In the morning Dylan and I played for a while in the parking lot after his feeding and then drove sixty miles as Josephine slept above. I wept tears of gratitude. I was two hundred miles from Atlanta and truly felt that I had been true to myself. I had experienced the road and traveled the inner journey from head to heart. One dream was ending and a new was being born. Later I would journal: Endings are really beginnings in disguise.

After breakfast at a Cracker Barrel restaurant, Dylan,

Josephine and I drove The Dub the remaining 180 miles to her home in Atlanta along Route 75, 675 and 285. Josephine had shared my last night and final day on the road.

Arriving around three in the afternoon on Monday, May 21st, we showered and napped. Later we would watch her show, *Ally McBeal,* and then fall asleep in each other's arms.

We were in Atlanta. The Dub was parked in the driveway, the road was behind me and our shared dreams were in front of us.

CHAPTER SEVENTY-NINE
SERIES OF DREAMS
"LOVE IS ALL THERE IS"

My writing is current. It's May 29, 2001, and tonight we celebrate our one year anniversary together and the start of my second week of transitioning from the road to Josephine's home. She is at work and I am sitting at the kitchen table writing these words. Over the past week, Dylan and I slipped into a new but familiar routine. We arise for a dream feeding. Later I eat, journal, and write. Around the middle of the day we get our run in. In the afternoon we share lunch and more writing. Josephine joins us for dinner and we spend our evenings together talking, reading, laughing, a little TV and some loving before falling asleep in each other's arms.

The first book I read as I came "off the road" was *On The Road* by Jack Kerouac. I reminisced about my times in The Dub and my life on the road as Sal Paradise and Dean Moriarity raced around the country from the northeast while stopping in Denver, San Francisco, New Orleans, and all points in between. The summer in Georgia will be my transitional months of adjusting to life off the road. In September we will implement the "Beach Relocation Plan" and plan for a move to Folly Beach, South Carolina. I am done with the road. We still have trips planned, but the lifestyle is behind me. I feel I have completed what the road called for me to undertake. While the external journey changes, the inner journey simply continues. I'm free to live new dreams.

Sara's birthday is June 12th and Father's Day is the 17th.

My plan is to drive The Dub north and deliver her to the kids, to be used as a clubhouse in their backyard. They are extremely excited about this and as for me, I couldn't think of better new owners.

The last weekend in June, G from Detroit is hosting a gathering for the downtown Detroit/Windsor fireworks celebration just before the 4th of July. Josephine and I already have our roundtrip plane tickets. While many of my friends are disappointed The Dub won't be there, I know she will be safe in New England.

In July and August we hope to take a few weekend trips to the Charleston area and also spend a week or two in New England with the kids. Perhaps we will take The Dub to my sister's home on Cape Cod. Sort of a reunion weekend.

I called The Big W my home for three years. It was my sacred space. I traveled 55,000 miles and ventured into 41 states. I saw the mountains, the desert and the beaches of the United States. I ended my relationship with Lily and shared seasons with Corrina, Jane, Johanna, and Angelina. I was able to visit many of my friends scattered throughout the country and meet many new ones in my travels. But mostly, I honored the tugging on my soul. I ventured into the unknown. I stepped out of my comfort zone. I shared moments of companionship, endured moments of loneliness, and rejoiced in solitude. When I left for the road I didn't know why I was going, for how long I was going, or where I was going. Now the road journey is completed and I know deep within that the inner journey never ends. I am with Josephine and our dreams of a life together. And as I sit in her home and dream of writing, the beach, a home, the Jumbo Dub, and of love, I reflect on all that as transpired and all that has made it to paper.

I look back on what I have written. Much of it feels like it is from another lifetime, yet I know it's the path I walked. I'm shocked as I read chapter one. Should I delete the chapter about my penis? Is it "TMI", too much information?

No. It's a real tape. Deep within men try to prove their "worth" based upon their penis length and Olympic performance in bed. I, too, am aware that women suffer terribly about their body images based upon the messages promoted and ingrained upon us by society. Are their breasts big enough? Is their butt too big? No. The chapter is real and the tapes run deep. We all must travel from head to heart and discover our bodies are not who we are, but simply where the spirit dwells in this human experience.

Reviewing my text further I am plagued with momentary self-doubt. The polluted mind re-emerges and questions my ability, my style, and my purpose. The heart gently encourages me to finish, "This is your journey, these are your thoughts, this is your style, its okay to share, remember we must all walk the walk."

I had read Stephen King's book *On Writing* in which he writes that we each must find our own style of writing and be true to it. In the movie *Wonder Boys* Michael Douglas's character states that each writer must find his or her own voice and use it. What I've written is part of my voice, part of my style and as I traveled I discovered, like Rilke, that I had to write. And finally, I identify with Michael Crichton in his book *Travels* as he declares, "If you're a writer, the assimilation of important experiences almost obliges you to write about them. Writing is how you make the experience your own, how you explore what it means to you, how you come to possess it, and ultimately release it."

Reading on, I reflect on the teachers along my path. All lovers, all friends, all connected on a soul level.

Lily taught me that I could love again. We shared different visions of life and I parted for the road in The Dub, knowing full well I was capable of love even after a failed marriage.

Corrina showed me love was not the caging of a spirit, but the releasing and letting go of that spirit so it could soar. Our season was brief, but I believed I mastered the lesson. When our time to part was upon us I didn't need to play the victim, but rather I could cherish the time we shared and honor both my own inner voice and her inner voice.

Jane revealed the lessons of self-care. She taught me how

to stand up for myself. She guided me in a new direction in the spirit world and introduced me to the concept of other lifetimes.

Johanna enforced the lesson that it is not enough to just be aware and listen to one's heart voice, but also that one must express it, trust it, and live it. We dated for ten months and now over a year later I can see how blinding physical intimacy can be. Lessons I thought I had mastered were ignored.

Angelina was a distraction, but she showed me I must live in the truth, because only the truth will set me free. Our season of laughter was real, honest and playful.

Each moment shared with these lovers helped shape and mold me into who I am today and led me to Josephine. There are no mistakes. The lessons of my past can now be applied in my present and new lessons will emerge if I stay close to my heart.

As I look towards the future, I wonder of alternate realities. Did each decision I made create an alternate Napoleon?

Is there a Napoleon who settled down with Lily and never ventured to the road? Did she ever find a husband for her and a father for her daughter?

Is there a Napoleon who traveled the beaches of the world with Corrina? Did she spend time alone? Did she walk her path? Did she honor her heart voice?

Is there a Napoleon still fighting with Jane? Is she fighting with another?

Is there a Napoleon who was happy with Johanna in New England? Did she go to school? Did she find a husband? Did she have a baby?

Is there a Napoleon with Angelina as she graduates from law school and prepares for the bar exam? Will she be a successful lawyer? Did she find a relationship based upon love and playfulness or did she settle for money instead?

I wish each of them happiness, joy and laughter and am grateful for the seasons we shared and the lessons presented.

Again, are there alternate realities and parallel universes? I can't say. But if there are, I wonder which version of this adventure you are reading.

So I sit at Josephine's home and continue to reflect. As I drove through Orlando, Florida, with Josephine I remembered the seminar I attended in the beginning of my travels and how Tony Robbins emphasized that it is the quality of the questions we ask ourselves which will ultimately shape and transform our lives.

My attempts at astral travel failed. Does that mean it's not real? I'll keep practicing and keep you posted.

Was there a continent known as Atlantis? Do the Akashic Records exist? I do not have these answers, but as Edgar Cayce emphasized, it is the present moment that counts.

And what of aura's and chakras, do they exist? I am aware that certain places and people give me energy, while at other times I feel drained.

My experience with past lives, are they real? Was it a coincidence that I began crying outside of Tecumseh, Oklahoma? Do we have past lives?

Does the spirit live on after the body dies? Are we really spiritual beings having a human experience? Is the spirit immortal? Does the journey never end?

I know the entanglements of everyday life easily distract us from walking our paths, but I sense the journey of the soul is real. The lessons of love are real.

Are there soul mates, soul groupings? My experience leads me to believe many of my friends and lovers have interacted before.

Is channeling, mediumship, and communication with the spirit world real? The evidence seems to be mounting in support of the realness of these activities.

I know the answers for me. You must decide for yourself. The journey of the road in The Big W allowed me to create a world where I could slow down, silence the noise, eliminate distractions, listen to my heart, reprogram my mind and participate in Soul School-Playground Earth.

I honored the tugging on my soul. I journeyed from the limited programmed mind to the limitless voice of my heart and discovered my dreams and my true inner divine self. I gave up the illusion of control, of security and took a chance. Now I sense a new tugging on my soul, a new adventure in love with Josephine.

Perhaps there is a tugging on your soul. My dreams, my lesson, my path, my journey in The Dub, may not be your dream, your schoolroom, or your path. That's up to you to discover. I encourage you to be still. To listen to your heart, express your heart, trust your heart, believe in your heart and live by your heart.

I discovered it's difficult to be myself in a world that encourages me to be like everyone else. I continue to challenge myself by asking myself questions such as:

Is my now creating the future I envision?

What price am I willing to pay for the luxuries I demand?

How do I define success?

Am I living in the truth or believing a lie and living in illusion?

Am I focused on limitations or do I honor the divine power of creation?

Who and what am I allowing to feed and program my mind?

Do I believe in my dreams?

Do I practice self-care?

What can I bring to a situation or a relationship?

Is it time to let go of negative people, things or places?

How would I like to be treated?

What makes me happy? Do it.

What makes me unhappy? Don't do it.

Am I walking my path, living my dreams, or am I part of the herded masses?

As Dr. Patch Adams instructed, "We must learn to see beyond the world of conformity." We all must walk our path. We are free to walk our path. We are free to be individuals. We are free to dream.

Again, I think of Mr. Robbins and ask myself what I believe? What's important to me? What are my dreams? What's holding me back? Which fears do I insist on clinging to? Who supports my journey and who distracts me?

I believe the power of the Universe, the power of God, is ours for the asking. Experience is our greatest teacher. If I am still, the voice within will speak. The answers lie within not without. Each moment counts. There are no meetings by chance. We are all teachers. We are all students. Life is a playground called Soul School-Playground Earth. We are here to learn, play, dream and love. We are all spirits born pure. Somehow our minds become programmed with shame, fear and limited thinking. Our human experience is a journey back to our heart, back to spirit nature, back to love. Life is good and we should enjoy the ride. We are love and need not fear love. The journey is real and never ending. There are many distractions and illusions of security and happiness, but I've come to believe that love is really all there is.

The Dub is parked out front, Dylan is in the backyard chasing birds and I am about to finish my first book. I have new dreams and will continue to co-create my destiny with the Universe and in my heart I am happy, joyous and free.

I have put closure on the road and will always treasure my three years in The Dub. Now I am ready to walk a new road with new lessons and new dreams. There is only one question remaining to be asked:

"Josephine, will you marry me?"

CHAPTER EIGHTY
HONEST WITH ME
"EPILOGUE"

Josephine and I spent the summer and fall of 2001 at her home in Atlanta. In December I had a chance to get my old appraisal job back in New England. I commuted from Atlanta to Worcester for six months. For the summer of 2002, Josephine and I rented in apartment in the Worcester area, and enjoyed working, saving, exploring and playing with Joey and Sara.

On October 12, 2002, we were married. About 100 of our friends flew into town and witnessed our declaration of love. The invitation read:

Josephine Bolton
And
Napoleon Zimmerman
Invite you to celebrate Love
as they commence to create
the Life of their shared Dreams.
The ceremony will begin
at seven-thirty in the evening
Saturday, the twelfth of October
Two thousand and two
Vecoma at the Yellow River
4400 Vecoma Lane
Stone Mountain, Georgia
Reception Dinner to follow

Three days later on October 15, 2002, we moved to Folly Beach, South Carolina.

ABOUT THE AUTHOR

Napoleon Zimmerman lived the script handed down from generation to generation: college, career, wife, children, home, and white picket fence. But something happened. At age 36, divorce shattered that world. Broken, bewildered, and disillusioned, Zimmerman purchased a small RV and ventured into the unknown in search of himself.

ABOUT GREATUNPUBLISHED.COM

www.greatunpublished.com is a website that exists to serve writers and readers, and to remove some of the commercial barriers between them. When you purchase a GreatUNpublished title, whether you order it in electronic form or in a paperback volume, the author is receiving a majority of the post-production revenue.

A GreatUNpublished book is never out of stock, and always available, because each book is printed on-demand, as it is ordered.

A portion of the site's share of profits is channeled into literacy programs.

So by purchasing this title from GreatUNpublished, you are helping to revolutionize the publishing industry for the benefit of writers and readers.

And for this we thank you.